D1545854

Uncanny Modernity

Uncanny Modernity

Cultural Theories, Modern Anxieties

Edited by

Jo Collins

and

John Jervis

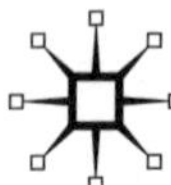

First published 2008 by
PALGRAVE MACMILLAN
Houndmills, Basingstoke, Hampshire RG21 6XS and
175 Fifth Avenue, New York, N.Y. 10010
Companies and representatives throughout the world

PALGRAVE MACMILLAN is the global academic imprint of the Palgrave Macmillan division of St. Martin's Press, LLC and of Palgrave Macmillan Ltd. Macmillan® is a registered trademark in the United States, United Kingdom and other countries. Palgrave is a registered trademark in the European Union and other countries.

ISBN-13: 978–0–230–51771–4 hardback
ISBN-10: 0–230–51771–4 hardback

This book is printed on paper suitable for recycling and made from fully managed and sustained forest sources. Logging, pulping and manufacturing processes are expected to conform to the environmental regulations of the country of origin.

A catalogue record for this book is available from the British Library.

Library of Congress Cataloging-in-Publication Data

Uncanny modernity: cultural theories, modern anxieties / edited by
Jo Collins and John Jervis.
p. cm.
Includes bibliographical references and index.
ISBN 0–230–51771–4 (alk. paper)
1. Psychology. 2. Experience. 3. Supernatural. 4. Culture—
Psychological aspects. 5. Postmodernism.—Psychological aspects.
I. Collins, Jo, 1978– II. Jervis, John, 1946–

BF57.U53 2008
155.9—dc22 2008000186

10 9 8 7 6 5 4 3 2 1
17 16 15 14 13 12 11 10 09 08

Printed and bound in Great Britain by
CPI Antony Rowe, Chippenham and Eastbourne

Contents

Notes on the Contributors vii

Introduction 1
Jo Collins and John Jervis

1 Uncanny Presences 10
John Jervis

2 Night and the Uncanny 51
Elisabeth Bronfen

3 Uncanny Reflections, Modern Illusions: Sighting the Modern Optical Uncanny 68
Tom Gunning

4 As It Happened ... *Borderline*, the Uncanny and the Cosmopolitan 91
James Donald

5 Access Denied: Memory and Resistance in the Contemporary Ghost Film 112
Scott Brewster

6 The Uncanny After Freud: The Contemporary Trauma Subject and the Fiction of Stephen King 128
Roger Luckhurst

7 'Neurotic Men' and a Spectral Woman: Freud, Jung and Sabina Spielrein 146
Jo Collins

8 The Urban Uncanny: The City, the Subject, and Ghostly Modernity 168
Julian Wolfreys

9 Profane Illuminations, Delicate and Mysterious Flames: Mass Culture and Uncanny Gnosis 181
Michael Saler

10 Terrorism and the Uncanny, or, The Caves of Tora Bora 201
David Punter

11 Document:
'On the Psychology of the Uncanny' (1906): Ernst Jentsch 216
Translated by Roy Sellars

Index 229

Notes on the Contributors

Scott Brewster is a Senior Lecturer in English at the University of Central Lancashire. Author of numerous articles on the Gothic and psychoanalysis, he also edited *Inhuman Reflections: Rethinking the Limits of the Human* (Manchester University Press, 2000) and edited and introduced the 2002 Wordsworth Classics edition of Wilkie Collins's *Woman in White*.

Elisabeth Bronfen is Professor of English and American Literature at the University of Zurich. Her publications include *Over Her Dead Body: Death, Femininity and the Aesthetic* (Manchester University Press, 1992) and *The Knotted Subject: Hysteria and Its Discontents* (Princeton University Press, 1998). She is currently working on a cultural history of the night, forthcoming with Columbia University Press, 2009.

Jo Collins is a Teaching Assistant in Cultural Studies and English and American Literature at the University of Kent. She has published articles on Australian Literature and colonialism. She is currently researching and writing in the field of the colonial uncanny.

James Donald is Professor of Film Studies at the University of New South Wales. His publications include *Imagining the Modern City* (Athlone, 1999) and, with others, *Close-Up, 1927–33: Cinema and Modernism* (Cassell, 1998). He has also coedited *The Sage Handbook of Film Studies* (Sage, 2008).

Tom Gunning is Professor of Media and Film Studies at the University of Chicago. He is the author of numerous articles on early cinema and the culture of modernity, including the impact of spiritualism, and has published *The Films of Fritz Lang* (BFI, 2000).

John Jervis is a Research Fellow in Cultural Studies at the University of Kent. He has published *Exploring the Modern: Patterns of Western Culture and Civilization* (Blackwell, 1998) and *Transgressing the Modern: Explorations in the Western Experience of Otherness* (Blackwell, 2000). He is currently writing *Sensational Subjects: Modernity and the Spectacle of Feeling*.

Roger Luckhurst is a Senior Lecturer in English at Birkbeck College, University of London. He is the author of *The Invention of Telepathy* (Oxford University Press, 2002), *Science Fiction* (Polity, 2005) and *The Trauma Question* (Routledge, 2008), and has edited *Late Victorian Gothic Tales* (Oxford World Classics, 2005).

David Punter is Professor of English Literature at the University of Bristol. His books include, in two volumes, *Literature of Terror* (Longman, 1996), and he has edited the collection *Companion to Gothic* (Blackwell, 2000). He has recently published *Modernity* (Palgrave, 2007).

Michael Saler is Professor of History at the University of California (Davis). He has written articles on modern European intellectuals and cultural history and is the author of *The Avant-Garde in Interwar England* (Oxford University Press, 1999).

Roy Sellars is currently a Senior Lecturer in English at the University of Southern Denmark, Kolding. He has published on Hegel, Freud, Adorno, Derrida, and Bloom, among others; and his works include a co-translation of a major work by Renate Lachmann as *Memory and Literature* (University of Minnesota Press, 1997).

Julian Wolfreys is a Senior Lecturer in English Literature at the University of Loughborough. His books include *Writing London vol. II: Memory, Materiality, Spectrality* (Palgrave Macmillan, 2004) and *Victorian Hauntings: Spectrality, Gothic, the Uncanny and Literature* (Palgrave Macmillan, 2002).

Introduction

Jo Collins and John Jervis

The uncanny is an experience of disorientation, where the world in which we live suddenly seems strange, alienating or threatening. Our study proposes to examine and interrogate the qualities that characterise uncanny experiences and the cultural contexts which permit ostensibly rational people to encounter such unnerving feelings, exploring how these experiences have been portrayed in literature and film, and how they can be theorised. We ask – where does the uncanny come from? Why does it keep returning? Could it be that the uncanny is a distinctively *modern* experience?

While the uncanny has of course been significant as a theme in literature since at least the high Gothic, it is Freud's paper of 1919 that has become the key cultural resource. This paper itself led a suitably subterranean twilight existence for its first half century, then staging a dramatic return from the 1970s, becoming widely read throughout the humanities and cultural studies, on both sides of the Atlantic. Here it has converged with a second stream of influence, deriving most directly from Walter Benjamin – and ultimately from Marx – locating the uncanny in relation to the 'phantasmagoria' of city life, the transformation of the urban world into a visual and spatial spectacle inhabited also by the shadowy hauntings of the fleeting and insubstantial, in turn relating to what could be called the 'technological uncanny', the suggestion that photo, film and phone have all been resources through which the uncanny presence of a disturbing otherness is revealed. Given a further fillip by the publication of Derrida's *Specters of Marx* in 1994, the influence of the uncanny throughout the academy was such that by 1998 Martin Jay could refer to it as the 'master trope' of the decade.[1] The continued spread of 'uncanny studies' now involves a range of fields from the humanities,[2] through architecture,[3] queer studies,[4] and postcolonial studies,[5] to sociology and urban studies.[6] The upshot is that the uncanny has become a widely used figure for the simultaneous homelessness of the present,[7] and haunting by the past, that has been associated with modernity since at least the time of Baudelaire.

All this seems both to rest on, and reproduce, a certain sensibility or experience of the modern. While it seems likely that all cultures manifest spirit or ghost beliefs, this itself is not sufficient to characterise the uncanny. Rather, the latter seems to presuppose something like what Max Weber called the 'disenchantment of the world', whereby the 'supernatural', as a category, comes to contrast with the 'natural', as the realm of the 'real', object of empirical knowledge. The uncanny arises out of the supposedly and necessarily *empty* character of the supernatural as a category; it is not so much that the uncanny *fills* this category (with ghosts, *revenants* etc.) – though it may do this readily enough – as that it suggests a fundamental *indecision*, an obscurity or uncertainty, at the heart of our ontology, our sense of time, place, and history, both personal and cultural. And this uncertainty is both unsettling, even potentially terrifying, yet also intriguing, fascinating. Far from being 'abnormal', it seems to testify to something fundamentally alienated and dislocated that is pervasive within the modern experience and the modern construction of selfhood. As reflection and rationality become central cultural values, so the threats posed to them by these recalcitrant experiences, seemingly emanating from 'inside' (the 'unconscious') as much as 'outside', become all the more troubling. Thus we need to consider the possibility that the uncanny may be a fundamental, constitutive aspect of our experience of the modern. This will involve exploring the sense in which the uncanny testifies to a distinctive sensibility, a fusion of feeling and reflection, hence to a distinctive *aesthetics* of modernity, along with the wider psychological and cultural consequences of this.

Freud himself sets out to explore the uncanny as a 'province' of aesthetics, a rather 'remote' and neglected 'province' that inspires 'dread and horror'. His aim, clearly, is to annex this province to psychoanalysis. Now, we know from Kant that aesthetics already possesses one unruly province, threatening to disrupt its boundaries, namely the sublime. What if the uncanny, too, turns out to be another such unruly 'province', threatening not only the boundaries of aesthetics but those of psychoanalysis too? Freud's own experiences in exploring this province do indeed provide ample grounds for this suspicion. His meandering peregrinations are notoriously problematical and inconclusive, with his essentialising aim, to understand the 'common core of feeling' at the heart of the uncanny, unfulfilled even on his own admission. Far from conquering the uncanny, Freud's theoretical territorialisation always seems to be undermined by the fact that psychoanalysis, by the nature of its subject matter, must always encounter uncharted regions and foreign bodies both outside and within itself. The presence of the uncanny impels the drive to master the fear of the unknown while ensuring that the outcome can at best be partial failure. One can therefore feel that there is ample justification for Ellison's recent claim that the uncanny can be taken to be 'that force, that *energeia*, which, in pushing beyond clearly established boundaries of all kinds, ends up possessing the naively unsuspecting would-be possessor (interpreter)'.[8] More generally, the uncanny troubles the serene confidence of any explanatory or interpretive framework through which we seek to capture it, whether in everyday life, literary reflection or cultural theory.

The idea of the uncanny itself seems to have emerged into widespread use by the mid-nineteenth century.[9] It does not follow that the experience of the uncanny could not have existed before, though the secularisation of knowledge within eighteenth-century culture suggests it is unlikely to have emerged much earlier. Anyway, we have reason to believe that the very way these experiences emerge *and* are articulated implies an intimacy between these dimensions that is both very modern and central to the possibility of the uncanny itself. In particular, we can refer here to the way the conjunction of eighteenth-century rationalism, the disintegration of the early modern category of the marvellous, and the simultaneous internalisation, production and cultivation of 'affect', results in a self of insecure boundaries, capable of both disciplined and transgressive experiences, of the kind that duly emerged, in narrative, as 'Gothic'. And something along these lines is indeed implied in Freud's own account, since although he postulates a transhistorical 'castration complex' as one underlying causal mechanism, the other – the apparent experiential confirmation of 'surmounted beliefs'[10] – is by definition culturally specific to the modern (and could, indeed, be taken to imply that the former, *in itself*, is insufficient alone to generate a sense of the uncanny).

We can draw here on Castle's wide-ranging thesis, tracing the eighteenth-century 'invention' of the uncanny through the internalisation of the supernatural into the projections of the mind, a mind which thereby becomes both constituted and haunted by images, phantasmatic 'inner pictures'. She argues that 'the historic Enlightenment internalization of the spectral – the gradual reinterpretation of ghosts and apparitions as hallucinations, or projections of the mind – introduced a new uncanniness into human consciousness itself'. And, in consequence, there was now 'a potential danger in the act of reflection – a danger in paying too much attention to mental images or in "thinking too hard". One's inmost thoughts might at any moment assume the strongly externalized shape of phantoms.' These imagined images of the other are partially constitutive of the sense of community and 'the social' in this new-context of modernity; thus she adds that a sensitivity to these spectral dimensions gave one, as a refined, civilised person, a chance to 'display one's powers of sympathetic imagination'.[11] This modern self, carrier of civilisation and Enlightenment, thus emerges simultaneously as somehow shadowy, spectral. The self, and the mind which seems to be its governing principle, emerge as uncanny spaces of doubling and fracture. And the encounter with other selves, similarly and simultaneously embodied and spectral, opens up further possibilities for the uncanny, since any attempt at a reflexive grasp of this mutual imbrication of self and social involves a potential for precisely those uncanny figurations that people the world of culture and experience from the Gothic onwards, playing across the boundaries (internal/external, self/other), alien yet oddly familiar, testifying to the uncanny grounding of modern selfhood and the social, not necessarily experienced as such, yet always a potential source of unease, disquiet, even fear.

By the late nineteenth century, the effect of all this in the context of the challenges of the new experiences of urban modernity has produced a diffusion of the conditions under which the experience of the uncanny becomes possible and a cultural interest in associated phenomena such as ghosts has become reinvigorated. The spectacle of femininity had produced a spectre of the evanescent and the unreal: self-denial and 'purity' marked the feminine as death drive, and the woman was already half translated to the spirit world she was indeed adept at communicating with, the ideal 'medium'.[12] A sense of unease, linked to a loss of continuity with the past and the natural environment, is associated with a range of distinctively modern anxieties which become increasingly codified as neuroses; and some of these, notably disturbances of the spatial sense (claustrophobia, agoraphobia) prove both symptomatically and culturally to have pronounced affiliation with the experience of the uncanny. Explored extensively in the arts (Symbolism, the Gothic revival, early film), the uncanny is also a presence in modernism itself, a reflexive 'defamiliarisation' being central to its programmes for artistic reinvention and renewal: 'making the world strange' prepares the way for its inevitable return in disturbing, unrecognised form, in turn a central theme in Surrealism, along with its fascination with the dream, poised uncertainly between sleeping and waking.[13]

Enough has been said to show that modernity, indeed, is as much about imagination as about bricks and mortar, hence Donald's injunction to study 'the uneasy space between the physical and the imaginary' if we are to grasp it.[14] Whatever its other aspects, modernity can only exist as *process* rather than achieved state, and as such is inseparable from being grasped, appropriated as such; it is a form of cultural self-reflection. Cultures do not *have* to see themselves as 'modern', and doing so institutes reflexive paradoxes and problems of temporal experience. And methodologically, as hinted at previously, the notion of figuration can play a significant role here. Arguing that terms like 'phantasmagoria' are not just literary devices, but the material of experience, Highmore suggests that 'the figuration of the urban (its existence as a network of metaphors, metonyms, symbols and the like)' is not only representational, but is also 'a crucial aspect of the material experience of the urban' so that 'the *work* of urban culture is the proliferation of these complex figures to the point where it makes no sense to talk about urban experience as being free from the figural'. He adds that if novels and films are metaphoric, figural, then 'urban experience inhabits an uncannily similar realm'.[15] One might say that the point about figuration is that it goes beyond the figurative to challenge the distinction between the literal and the metaphorical, thereby suggesting the very ground of the uncanny.

In short, this approach presents modernity as a conjunction of those 'structures of feeling' whereby we live as moderns, and the workings of a 'cultural imaginary', drawing on the full resources of media-inflected narrative, imagery and sensationalism, through which these are experienced and articulated. And overall, the uncanny has become a key term for figuring the uncertainties, tensions and obscurities of modernity itself, which is what the studies in this book seek to explore.

One other aspect of modernity deserves further mention. As Sconce suggests, in *Haunted Media*, 'Sound and image without material substance, the electronically mediated worlds of telecommunications often evoke the supernatural by creating virtual beings that appear to have no physical form', and by bringing this 'spectral world' into the home, the equipment takes on the appearance of a 'haunted apparatus'.[16] However, it is doubtless the camera that carried this sense of technology as uncanny into the heart of nineteenth-century culture. Gunning writes that photography was experienced 'as an uncanny phenomenon, one which seemed to undermine the unique identities of objects and people ... creating a parallel world of phantasmatic doubles alongside the concrete world of the senses'.[17] Conveying the spectrality of self as image, image *of* the body yet separate from it, the photo, as an image of self-identity, becomes an emblem of the death of the body *as* the life of the self (or soul). The use of the photo in spiritualism becomes readily intelligible in the light of these considerations.[18] However, it is also worth remembering that 'messages from elsewhere', as a feature of the mediated culture of modernity, are also stimulated by the development of the telegraph and the wireless, the great electronic technologies of mass communication; and these, of course, are non-visual media. Hence that conjunction of 'disembodied voices' and 'disembodied images' that has become central to the uncanny substructure of modern experience. We encounter visions of a technologically generated autonomous world that threatens to replace this world, and certainly possesses power to influence it.

This runs readily enough into the themes of simulation and hyperreality that became central to the cultural impact of the postmodern in the 1980s and beyond. We no longer have the ether, but virtual reality and cyberspace are appropriate successors, with their obscure ontological status, and their own uncanny potential for disembodied messages in parallel worlds of simulation where material reality itself seems only to exist as a hallucinatory memory. The postmodern itself seems to exist somewhere uneasily between fantasy and reality, a state presided over by Jean Baudrillard, observing the 'dissolution of TV into life, the dissolution of life into TV',[19] making strange what seems familiar, reversing conceptual certainties. Presence becomes subsumed by signs which purport to represent reality, but actually only signify its disappearing point.

Whatever truth there may be in this, one can wonder about the fate of the uncanny. If there is a diffusion of uncanny potential, is there, conversely, a diminution in our ability to experience it? If everything becomes potentially uncanny, nothing is really experienced *as* uncanny, or as *sufficiently* uncanny. And yet ... it remains likely that the potential of the uncanny to disrupt our experiences and expectations is far from played out. This is a world where risk and unpredictability can have momentous consequences. In media technology itself, it is surely the computer virus that most vividly encapsulates this: the mysterious alien incursion from an unknown elsewhere, known as present only in the havoc it wreaks. As hitherto, then, the uncanny may yet insist on having the last (ghoulish?) laugh ...

* * *

This collection opens with John Jervis's chapter which aims to extend the discussion of some of the issues raised above, showing the difficulties of capturing modern experience in/as representation that result in uncanny fissures between past and present, reality and image, perception and cognition, and drawing on Poe, Benjamin, Djuna Barnes, Hoffmann and Hitchcock to reveal the centrality of the figural for the modern experience of the uncanny, where the aesthetic figuration of experience is also a slippage of our attempt to clarify and control.

This concern with conceptualising modern experience is also addressed by Julian Wolfreys's exploration of the 'urban uncanny' in Roeg's *Don't Look Now* and Descartes' writings on Amsterdam, presenting the city as that which refuses stability, hovering on the borderlands of what can be conceptualised and represented, thus presenting us with an urban self that is fundamentally dislocated. In Elisabeth Bronfen's article we also find ourselves in the cityscape, shadowing the wanderings of two *flâneur* characters from Schnitzler and Scorsese, exploring the uncanniness of the night as phantasmatic 'double' of the day. James Donald analyses the modernist film *Borderline* to reveal the anxieties surrounding modern rootlessness in the figure of the cosmopolitan and imaginings of racial difference. Issues around gender are raised by Jo Collins, who reveals how Sabina Spielrein was a crucial figure in the Freud/Jung relationship, who not only significantly influenced the thinking of both men, but also functioned, like the role of women in Freud's essay, as a kind of 'repressed feminine', simultaneously contributing to the origin of the theory of the uncanny while being rendered uncanny herself. Both Roger Luckhurst and Scott Brewster take up the theme of trauma through exploring Stephen King's writing and recent ghost films, suggesting, in their different ways, that key facets of uncanny experience and trends in trauma theory imply a need to revise or go beyond Freud's theory of repression.

Michael Saler's contribution examines works by André Breton, Philip K. Dick and Umberto Eco to show how the uncanny can be thought of as providing a legitimate, alternative gnosis, one that is not incommensurate with rationality, but partakes of mass culture and serves to make everyday objects and reality uncanny. David Punter also considers the relationship of the uncanny to knowledge, exploring the uncanny and terrorism, probing the conceptual ambiguities which resonate around the caves of Tora Bora, an underworld which ominously and symbolically resonates with echoes and traces of what might (never) be found, thus showing how the uncanny is recalcitrant to the interpretation it insistently demands. Gunning's contribution presents the 'uncanny optics' of the modern, examining film, literature and early magic shows to show how modern technological advances heralded new kinds of visual encounters with the uncanny, revealing vacillation between receptivity and scepticism towards the supernatural. Roy Sellars's contribution is a translation of Jentsch's classic paper,[20] which enables us to locate Freud's 1919 essay within its historical-intellectual context, showing how Freud's dismissal of Jentsch's ideas on 'intellectual uncertainty' returns to haunt his own argument.

Notes

1. M. Jay, 'The Uncanny Nineties', in his *Cultural Semantics: Keywords of Our Time* (London: Athlone, 1998), p. 157.
2. For a wide-ranging discussion with an invaluable bibliography, see N. Royle, *The Uncanny* (Manchester: Manchester University Press, 2003). Within literary studies, the influence of Derrida is apparent in such works as J. -M. Rabaté, *The Ghosts of Modernity* (Gainesville: Florida University Press, 1996) and J. Wolfreys, *Victorian Hauntings: Spectrality, Gothic, the Uncanny and Literature* (London: Palgrave Macmillan, 2002). D. Ellison, *Ethics and Aesthetics in European Modernist Literature: From the Sublime to the Uncanny* (Cambridge: Cambridge University Press, 2001), is significant for our understanding of the uncanny in modernism. On film, see S. J. Schneider, 'Uncanny Realism and the Decline of the Modern Horror Film', *Paradoxa* (1997) vol. 3, nos. 3–4. For a case study from history, see J. Richardson, *Possessions: The History and Uses of Haunting in the Hudson Valley* (Cambridge, MA: Harvard University Press, 2003).
3. See A. Vidler, *The Architectural Uncanny: Essays in the Modern Unhomely* (Cambridge, MA: MIT Press, 1992).
4. For example, T. Castle's *The Apparitional Lesbian: Female Homosexuality and Modern Culture* (New York: Columbia University Press, 1993); and J. Fletcher's 'The haunted closet: Henry James's queer spectrality', *Textual Practice* (2000) 14: 1, pp. 53–80. See also T. Castle, *The Female Thermometer: Eighteenth-Century Culture and the Invention of the Uncanny* (Oxford: Oxford University Press, 1995), ch. 11.
5. H. Bhabha's 'The Other Question' and 'Signs Taken for Wonders' in *The Location of Culture* (London and New York: Routledge, 1994) discuss the coloniser's confrontation with the uncanny.
6. See A. Gordon, *Ghostly Matters: Haunting and the Sociological Imagination* (Minneapolis: Minnesota University Press, 1997); J. Donald, *Imagining the Modern City* (London: Athlone Press, 1999) chs. 1, 3; S. Pile, *Real Cities: Modernity, Space and the Phantasmagorias of City Life* (London: Sage, 2005), chs. 1, 4. These also draw on examples from film and literature.
7. Outside the two traditions listed above, Heidegger's work on modernity as 'homelessness' is worth mentioning: see M. Heidegger, 'The Structure of Uncanniness', in *History of the Concept of Time: Prolegomena* (Bloomington: Indiana University Press, 1985 [1925]).
8. Ellison, p. 53.
9. Royle, pp. 21–3.
10. S. Freud, 'The "Uncanny"', in *Art and Literature*, The Pelican Freud Library, vol. 14 (Harmondsworth: Penguin Books, 1985 [1919]), p. 372.
11. T. Castle, *Female Thermometer*, pp. 17, 165, 123; and see chs. 8–10, *passim*.

12. E. Bronfen's *Over Her Dead Body: Death, femininity and the aesthetic* (Manchester: Manchester University Press, 1992) considers the uncanny in relation to femininity, through literature. For discussions on Freud, women and the uncanny see D. Jonte-Pace, *Speaking the Unspeakable: Religion, Misogyny, and the Uncanny Mother in Freud's Cultural Texts* (Berkeley, Los Angeles and London: University of California Press, 2001) and M. Sprengnether, *The Spectral Mother: Freud, Feminism and Psychoanalysis* (Ithaca: Cornell University Press, 1990).
13. On literary modernism, see Ellison, *Ethics and Aesthetics*; for Surrealism, see H. Foster, *Compulsive Beauty* (Cambridge, MA: MIT Press, 1993); for early film, see W. Paul, 'Uncanny Theater: The Twin Inheritances of the Movies', *Paradoxa* (1997), vol. 3, nos. 3–4.
14. Donald, p. 71.
15. B. Highmore, *Cityscapes: Cultural Readings in the Material and Symbolic City* (London: Palgrave Macmillan, 2005), pp. 5–6, 22.
16. J. Sconce, *Haunted Media: Electronic Presence from Telegraphy to Television* (Durham, NC: Duke University Press, 2000), pp. 4, 83.
17. T. Gunning, 'Phantom Images and Modern Manifestations: Spirit Photography, Magic Theater, Trick Films, and Photography's Uncanny', in P. Petro (ed.), *Fugitive Images: From Photography to Video* (Bloomington: Indiana University Press, 1995), pp. 42–3.
18. See P. Thurschwell, *Literature, Technology and Magical Thinking: 1880–1920* (Cambridge: Cambridge University Press, 2001), for an exploration of these and related issues.
19. J. Baudrillard, *Simulations* (New York: Semiotext(e), 1983), p. 55. See Sconce, *Haunted Media*, ch. 5, for a discussion of these concepts.
20. Originally translated by Roy Sellars in *Angelaki* (1995) 2: 1, pp. 17–22. This retranslation appears in this edition by the kind permission of Sarah Wood and Pelagia Goulimari.

1
Uncanny Presences

John Jervis

Fascinated by the paintings wherein Constantin Guys attempted to capture the essence of the modern, Baudelaire wrote: 'This seems to be the fear of not going fast enough, of letting the phantom escape before the synthesis has been extracted from it and recorded ...'.[1] What is the status of 'phantom' here? Bronfen's remark that the uncanny may well occur when there is 'an effacement of the distinction between literal and figural'[2] is suggestive, just as one might go on to observe that this traditional use of 'figural', referring to tropes as a 'figurative' dimension of language, has increasingly been supplemented, in recent scholarship – including this essay – by a use of 'figure' and 'figuration' in deliberately more ambiguous ways, indeed pointing to this very effacement to which Bronfen refers.[3] This encourages us to ask about Baudelaire's use of 'phantom' here, so as to understand how the figurative can, at times, vibrate the always insecure boundary that insulates it from the literal, and conversely, insulates the real from the fantasies that necessarily partake of it. And the 'synthesis', that has to be 'extracted and recorded'? This synthesis of a phantom, itself phantasmatic, reminds us both of the spectre of the past – apparently past yet with us still – and the fantasy construction of the whole in representation: the imaginary unity of the image, figuring what cannot coherently be grasped. The spectral can figure a state of ontological undecidability or tension, where there is an *insistence*, a *presence* of whatever resists us, recalcitrant to our understanding. What this little quote calls for, then, is an exploration of 'presence' as a possible object and context of experience; its relation to our sense of time; our ability to capture it through representation, particularly as image; the resulting instabilities in the experiential field that can generate 'presences' out of what is conventionally 'absent'; and how all this relates to our sense of the modern, of ourselves as modern.

'Presence', one might say, can only be experienced, not represented, which in turn means that even its status as experience is problematical; it cannot be known as experience, even as it is experienced. The gap that is opened up here, the 'empty space', is both a gap, a distance within the self, and is also the place of the image, as an attempted fixing of the present moment, giving us the imaginary plenitude of presence even as it disappears. This image always carries a past with it, that very past that is constituted through this disconnection from presence, the disconnection that renders the image free-floating, and thereby carries with it the permanent possibility of the uncanny. In a sense, then, the present is always an awakening, and this awakening is also a remembering. And history has to be understood as a stream of disappearing traces, each alienated in the very moment of its appearance, hence giving us that sense of modernist distance, in Baudelaire and beyond, 'as if the modern artist is committed to a moment in which he can never be properly inserted', for the heroic immersion in the now actually invokes a past, forever impossible to escape. Howells adds that 'what appears as a diachrony – a distancing of oneself from an earlier past, whether one's own or that of a previous "generation" – is in reality a synchrony – the inability to coincide fully with the present, that is, with presence ...'.[4] In this way, adds Rancière, modernity is 'not contemporaneous with itself', and is 'deprived of the categories of its own understanding'.[5] In effect, the possibility of the uncanny looms.

Freud defines the uncanny as 'that class of the frightening which leads back to what is known of old and long familiar';[6] this reminds us that it is first and foremost a sensation, a feeling, a shudder of apprehension or fear. It disturbs deeply held, taken-for-granted assumptions about what is real and unreal, or imaginary, about the world, and the entities within it; whether these entities are dead or alive, animate or inanimate, natural or artificial, self or other. And hence one can be disturbed by something, even when one is not necessarily sure that there is a 'something' there to be disturbed by. The uncanny shakes fundamental categories of knowledge and experience, while yet depending on them; it challenges the limits of experience and understanding, given the world we (think we) live in. We cannot, therefore, 'locate' the uncanny; we cannot ask where it 'belongs'. '*If* it belongs, it is no longer a question of the uncanny.'[7] Thus it disturbs our sense of atmosphere, makes us 'apprehensive' in our apprehension of 'presence', of the here, the now, of time, the taken for granted framework of experience. The uncanny therefore incorporates suspense, the experience of the possible presence of the past in the present, stretched out indefinitely, hanging between past and future, the present as impossible infinite. One 'apprehends' the present, reaches out for it, 'apprehensively', experiencing it as troubling, a troubling that brings into play that dimension of experience that does not recognise boundaries, hence does not acknowledge the boundary-defining aspect of thought: 'experience' as that which is neither inside nor outside, self or other, or both at once. Thinking always involves categories; experience just *is*, even as it escapes through the very act of being 'grasped', apprehended. Thus the very *registering* of these experiences as experiences can contribute to our regarding them as 'uncanny'. And it is the particular boundary between epistemology and ontology, between the 'real' and the 'known' as apprehended in experience, that seems to be crucial for our sense of the uncanny as atmosphere, underlying the manifestation of the uncanny in more specific 'presences'.

If we return to Guys, we can recall that he was *painting* the modern, in an era when the photographic image was already coming to be seen as offering greater potential for capturing the sought-for immediacy, the presence of the present. Yet no more than the painting can the photo represent the very absence that makes it possible, the presence of the present, for it can never overcome the gap in time, space and experience that constitutes its very ability to purport to represent presence, but renders presence forever inaccessible. This gap corresponds to a well-known paradox of the image: its capacity to represent what it, itself, is not; its capacity to replace, defer the real, in the very act whereby it calls attention to the real, 'presenting' it to us even as it aspires to abolish its own role, render itself transparent, the invisible film over the surface of the real. Mapped onto linear time, this 'difference' of the image becomes a necessary inability to attain presence; hence the pastness of the image becomes its own explosive presence, locking it into a reality that is neither – or both – past and present. Given the modern sense of a discontinuity in the nature of the image – its status as 'mere' image, separate from the real – the image has a resultingly obscure ontology, a place in the twilight, caught between past and present, real and unreal, always liable to float free of its moorings, always potentially phantasmatic. Haunting the tracks of the modern experience, the uncanny thus reveals *presences*, traces of the past in the present, and of the other in the self. It suggests an atmosphere, concentrated in a 'presence' located uneasily between time and space, and between material and immaterial, real and unreal – a sense of the world as unfamiliarity, of our own presence in it as 'unbelonging'. It reminds us of our own inability to be sufficiently present to ourselves, the limits of reflexive awareness, suggesting that there are always potential surrogates, 'presences', for this necessarily absent presence, particularly what are, in secular modernity, those necessarily absent or displaced presences: the dead, and one's past self. These possible experiences of the uncanny are linked closely to the role of the image as a product of modern technologies of the visual, involving a sliding of representation into experience, their mutual penetration as inherently productive of the uncanny. And we will see that this technological figuring of the uncanny, mapped onto the idea of 'absent presences', serves further to introduce the 'mechanical' uncanny, of dolls and automata, where representation becomes reproduction, nature becomes artefact, and the result hints at 'unnatural' life.

Apparitions of the self

In his story *The Oval Portrait*, Edgar Allan Poe narrates an encounter with a painted image, and the history of its subject. In a dark, obscure corner of a chateau, the flickering light of a newly moved candelabra illuminates a hitherto-unnoticed portrait, to startling effect. Among a roomful of 'very spirited' paintings, this one was particularly so: a portrait of a young girl 'just ripening into womanhood', her features emerging radiantly out of the 'vague yet deep shadow which formed the background of the whole'. So intense is this, that the narrator is initially shocked into closing his eyes; but on recovering his composure, being startled into 'waking life', he subjects the portrait to the full intensity of his gaze. He never doubts that a portrait is indeed what it is – despite his previous drowsiness, he never mistook it for a living person – but he concludes that the spell of the picture lay in 'an absolute *life-likeliness* of expression', which had 'confounded, subdued, and appalled' him. Turning to the little book he had found nearby, which purported to describe the pictures, he learns that the depicted maiden had married the painter, who, alas, had 'already a bride in his Art', and who insisted on painting her; despite her jealousy of this 'other bride', she submits. So obsessed was he, as he continued painting, that he would not see that 'the light which fell so ghastly in that lone turret withered the health and the spirits of his bride, who pined visibly to all but him'. Those who caught sight of the emerging portrait regarded it as a 'mighty marvel', and proof of his love, as well as his skill. Time went on, and still he would not see that 'the tints which he spread upon the canvas were drawn from the cheeks of her who sat beside him'. Finally, it was finished. Seeing, aghast, that it was '*Life* itself', he turned to see that his beloved was dead.[8]

It is made perfectly clear by the narrator that the portrait itself derives its power from its properties as an image. It is not mistaken for a real person. At the same time, it is a kind of apotheosis of the image: its attributes, like its powers, the vividness of its presence, constantly strain towards the real. Hence it is uncanny, apparitional. Indeed, if the narrator, in his overawed confusion, holds fast to the distinction between 'life-likeliness' and 'life', the painter himself goes the other way: 'This is indeed *Life* itself!'. And all this is true to the uncertain status of the image, poised uneasily between representation and reality, its 'presence' paradoxically drawing on both the reality of its materiality and its power to double the object or experience it 'represents', while purporting, through 'presence', to abolish the very gap that makes its power possible. This oscillation of the image is what renders it permanently a liminal phenomenon, disturbing the neatness and clarity of the real/unreal boundary whose very difference makes it possible.

This boundary is made all the more problematical by its relation to another, that of depth and surface, fundamental to the modern ontology of self and self-identity. Indeed, the self is a very difficult organising construct of the Western tradition. This self is nebulous, unseen: so how are we to represent it? The problem can hardly be avoided: 'some form of manifestation is always necessary', Cadava reminds us,[9] but this mysterious 'manifestation' is always difficult to map onto the self from which it purportedly 'emanates'. The self is poised uneasily between the function of the subject, a bearer of linguistic location in an essentially grammatical, non-material way, and the body, inherently material, organic. The self is postulated as the mode of existence of the body that enables us to refer to 'personal identity', but a mode of existence that designates a theatre of depth, an ontology of personal identity as the deep principle of integration of body and mind. Although referring to depth, to a sense of 'underlying character', for example, such a self can only be represented as surface, as image; and, given the necessary individualism of 'personal identity', it cannot have the featureless generality of the pre-modern 'soul'. As such, the image of self can only be that of body itself, body as adorned, presented in culture, the encultured body as mine, as me. The representation of myself is *as* my body: myself as representation is the absence of body in its very appearance as representation. Thus the spectre can be seen as the appropriate representation of myself as self, *my*self. And thus also the problem that seems to arise when the image, as 'mere' surface, seems to take on the features of depth, since this maps it, again, as spectral. In her comments on the story, Bronfen remarks that 'A sense of the uncanny is provoked when depth, the one dimension that differentiates model from copy, seems to have been added to the imitation'.[10]

This can serve as a foundation myth, then, of the emergence, the 'emanation' of the self, from the murky depths; of the production of the image from the obscure background, the dark turret of the real; of the creativity of the artist as mysterious, self-generating charismatic power. And in this story – as generally – it is the male artist, whether as the painter or his double, the narrator of the book, or redoubled, as the author of the story himself. These doublings cover over, but simultaneously repeat, the paradox of the initial situation. And the story gives a further twist, for these productive doublings are also destructive: the life of the beloved is sacrificed to the life of the image, and thus to the celebration, the very possibility, of masculine procreative power. The spectral power of the image emerges as the appropriate mode wherein these paradoxes, of real and unreal, literal and figural, depth and surface, can be 'resolved' through being revealed.

There is a strong hint here of an intimacy between the lives of the self, the image, death and the spectral. It has already been implied that the object must die, for the image to be truly alive. And this corresponds to a truth of the image: that only by establishing a precarious distance from the object of representation can it exist as image. Once again, as we have seen, it is real and unreal, both or neither, intensely simulacral. And when it is the self that is being represented, the image is challenged in another way. If the image conjures up the death of the self, this death cannot, for all that, be represented. We are forced to represent death indirectly, again through its effects in the body. Death in representation is death as illness or violence, figured as the corruption or dismemberment of the body which must nonetheless remain recognisably *mine*. It is death as violence that most clearly marks the necessity to destroy the body, as essential vehicle of the self. The self can thereby be 'seen' to die; except that its death, like its life, can never be 'seen' anyway. Or rather, it can only be 'seen' as spectral; for the spectre, as pure appearance, appearance divorced from matter, yet in identifiable, personal form, is exactly the self as imaged, the form of life appropriate to it *as* self, a form of life that is neither life, nor death either.

At the same time, the spectre can be a decisive mark of death, of *my* death; Baudrillard reminds us of the commonly encountered idea that 'Whoever sees his double, sees his death'.[11] The self, as representation of itself, has become too 'other'; all that can be left is the death of the body, of my body, me in 'myself'. So Bronfen adds that this lack of distinction between representation and reality, whereby the representation seems to take on a life of its own, is both productive of the uncanny and 'metaphorically figures the experience of one's own mortality'.[12] We see the impossibility of representing *my* death, the death of me, my*self*, the spirit that animates the body and that can, itself, only be represented as *separate*, in its impossible separation from the body, an impossible separation that is, nonetheless, opened up as possibility by representation itself, its non-existence as that *through which* and *by which* a reality beyond is pointed to, so that if the pointing succeeds, the gesture abolishes itself. By that very same token, representation makes itself real, abolishes reference, asserts its self-sufficiency. It oscillates between real and unreal – like the ghost; and the self. Thus Cixous suggests that the ghost, as the 'direct figure of the uncanny' is the 'fiction of our relationship to death', and that 'What is intolerable is that the Ghost erases the limit which exists between two states, neither alive nor dead.'[13] We can superimpose the impossible materiality of representation on the impossible immateriality of the self, producing the represented self as spectral body: the very image of death.

In the story, Poe offers us a narrative, but it is a narrative that exists in a relation of some tension with what it is about: a portrait, an image. Reality – the artist's wife, the 'beloved' – has to be subjected to being painted, presented in a portrait. Then, she has to be re-subjected, to the anonymous narrative in the book that purports to tell us the truth of her 'story'. Finally, obsessively, she has to be subjected to a further narrative, that of the storyteller himself, rediscovering, redoubling, her story. Thus is the 'truth' of the image revealed, as an obsessive subjection and resubjection to narrative, desperately seeking closure: not just endless narrative, but endless narrative that aspires to end in the revelation of the 'secret', the depth that explains the surface, the mystery of the self at last revealed. And yet, at the end of it all, the portrait of the woman is still there, staring back, enigmatic, spectral, yet so full of life ...

If narrative is productive of the fictional self, this is true in both senses: the self in fiction, and the self as fiction. And this narrative productivity is always troubled, for if our sense of self is inseparable from the images through which memory is constituted and accessed, then these images will not coexist seamlessly with the narratives wherein we seek to recuperate them. This will seem all the more true of images coded as 'unconscious'. Indeed, this brings into play the fundamental obscurity of the unconscious, whether as concept or as the ostensible object designated. It is only within the modern, spatial, depth/surface model of the self, codified in the Freudian topography, that we are compelled to locate an unconscious 'inside', as it were; and this is, indeed, powerful imagery, carrying with it the idea of deeply troubled depths disrupting the placid surfaces of rational self-understanding. But this is no less powerful if it is allowed to trouble the inside/outside boundary itself; as Royle suggests, the uncanny 'disturbs any straightforward sense of what is inside and what is outside', and is hence 'an experience of liminality'.[14] If the self has obscure boundaries, developing out of the darkness of its background, this 'background' could as well be external as internal, opening up a 'space' for uncanny encounters as much as for unsettling eruptions from the depths. The unconscious cannot 'explain' the uncanny; rather, they are both cut from the same cloth. If the uncanny is a projection of the unconscious, this is only because the unconscious is already an internalisation of the uncanny.

Ghosts and soft furnishings

This inside/outside tension can also be troubling in the context of the home. We are told of Benjamin's experiences as a child in the photographic studio, learning dissembling and disguise, doubling himself through the props and furnishings that become as lifelike and demanding of him as he becomes objectified among them.[15] Asendorf reminds us that the interior of the bourgeois home of the 1870s and 1880s was 'sunk in twilight', full of elaborate tapestries and fussy, excessive furnishings, and quotes an observer at the time who refers to the 'faculty of delusion' necessary for us to 'feel at home', which gets pretty close to a sense of the Freudian uncanny. Thus we find, adds Asendorf, a 'transparently delusory life insurance, the compulsively stuffed interiors a kind of "magical defence"'.[16] Defence against what? The ghosts that their very atmosphere calls up? Ghosts prefer their apartments to be furnished, it would seem. And as homes, these excessive furnishings remind us of another excess, the excess of domestic feeling, the intimacy and affection that is so central to the ideology of the domestic sphere. Indeed, this suggests a sense in which the sentimental and the uncanny entail one another, as necessary opposites. Just as the uncanny is the strange in the ordinary, the ordinary extended into the strange, the ordinary rendered other, so the sentimental is the ordinary brought closer, the other rendered homely, the excess of the homely.

These rooms can also be locations for the tragic and the decadent. One can recall Renée Vivien, a leading figure of the 'Sappho 1900' movement of turn-of-the-century Paris, dying alone, in her twenties, of anorexia, consumption and soft furnishings, in her luxurious apartment, surrounded by oriental drapes and tapestries, the ornate curtains permanently drawn to exclude the threatening, unwanted sunshine.[17] That there could indeed be a relation between decadence and the uncanny is suggested by the way decadence seems to encourage, or imply, the spectral. At the most overt level, decadence performs the modern alienation of nature, taking it to extremes: nature is rejected in favour of style, artifice, cultural excess. Yet this very extremism also incorporates a return to nature: nature now as sickness, the irreducible 'other' side to life, inseparable from it, even an indicator of a 'healthy' attitude to, and practice of, life itself. If life is inseparable from death, that death must be incorporated in it, lived in it. Decadence is an excess of both culture and nature; the modern lived as abjection and excess. Decadence haunts the modern, then, and this spectral presence comes out in two ways: the urge to transcend nature and natural limitations produces a mode of life of the person as a spiritual presence in culture, an ethereal transcendence; and the urge to explore the 'other side' of progress, the sense in which it represents a sickness of culture, or rather, has to be explored as a route to cultural health through sickness and death, now resulting in the person as the abjection of culture in the sick, enfeebled body. Either way, the decadent is already only half-alive – pale, shadowy, intense – and this spectral death-in-life is thereby presented as a condition of creativity.[18] If, as de Certeau tells us, 'Haunted places are the only places people can live in',[19] we can see that they are appropriate places to die in, too.

In these over-stuffed rooms, the objects that jostle jealously for space are never sufficiently accountable in terms of their function, even if they have one at all, yet their obsessive, insistent presence makes demands on people, reducing them to props, doll-like, simultaneously real yet mysterious, like everything else in the twilight. 'The things that are not needed begin slowly to appear as strange ... They simply sit there, like untouchable images of the divine in an imaginary cult of boredom.'[20] These objects conjure up memories, a past; their vestments, always slightly faded, and dated, remind us of those who came before; they embody dreams, delusions of presence now past. They possess aura, or transmit live memories of aura under the aegis of its decline. They remind us that aura in modernity is 'experienced primarily in its withdrawal or destruction. This is why the aura is always a matter of ghosts and specters.'[21] And one can see the closeness of the links between aura, the uncanny and the sentimental by recalling that aura is, for Benjamin, 'the unique phenomenon of a distance, however close it may be'.[22] Hence Cadava on 'auratic darkness', namely that 'what is nearest to us is the distance that keeps us from ourselves',[23] further implications of which will need to be explored later. We can see what Benjamin means by referring to 'the immense forces of "atmosphere" concealed in these [everyday] things'.[24] 'Atmosphere': a distinctive presence that materialises into presences, poised between the real and unreal in the liminal experience of twilight.

And inside these rooms, we encounter the miniature microcosm of the home itself: the doll's house. This period of the late nineteenth and early twentieth centuries was the great age of this condensed spectacle of domestic theatricality, small in extent but resonant with symbolic coding. Stewart reminds us that the doll's house reveals the house's articulation of a tension between inner and outer, exterior and interior: it is 'center within center, within within within'. It is a 'materialized secret', with the promise of an 'infinitely profound interiority'.[25] And, one might add, the promise that it might come alive; at night, perhaps, when its inhabitants surge forth, uncanny others of those who appear to use it – play with it – in the daytime. And the doll itself? A simulacrum of the living being, a supplement or substitute for life itself, generally on a scale with the child playing with it, the doll does not seem to threaten the child with its potential for seeming – or being – alive, as indeed Freud remarks. That may, after all, be part of the doll's fantasy identity for a child, part of the point of it; you can have a *relationship* with a doll. It is only later that the 'living doll' becomes potentially uncanny, *after* the child has internalised the key distinctions that set in place the modern ontology of the real: the distinctions between living/dead, organic/inorganic, natural/artificial. If the ghost is uncanny through raising issues of life as representation, the self as spectral, as living image, the doll attains this status through raising issues of life as reproduction, the body as inorganic, as mechanism.[26]

The doll can also be a powerful signifier, carrier of fundamental messages, of child and adult, self and other, and of gender, which can be mapped on to one another to reinforce this uncanny potential. In her modernist – yet simultaneously decadent – classic *Nightwood*, Djuna Barnes makes the doll a key player in the relation between Nora and Robin, and it also serves as a figural resource drawn on in other contexts. Above all, it signifies forbidden love, the 'third sex': here, the doll can resonate with a sense of the 'unnatural', a loaded term that can incorporate both ontological and moral assumptions, and that seems to apply to so many of the situations that can produce a sense of the uncanny. Nora says to her confidant, Dr O'Connor, that when a woman gives a doll to a woman 'it is the life they cannot have, it is their child, sacred and profane', to which he replies that 'The last doll, given to age, is the girl who should have been a boy, and the boy who should have been a girl', since 'The doll and the immature have something right about them, the doll, because it resembles, but does not contain life, and the third sex, because it contains life but resembles the doll'. And we learn of Frau Mann, highly 'unnatural', her costume stitched so tightly that she was 'as unsexed as a doll. The needle that had made one the property of the child made the other the property of no man'.[27] Some light is cast on this by Stewart's comment that 'the body of the child is a body erased of its sexuality – the seamless body of the doll',[28] which reminds us of the way the 'third sex' could be characterised both as 'illicitly sexed' and as 'sexless', because non-procreative, and, in *this* sense, child-like. Overall, then, for Barnes, explorer of the transgressive uncanny, 'Decadence inhabited the domestic; the apartment was a world in which moral and sexual codes were reversed',[29] a place in which luxury and soft furnishings cohabited easily with perversion. For her, home becomes 'the figure for universal loss, grief, and desire',[30] a place of familiarity where the secrets invariably raise the spectre of taboo and transgression, with their profound consequences for identity.

Uncanny intertextualities

It is hardly possible to avoid *The Sandman* when contemplating the uncanny, not only because of the central importance of the Hoffmann text to Freud, but because it has become widely read in its own right. Having recently read it myself, in its entirety, for the first time, I found my mind wandering off, thinking of parallels. I had already earmarked *Nightwood* as a possible text to use, as its perverse atavistic 'modernism' seemed to give it uncanny qualities, but now certain more specific parallels with the Hoffmann text struck me, notably a certain resemblance between the doll Olympia, with whom Nathanael is infatuated, and the somewhat doll-like Robin, Nora's beloved. Then, out of the blue, that final scene in Hitchcock's film *Vertigo* (1958) hit me, and its similarity to the end of *Sandman*. At the time, I experienced this as decidedly 'uncanny'. Finding such parallels and repetitions *myself*, thus experiencing the findings as *encounters*, as real experiences, marked them as uncanny – irrespective of whether the parallels are 'really' there (whatever that might mean). That is, the *experience* of them as *resemblances* – involving both subject and object, form and content – constituted these experiences of resemblance, this *fusion*, as uncanny. It is as though the experience threatens to entail its own impossibility by threatening the boundaries that mark the independence of the self as its necessary location. It is the fusion that challenges, that disturbs, precisely because it seems to lie astride these powerful, taken for granted distinctions – self/other, subject/object, same/different – that are central to the spatio-temporal coordinates of identity. Hence the sense in which a certain instability of experience itself is suggested – or precipitated – by the uncanny, as in Royle's characterisation of it as '*the continuing experience of an uncertainty*, or as a *decisive suspension of experience*', adding that, as *déjà vu*, it seems to involve 'the experience of experience *as* double', as 'a trembling which is the trembling of experience itself'.[31]

Barnes may have been familiar both with the original Hoffmann story, and the Freud paper in which it is analysed.[32] The figure in *Nightwood* to whom the aura of the uncanny clings most strongly is, as implied above, surely Robin. Indeed – reminding us of the original sense of 'aura' as a kind of physical emanation or envelope surrounding a person – Barnes has to run through the whole sensorium to describe its presence in Robin, 'the pretty lad who is a girl',[33] beloved by all, men and women, possessed by none, ever elusive, unattainable. Her body exudes a perfume of 'earth-flesh, fungi', her flesh is 'the texture of plant life'; around her head 'an effulgence of phosphorus glowing', as if her life lay in 'ungainly luminous deteriorations', as is appropriate for 'the born somnambule, who lives in two worlds'.[34] And these 'two worlds' shift and alter. If she is decaying plant life, yet human, she is also animal, 'a wild thing caught in a woman's skin', and she is also not nature at all, but culture, an artefact, 'gracious and yet fading, like an old statue in a garden'. Robin is ageless, yet as old as history, or nature itself; as their unwanted presence in modern culture, she has nowhere to go, a figure superficially attractive yet doom-laden, 'the infected carrier of the past'.[35] She resembles one of the objects in the museums, wonder cabinets and flea markets that she and the other characters are obsessed with, doomed to fragment and disintegrate as ageing memorials, rather than being subject to a natural death. She becomes an allegory of a modernity ill at ease with itself, eternally young even as it disintegrates within. And she carries an evasive promise of redemption: 'Crossing the boundaries between beast and human, between female and male, between night and day', claim Gilbert and Gubar, Robin thus 'enacts and sanctifies a myth of herself as an invert who recaptures the chaotic, chthonic energies that have been debased by culture'.[36]

For the Count, Felix Volkbein, who impetuously falls for her, as comprehensively as Nathanael does for Olympia, Robin does indeed have doll-like qualities. Felix found her eyes expressionless yet mysterious;

when he walked with her, she was 'so silent'; her movements were 'slightly headlong and sideways; slow, clumsy, and yet graceful'. She had a 'childish face ... her eyes fixed ... she opened her mouth but no words came'.[37] It is, indeed, all oddly reminiscent of Olympia. And she is accompanied by a warning: 'The woman who presents herself to the spectator as a "picture" forever arranged is, for the contemplative mind, the chiefest danger'; she may turn out to be 'beast turning human', and her every movement 'will reduce to an image of a forgotten experience'.[38] So here we have it: the woman who exists in the male gaze may be dangerous even in her passivity, her existence as fantasy precipitating the uncanny return of the unresolved mysteries of the past. The man of the obsessive gaze may thereby be prevented from seeing. It may be added that this affliction seems to be congenital in the Volkbein household. Felix's father had a home 'peopled with Roman fragments, white and disassociated', with 'blind bold sockets' as eyes. As for Felix, into one eye was set 'this monocle which shone, a round blind eye in the sun';[39] and his son will turn out to need heavy lenses, making his eyes bulge forward.

Where Felix seems visually impaired, Nora sees too much, but this excess does not give her a clear vision either. Her eyes were 'large, protruding and clear', but succeeded only in reconstructing what she looked at 'in her own unconscious terms'. She does not recognise her own role in constructing the Robin she relates to, and in the end the relationship is doomed. As O'Connor subsequently said to her, she had 'dressed the unknowable in the garments of the known'.[40] But for a while, Robin is alive to her, happy with her, her gaze more active. On her night time jaunts alone, Robin's eyes searched for 'the sculptured head that both she and Nora loved', a Greek head 'with shocking protruding eyeballs',[41] which reminded her of Nora's love, ultimately impossible in its excess. While Olympia seems to exist, as a person, only in Nathanael's gaze, Robin's identity is more nuanced, shifting with her relationships, never resolved. In a sense, the repetitions and fragmentations present in the Hoffmann text – Coppelius/Coppola/Spalanzani, Clara/Olympia – are here used to disintegrate notions of identity, including gender identity, by internalising them in each character, shifting the register of the uncanny more towards the 'nightwood' of everyday life.

And then, when the affair is over, there is, finally, Nora's dream. She stands at the top of a house, looking down, into the house, and sees Robin, in a company gathered below, in a scenario uncannily reminiscent of Nathanael looking down from the tower and seeing Coppelius in the crowd. First, though, he has looked through the spyglass, and seen Clara, the act that precipitates his final suicidal madness. Does he, at that moment, see Olympia in Clara? He is, after all, using the spyglass Coppola sold him, the spyglass through which Olympia came alive for him, as the object of his obsessive love. And, by comparison, we are told that when Nora looked down at Robin, she seems to recede: it was as if she and Robin 'were a pair of opera glasses turned to the wrong end, diminishing in their painful love'. Then, at the end of the dream, going towards the statue in her garden, she catches sight of Robin and the 'other woman', the Coppelius/Clara equivalent, so that her eyes 'dropped from their orbit by the falling of her body',[42] a 'fall' not into the literal death that met Nathanael, but into the knowledge of the death of her relationship, and the blindness of mourning a love she can never understand, and never terminate.

That both stories also contain a confused mesh of relationships, in which family, love and gender identities somehow fragment, fade, reappear, superimpose themselves, reduplicate, is also suggested in this dream. The location at the top of the house is 'Grandmother's room', and Nora hears herself saying 'Come up, this is grandmother's room', yet knowing this was impossible to do, as the room was 'taboo'. So we encounter grandmother, who is and isn't there (the room was 'the absolute opposite of any known room her grandmother had ever moved or lived in', but 'saturated' with the 'lost presence of her grandmother, who seemed in the continual process of leaving it'); Nora, who is and isn't her own grandmother – a grandmother who was also 'for some unaccountable reason, dressed as a man' – and who now summons Robin, who is and isn't her grandchild,[43] to engage in what would and wouldn't be incestuous acts of love. And here, we must indeed remember that 'Robin is incest too, that is one of her powers'.[44] A full gamut of possibilities is opened up here: that the boy-girl Robin, as Nora's lover, might be her child, that Nora in turn might be *her* child or wife, always there when Robin, father-husband, comes in at night; that Robin might be a projection of herself.[45] And over all these, contributing to making the superimpositions uncanny, hangs the shadow of the past, the 'lost presence'. Thus the oracular Dr O'Connor can pronounce that 'In the acceptance of depravity the sense of the past is most fully captured. What is a ruin but Time easing itself of endurance? Corruption is the Age of Time. It is the body and the blood of ecstasy, religion and love.'[46] And hence *Nightwood* indeed emerges as a master work of the transgressive uncanny; and Marcus can conclude, of Barnes, that 'her articulation of the female uncanny and its relation to writing in a complex of signs around images of dolls and eyeless statues participates in female modernism's larger interrogation of gender and the writing self under the male gaze'.[47]

And in *The Sandman*, too, we have the same frenetic oscillation of possible and tabooed identity positions. For the moment, maintaining a certain focus on Olympia, one can just observe that Freud must, of course, be partly right in presenting her as a projection of Nathanael's fantasy, though this could also be partly true of Clara. Her coldly rational side marks her as a possibly prohibited love object: she is, after all, given her place in the same domestic unit as Nathanael, positioned structurally as his sister. Juxtaposed, Olympia and Clara seem like two broken halves of a femininity that never comes together, just as, for Felix, Robin seems to be the 'converging halves of a broken fate';[48] superimposed, though, a degree of assimilation is apparent. After all, the coldness of Olympia – before she is warmed into life by Nathanael – is several times remarked on, and 'cold' is used just as repetitiously of Clara. But this reminds us of other 'broken femininities', doublings; this time, in *Vertigo*.

The slightly uncanny, dream-like quality of the film overall is particularly brought out when Madeleine is on the screen. And there is surely something doll-like about Madeleine. She, too, barely speaks; one of the most striking features of the film is how little she speaks, given the length of time she is on screen. And it turns out that her speech, her whole identity, are constructs: she is a puppet, reading Elster's script, there to fool Scottie and serve as a cover for Elster's murder of his wife; but she also becomes Scottie's obsessive fantasy, just as surely as Olympia does for Nathanael. The brief point at which she seems to depart a little from the script, revealing something of herself, turns out to be the moment that precipitates her 'death', the apparent fall from the tower. And this returns later: for Judy, supposedly the 'real' figure underlying the phantom Madeleine, is herself made doll-like by Scottie, desperate to make her into as close an approximation to the 'real' Madeleine of his fantasy as he can.

If we bring in Midge – the homely 'friend' who would seem, like Clara, to be more like a sister than a love object – we can perceive two successive sets of contrasted pairings here: Midge/Madeleine and Judy/Madeleine, with Midge leaving the film as Judy enters. These two sets of contrasts seem to map onto Clara/Olympia reasonably well. And we could also map the underlying dichotomy as that of reality/fantasy. This is revealed in the outcome, whereby fantasy wins out, and 'destroys' – literally or metaphorically – the 'real' person or pole of each dichotomy. Madeleine destroys Judy both through Scottie's inability to accept the 'real' Judy, with her history (just as Nathanael is unable to accept Clara), and, more speculatively, through the *way* the finale in the tower develops. This episode – with Judy falling to her death, this time for real – could reveal Judy reverting to her Madeleine identity, under the continued psychological pressure from Scottie, or in the sudden fear precipitated by hearing the footsteps of the nun, who might, after all, have been the returning Elster; hence the panic reaction that kills her.[49] If we recall the 'grey bushes' spied from the tower by Clara, the bushes that recall the bushy eyebrows of Coppelius, heralding his possible return – the bushes that lead Nathanael to get out his spyglass and look at her one last time – then the nun/bushes and Elster/Coppelius symmetries are striking indeed.

Strange powers

'Do you believe that someone dead, someone out of the past, can take possession of a living being?' This question clearly has a resonance for Scottie and Madeleine/Judy; but, asked early in the film, it ostensibly refers to the alleged obsession of Elster's wife with the figure of her great-grandmother, Carlotta. It is actually Carlotta's necklace that seems most important here. It plays something of the same role in enforcing the return of the past as a haunting presence in the present as does Coppola's spyglass in the Hoffmann text. It is Judy's wearing of the necklace – 'careless', yet deeply motivated in the structure of the film – that enables Scottie to 'see' Judy-as-Madeleine, through his instant recall of the image of Carlotta's necklace in the portrait, just as the use of the spyglass by Nathanael always transforms his vision, enabling him to 'see' Olympia, and, at the end, Clara-as-Olympia. These objects – Carlotta's necklace, Coppola's spyglass, Nora's opera glasses – all raise questions about vision and the image, about power and powers, that can certainly be answered within the modern world view, but also implicitly question it, suggest certain unresolvable, underlying tensions that can be a powerful carrier of the uncanny.

Going back to the earliest story, we can recall that Coppola is described as a 'barometer-seller', an innocuous enough description. But Castle points out that barometers and thermometers seem to have led an active cultural life in the eighteenth and early nineteenth centuries. They were thought to register not just physical, but also psychological states. Placed in proximity to a woman's body, her emotional state could be measured, as if the heightened state of the thermometer reading would testify to the sexual arousal of the woman. And, as wits of the time noted, it was by no means impossible that the actual use of such equipment could help precipitate what it ostensibly measured. A spyglass, in turn, would not necessarily be innocent of such a potential to bring about what it ostensibly only recorded, especially given the state of the person using it. And in this specific case, 'Coppola's weatherglasses may be taken indeed as a metonymic sign of those wild mood-swings and disturbing sensitivities he provokes in his victim'.[50] One could say that one of the most intriguing and problematical aspects of the modern cultural imaginary – a strict distinction between a subjective, psychological realm of affects, thoughts and images, and a physical realm of causal determinism – is by no means decisively established at this period.

In effect, this psychological realm, this theatre of affects and images, is what we think of as 'mind', how we picture it; but, in some tension with this, its function is to provide the direction, the guarantee almost, of individual self-identity. It provides the grounding of the idea of the self as self-creating, undetermined, not a mechanism that runs automatically or at the behest of some external force or programming power. This is an aspect of the project of modernity, the idea that mastery of the world requires mastery over the self, by the self, a self that must, in this sense, be logically separate from the world, irreducible to its laws. Hence 'the Enlightenment belief in the essential coherence of the self as will',[51] a will that has to be one's own. But how can one know this to be the case, how can one be sure? After all, the mythical postulate of the unique will has to coexist with our acceptance of science, which is cast in the language of causal mechanisms, without residue. The ultimate recalcitrance of will to phenomenological understanding – my inability to know it as mine – appears to entail the possibility that neither I nor the other may necessarily be what we appear to be; that what appears to be a human being may turn out to be an automaton. When enough happens to bring this theoretical possibility closer to realisation, the uncanny gleams through.

This surging of the uncanny happens in both the story and the film. Olympia seems, right from the start, both doll-like and automaton-like, alternative versions of the mechanical simulation of life. And if it is the Spalanzani-Coppola pair that constructed Olympia – Spalanzani providing the basic mechanism, Coppola adding the eyes – then just as surely Elster and Scottie make Madeleine, Scottie adding the power of the gaze without which Elster's deception would not work. Scottie is thus both a participant in creating Madeleine and also the victim of Elster's plot, through his own obsession – which is where Scottie comes to play the Nathanael role. Here again the issue of free will and determinism is raised: for both Nathanael and Scottie, through their obsessions, become 'taken over', mechanical automata in the grip of a power they cannot control. They become entirely suitable subjects for the objects of their fantasy.

In the case of Nathanael, this can all be taken further. Early in the story, Coppelius dislocates and replaces the child Nathanael's limbs. In thus implying that Nathanael himself – and each of us? – could be an automaton, Hoffmann is simultaneously genuflecting to the power of the scientific world view and yet also pointing to its subversive implications for our notions of free will. The fear that this spectre of determinism could indeed reveal itself anywhere is brought out light-heartedly in another episode in the story. Following the unmasking of Olympia as an automaton, we are informed that partners felt impelled to test the ontological status of their lovers: might one be in love with a wooden doll? One's beloved should preferably say something unpredictably meaningful from time to time ... Quite an insightful parody of the mix of eccentricity and transgression to which the modern individual is pushed in order to manifest its necessary autonomy, as a self in charge of its destiny.

In the wider context, this is reminiscent of Marx's analysis of the fetishism of commodities, and his claim that commodities become 'autonomous figures endowed with a life of their own'.[52] Derrida's lively account[53] brings out the animism/mechanism nexus here, whereby, in effect, we find a world peopled with Olympia figures: we can become thing-like, just as forces can work on us *through* things, which 'figure' these forces; and, in turn, the constructions of novelists and film-makers can reconfigure them, all the more dramatically. And when Gordon refers to 'the fundamentally animistic mode' by which 'worldly power' makes itself felt in our lives,[54] we return to one of Freud's two key perspectives on the uncanny – but this time, the repetitive, atavistic quality is produced and reproduced within the modern itself: Freud read in the light of Marx, the Surrealists, or Benjamin ...

But where there is determinism, there can also be manipulation: the scientific drive to understand is also a drive to control. Throughout the story, one has the sense that Nathanael is being manipulated, at the mercy of forces, whether from outside or from his unconscious, forces he can neither understand nor control, and which work both against him and through him. But we, as readers, may also have this feeling – the author, Hoffmann, as arch-manipulator, we as puppets, not so different from poor Nathanael. The storyteller is also the ironic manipulator of the text, and as much of the reader as of the characters in the narrative. This is even more obviously true of *Vertigo*, which is after all a product of the master manipulator himself: Hitchcock is known to have enjoyed plotting the involvement of his audience; his surveillance incorporates the viewer, not just the characters.[55] One of the uncanny moments in this film brings this out: Madeleine's arrival at the McKittrick Hotel, followed later by Scottie, who is informed by the receptionist that she has not been there, that her key has not been taken that day, and that her room is undisturbed ... This is set up in such a way that one could construct a rational explanation, but it retains that uncanny feel, and is clearly designed specifically to this end. Again, the Elster phone call, during the brief conversation in Scottie's apartment after the 'attempted drowning', conveys the sense that both Madeleine and Scottie are puppets, dancing to Elster's tune. There is also a resonance here with *Nightwood*, where part of the uncanny feel comes from the way the words seem to 'pass through' the characters, rather than being meaningfully 'spoken' by them. So we encounter a dialectic of conspiracy/deception and mechanistic determinism, conveying the sense that scientific demystification of the world, the drive to understanding, is always potentially an exercise in re-mystification.

In their potential for an 'uncanny effect', mechanism and the temporal structure of experience can work together, through the idea of the hold of the past, the insistence of the past in the present. Barr refers to 'the film's intense and rather magical quality of rootedness: in the city and its environs, in its historical past and in the uncanny dimensions waiting to be explored within and around it', adding, more generally, that 'The more anchored they are in the real, the more convincingly the interior and exterior environs can add up to comprise an alternate world of subjectivity and dream'. He also observes that 'there is no *division* between worlds, but rather a hesitation':[56] a hesitation within which the whole world of the uncanny, the world *as* uncanny, resides. We could refer here to 'uncanny realism': the world has to be fundamentally *ordinary* before being invested with an uncanny aura; or, the uncanny works *through* the ordinariness of the world, even produced *by* it, as though a de-sacralised, disenchanted world becomes uncanny in its very essence. And many of the 'tricks' associated with a sense of the uncanny, from the original phantasmagoria magic show, through early film and beyond, convey the sense of an ordinary world rendered extraordinary through perfectly ordinary mechanisms that we can manipulate but can never understand sufficiently to ensure closure, hence condemning us to an uncanny awareness of the issue of free will and determinism through our very immersion in such a world, a world where experience always exceeds our reflexive grasp, where 'presence' always implies the possibility of the continuing hold of a spectral past.

Production, reproduction, representation

Mastery is also creativity: the god-like ability to realise will is a modern way of mapping the mysteries of creativity and origin, production and reproduction. Nathanael's father, Coppelius, Spalanzani, Elster – but also Hoffmann, Hitchcock – are engaging in male procreation. The most dramatic instance is clearly at the beginning of the tale, in the dramatic scene where the frightful Coppelius, and Nathanael's father, with the 'hideous, repulsive mask of a fiend',[57] are working together at the furnace into which the domestic hearth has been transformed, endeavouring to produce humans, real or simulated. Here we see the scenario of modern creativity, as imaged in the early nineteenth century in terms of fire, smoke, smelting, foundries – the 'palaeotechnic' vision of the First Industrial Revolution[58] – brought into the heart of the 'female sphere' of the home, where it is most alien: the strange in the familiar, indeed. And the exile of women resonates at several levels, here and elsewhere; notoriously, the Olympia creation scenario again involves two male parents, Spalanzani and Coppola. And while this may be fundamentally patriarchal, it also superimposes the modern myth of the self-created self, and the paradoxes that necessarily flow from this. After all, this initial episode could be seen as Nathanael's birth scenario, and an implicit denial of parentage. In successfully *not* losing his eyes, and managing to run from the room, Nathanael becomes self-created, born in trauma, a trauma that will shape his future through unresolved avoidances and repetitions of his origin, simultaneously horrific and impossible. There is a parallel here with the film: Scottie, hanging from the building in the very first shot, apparently about to plunge to his death, has as traumatic a 'birth' as one could envisage; and that it *is* a birth is made clear in that we are carefully informed of his resulting lack of a job, and of any apparent family. The former Scottie is no more; but the new one, it turns out, will be just as traumatised as Nathanael, just as unable to find successful resolution.[59] Both episodes code birth as rebirth, the emancipation of the self into culture from nature, with all that entails (particularly, of course, the devaluing of the female role in procreation).

Birth and rebirth, creator and created, representation and the represented: all reveal issues around legitimacy and the twin senses of 'reproduction', as reproducing/representing the real, and as procreation. How closely should the result resemble the source? Should the 'reproduction' – in either sense – be indistinguishable from the 'original'? It seems fair to say that when the two move 'sufficiently' close – and clearly the precise point cannot be specified in advance, if at all – then this produces a sense of the uncanny. In effect, this excessive proximity subverts the necessary spatio-temporal distance between the separate entities; it questions, threatens their separate identities through an excess of presence, disturbing the boundaries. And it is not just individual entities, but categories that can be at stake here, notably the distinction between organic and inorganic, real and artificial. 'Legitimate' representation and reproduction must respect the necessary distance, the necessary boundaries. Hence, again, we recall the reaction of the citizens to Olympia's unmasking, propelling themselves into individuality and therefore authenticity, each asserting a distinctive 'signature'. Huet indeed brings out the parallels with art by suggesting that 'legitimate' representation, involving a proper lineage, might be taken to involve a degree of imperfection, and an artist's signature, since perfection would abolish the space between model and image. A representation that does not offer itself as such, that takes the place of the model or the origin, is 'monstrous or fantastical'.[60] Hence Olympia, and the portrait in the Poe story.

But a further twist is added, if we take the portrait of Carlotta in the film, with the necklace, which are together supposed to help validate Madeleine's story, as the wife of Elster. For it turns out, at the end, that although 'great-grandmother' Carlotta did have a child, this child died without offspring. Neither portrait nor necklace give any real link to the past, neither validates a line of descent.[61] (And, once again, we find the woman's procreative role eliminated in favour of the cultural myth of autogenesis.) We also saw that Nora's contradictory dream of her own grandmother signalled its own unreliability. These identities are never really knowable, these guarantees are never worth much, as the presences reveal their absence in their very assertions of presence. Identities, guarantees: these exist to produce something that, if it existed, would be the opposite they seek desperately to avoid, the representation that replaced the reality through its very identity with it.

Identities, boundaries: that the subversion of these is connected to a sense of the uncanny can be further illustrated by a return to the role of eyes in the Hoffmann text. Subsuming both the flaming eyes of Coppola's spectacles and the ones thrown at Nathanael by Spalanzani, and the spyglass Nathanael actually buys from Coppola, under the term 'optical supplements' or 'detached eyes', we could say, following Møller, that these constitute a third term, between 'eyes' and 'no eyes': they are neither, or both. 'They are related to insight as well as blindness, to life as well as to death'; they reveal 'the desire to create and to animate, both figuratively and literally speaking, and the desire for knowledge and insight'. And it is a desire for mastery, transgressive in involving the modern – and male – quest for power beyond limits, beyond boundaries. The optical supplement is the eye of the other, the transformative vision that risks madness and death: if Nathanael refuses it, out of terror, Clara denies its very existence.[62] And for the reader, this is a text that conveys contradictory imperatives too. We are encouraged into the narrative, invited to use the spyglass, experience the *frisson* of the uncanny; but we are also invited to stand back, take our distance; most dramatically, by the 'professor of poetry and eloquence':

'The whole thing is an allegory – an extended metaphor!'

This apparently reflexive comment is inserted innocently enough into the text – it is easy to pass by without really noticing – but is surely worth pondering. Firstly, though, we can see the professor's comment as being of a piece with the author's style, which at times inserts a vein of irony into the text. Irony, in this respect, could be counterposed to the uncanny: it defies experience in the interest of reflexive distance, simultaneously lamenting the inability of language to capture the plenitude of experience while celebrating this very inability, this distance, as a form of superiority. A condition of such an ironic reading is to separate out levels of the text: the ironic distancing of language from experience is mapped onto an ability to read this *in* the text, which in turn leads us to recognise that this is an ability that Nathanael does not seem to possess, an important key to his fate. Bresnick suggests that 'To recognize irony, then, means to be able to perform the act of critical negation that would separate the literal from the figurative; yet it is precisely this negation that proves impossible for Nathanael', who is 'invariably swayed by the positivity of his fantasy'.[63] Yet there may be more to this than an inability to master irony.

So, if we now follow the professor's advice, and read allegorically, can we see Nathanael as the tragic Romantic hero? In a sense, after all, this hero has to refuse these commonplace distinctions (such as literal/figurative) in the intensity of his insight; his 'tragedy' is that he must either betray this insight, in the act of writing or painting – to communicate it is to corrupt it – or be trapped by it, unable to function in everyday life, where these distinctions are fundamental. He seeks obsessively to create unity out of these separate spheres, integrate the distinctions into an unattainable whole, the irrecuperable sublime of the Romantic aesthetic quest. He knows his will is not his own, that the 'autonomy of the will' is a chimera; he does not fall for *that* hoary Enlightenment myth. To use Nathanael's own words, he feels himself a 'plaything for the cruelty of dark forces'.[64]

Nathanael's poem seems crucial here. It is a poem centred on a vision of an attempt by Coppelius to destroy the love between him and Clara. In his earlier writing, Nathanael is presented as lacking in talent; but this is different. On reading the finished work aloud to himself, he is gripped by terror, and shrieks: 'Whose hideous voice is this?' He does not recognise it as Coppelius; we, as readers, are bound to see it as having some relation to the latter, whether as 'return of the repressed', as alienated other, or as the Romantic-demonic voice of creativity. What is clear is that he does not recognise it as in any sense *his*. So his tragedy is perhaps that he is not *sufficiently* the Romantic hero: he cannot perform the transition from the pre-modern to the modern that is implicit in the very possibility of Romanticism and the status, powers and limits of the modern imagination. He unwittingly embodies an important aspect of the uncanny itself, reminding himself, and us, of a world of portents, signs and powers that might once have been meaningfully reinforced as part of the cultural imaginary but has now become an atavistic return of something uncomprehended, strange. He takes the 'dark forces' as straightforwardly literal, rather than metaphorical, and remains trapped in this polarity that he cannot 'master'. It is precisely the Romantic notion of the transfiguring power of the imagination, mediating the absolute terms of that opposition, that is not available to him. If Coppelius could be taken to represent the terrible gift of creativity – beyond law, morality, even culture itself – then Nathanael could be said to disavow or betray the gift, through fear and horror.

If Nathanael is doomed to carry the torch of nascent Romanticism, Clara is clearly his opposite: she allegorises the project of Enlightenment, even in her name.[65] She articulates, very cogently, what is in effect the 'official' modern view of these matters, together with the practical emphasis on how to deal with the problem of false or archaic beliefs. Her view is indeed very close to that of Freud himself, whose psychoanalysis is essentially a more elaborate framework built on these foundations.

Clara argues that if there is indeed a 'dark power' that 'places a thread within us', then 'it must take the same form as we do, it must become our very self'; only then can we come to believe in it. If we can recognise these 'alien and malevolent influences for what they are' and be resolute, then 'the uncanny power must surely perish in a vain struggle to assume the form which is our own reflection'.[66] While rather complex in form, this argument has the ring of everyday plausibility, of common sense; but it is worth pausing to note just how strange and tension-laden the argument actually is. Clara is purporting to argue *against* Nathanael's belief in 'dark powers', yet she seems to agree with him in giving them at least a twilight reality. This power doesn't exist; yet it 'places a thread within us', it 'struggles' to assume our form, and we can destroy it. It has to be in some sense *there*, so that we can vanquish it, yet it is never really there at all. We must destroy it before it really exists; once it *does* exist, it does so as 'our very self', so again, either it does not really exist, or else our 'self', in being identified with it, is threatened by the same state of non-existence, or of existence as what we could call 'alienated other', no longer *our* self at all. And this acute tension speaks to the very tension in the Enlightenment approach to the ontological status of self, other, and those problematical presences that threaten the purity and clarity of the everyday disenchanted modern world view: dreams, visions, fantasies, hallucinations, ghosts. They all 'exist', as contingent realities of consciousness from time to time, just as they cannot 'really' exist, beyond these forms of consciousness themselves. We are in the world of phantasmagoria and the other innovations of visual technology around the time Hoffmann was writing: visual phenomena whose appearance as 'real' could be conceded, but only on condition that they could be 'explained' by being 'explained away', rendered unreal, 'mere' projections of mind, like the images projected by the magic lanterns in the phantasmagoria magic shows.[67]

Clara herself, in her own developing argument, emphasises the way such projections can be superimposed on 'the other': if we surrender to the dark psychic power, it draws 'alien figures' from the outside world into our 'inner selves', so we ourselves give life to the 'spirit which our strange delusion persuades us is speaking from such figures'. So the other becomes, in effect, the 'phantom of our own self'; such power as Coppelius/Coppola may have is a function of this phantasmatic projection: 'his power consists only in your belief'.[68] Again, the self is conjured up, only to disappear into the other; it is difficult to see what residue can be left, to what subject such 'beliefs' can be attributed. But if we do accept this oscillation, whereby power returns to the self as 'belief' in order to deny power to the other, then this power of belief must be extraordinary indeed, if it can produce such phantoms with malevolent power to harm or even destroy the self. Is this so different from Nathanael's attribution of influence to 'dark forces' from *outside* the self? In swinging between outside and inside – or *from* outside *to* inside, as is required by the modern view of the self – the ontological structure remains (uncannily) intact, continuous. Nor, as we have seen, is it so easy to ensure that the transition from 'external' to 'internal' is so straightforward: the boundary is unstable, and the direction is always in principle reversible. Indeed, as we have seen, even on Clara's own argument there are grounds for thinking that the location of the 'dark power' is necessarily *indeterminate* between these possibilities.

As for the Enlightenment in practice, it has to be remarked that occasions when Nathanael actually follows Clara's advice, or takes into account how she would look at the situation, invariably seem to presage disaster. For example, only when she reminds Nathanael of Coppelius's existence, by bragging about how they have driven him off, does he remember his poem; and, towards the end, it is she who suggests going up the tower (to get a good view, see the town in all its clarity before leaving – a typical Enlightenment-panoptic conceit), spots the bushes, and thus precipitates the final disaster. The down to earth, literal-minded Clara is resolute in driving away any hint of the figural or phantasmagorical: thus she is always trying to separate the phantom Coppelius from the 'real' Coppola, and reduce him to his appropriate state of unreality altogether. But Nathanael cannot resolve this either: to accept the figural and the phantasmatic as real, to grant the reality of spectral presences *simpliciter*, is again to miss the point, and remains just as one-dimensional. Both Clara and Nathanael are slaves to the literal, in their contrasting ways: for Nathanael, the 'dark power' is literally there; for Clara, it is purely imaginary, not-there. At best, it can be mere misleading metaphor. Neither shows any adequate grasp of the 'real' possibilities (and limitations) of the figural. Clara consistently applies rationalist criteria in all situations, and always seeks the explanation that explains away. She pursues *closure*, the dream of total presence, total transparency, just as obsessively as Scottie in the second half of *Vertigo*. Determined to banish Coppelius and Olympia through rigorous, reductionist logic, she ensures their return. This will to absolute understanding and absolute control suggests a model of the Enlightenment as death drive; perhaps it is appropriate that, at the end of his dream-poem, when Nathanael manages to gaze at Clara, 'what looks at him from Clara's kindly eyes is death'.[69]

Fantasy, one might say, should not overcome or displace the 'real', but reminds us that the latter can only be grasped in transfigured form. One might say that reality lies in the gap between the real and the unreal, or the superimposition of the one on the other that enables us to appropriate it through constituting it through the imagination of the figural: and it is from this gap, or out of this superimposition, that the uncanny emerges, the unresolvable in the modern, the presence of presence in its very displacement.

The self, the image, the darkroom

These issues raised by the contrasting perspectives of Clara and Nathanael can seem like a re-run of debates on 'spectral evidence' that had occurred a little over a century before, during the Salem witch trials of 1692. These debates focused on the 'evidence' that the shapes, the forms, of the accused had actually appeared to the bewitched, the victims of the witchcraft attacks. Pudaloff presents this as 'the Lockean moment, when argument and interest shift from the powers of supernatural beings to the role of human senses in gaining knowledge and their reliability in evaluating it'. Both advocates and sceptics of the claims around 'spectral evidence' agreed that one should 'trust the senses and the self as the bases of all knowledge'.[70] In effect, the demise of witchcraft beliefs and trials involved the gradual 'explaining away' of the sensory evidence by relocating it decisively on the side of the subject, as a matter of fantasy, dream, or delusion – though, as we have seen, the 'decisiveness' turns out to be not so simple after all. So the challenge for the Enlightenment in this area became, as Castle suggests, 'how to explain away the supernatural without "inventing the uncanny" in its place'[71] – a challenge it never really succeeded in meeting.

Let us now take the crisis of belief and representation. Both the category of belief, and the nature of the image as a product of imagination, have in common a difficulty in conveying negation, though the nature of the problem differs. 'Surmounted' beliefs, such as those in spirits, witchcraft, etc., pose the problem that even the assertion of disbelief seems to covertly self-refute: 'not believing' seems to posit the object of disbelief even in denying its existence. And when something happens that seems to 'confirm' the old belief, this counts as uncanny. Again, as mentioned earlier, in connection with presence and absence, 'imagined entities' have an obscure status, neither properly existing nor not-existing; and the uncanny is the mode of existence of the imagined 'unreal' or absent. And these can be linked together: not believing in what we see is still seeing. It is still an experience. The uncanny is the presence of the absent and the 'not real'; the implicit presence of disavowed, transgressive forms and locations of personal experience. We see here that any culture that insists on a strict categorial distinction between 'real' and 'unreal' as basic to its ontology will have problems. After all, 'unreal' is at least as paradoxical as 'undead', since it pretends to the status of absolute negation but actually can only function as mediator, hinting that the unreal cannot be *wholly* so, for it could not be known or labelled as such, without becoming at least 'slightly' real, which contradicts its point. Nor can the 'real' be insulated here; if there are problems with the 'unreal', there must be with the 'real', too. One could, for example, say that the real defies its own adequate representation; its representation is always inadequate, poised between *adding* to the real, and the nothingness, the paradoxical 'unreality', of mere representation. As we have seen, as representation moves closer to the real, either it, or the real, becomes uncanny, a spectral doubling. And to this 'other', uncanny side of the world, corresponds the allegorical. The world as allegory is the world doubled, with overt surface and hidden depth of meaning, but the modern world is no longer straightforwardly legible because these are no longer so securely fixed together, hence no longer existing save in fragments. And the 'doubling' of allegory reinforces the uncanny, as a sense of an absent presence: an occult materiality present in the world, potentially able to spread anywhere.[72]

Recalling that list of 'problematical presences' – dreams, visions, fantasies, hallucinations and ghosts – it is clear that what they have in common, whatever their differences, is an involvement with the image. The demise of 'spectral evidence' in effect gives enhanced scope for the imagination, resulting in the production of the mind as a phantasmagoria, an inner theatre of the imagination, populated with images that could come to have a powerful reality of their own. Castle elaborates the consequences of this increasing emphasis, during the eighteenth century, on the internalisation of the self as a theatrical space, with boundaries, an 'inside' to the 'outside' of the body and its communication with the rest of the world through the senses. Rationalism thereby produced 'a new human experience of strangeness, anxiety, bafflement, and intellectual impasse', because the 'demystifying project' was seriously compromised from the start: the rationalists 'did not so much negate the traditional spirit world as displace it into the realm of psychology'.[73] If ghosts were thoughts, thoughts in turn became images: ghostly, haunting. Ferriar, propounding his theory of hallucination in 1813, claimed that normal thought itself has a spectral side: memory is a process of 'spectral representation', since 'From recalling images by an art of memory the transition is direct to beholding spectral objects, which have been floating in the imagination'.[74] And as a vivid illustration of the continuities with the time of Salem, we can recall the intriguing episode at a phantasmagoria show when a man strikes in fear at a phantom with his stick – just as, a century earlier, 'there were several instances of striking at spectres'.[75] This, then, is the context – of a lively imagination of the spectral, in both popular culture and Romanticism, and a counteracting, sceptical Enlightenment attitude – in which Nathanael's misadventures take place.

This period – the late eighteenth and early nineteenth centuries – is also one that Batchen has identified as manifesting an endemic 'desire to photograph', a precondition for the subsequent invention of photography itself. This desire can be characterised as a desire for the mechanical transcription of nature, but not cast exclusively, or even primarily, in the language of representation as domination. Rather, the conception seems more consistent with Romanticism, a conception in which representation and reproduction seem totally entwined: the representation *of* nature is simultaneously reproduction *by* nature. The inventors of photography present the photographic process as a mode of representation that is 'simultaneously active and passive, that draws nature while allowing her to draw herself, that both reflects and constitutes its object, that undoes the distinction between copy and original, that partakes equally of the realms of nature and culture'; a mode of representation that had become implicit and frequently explicit in late eighteenth century views of the relation between the viewer, vision and landscape. The viewer is inherently caught up in this process whereby 'viewing' is also 'reproducing', so the viewer becomes 'a being who is for the first time both the subject and the object of representation'. With authors like Coleridge, 'mind came to be regarded as something constitutive of the self rather than simply reflective of the outside world',[76] with the imagination playing a central role in this shift of emphasis, so momentous in its consequences.

In effect, what we encounter here is an essential continuity, or homology, between two processes, along with the models we construct to understand them: the production and reproduction of nature through the photograph, and the production and reproduction of the self through the image. Cadava suggests a model of the body as space, with 'an interiority devoted to the production of images', such that 'the body is a kind of darkroom',[77] basing this on hints in Benjamin, such as the latter's brief deployment of the concept of 'image-space' in his paper on Surrealism.[78] This spatialisation of the image involves a fixing, a kind of trapping of the image *in* time that simultaneously telescopes time into the image. The photo attempts to 'fix' the present moment, but inevitably embodies the paradox of the difference of that very presence.

Something of this is captured in the term itself, the linkage of light and writing in 'photography': the instantaneous quality of light impossibly transcribed in the textual temporality of inscription. Thus Batchen refers to photographic desire as entailing 'the desire for an impossible conjunction of transience and fixity'. And this of course implicates the viewer, so that 'The present during which we look at the photographic image is but a staging point, a hallucinatory hovering that imbricates both past and future'.[79]

What we 'fix' in the image is necessarily both a construction and a projection. If we cannot simply 'reflect' nature outside, as we are intimately involved in the production whereby it is fixed as image, no more can we reflect nature inside, the self and its experiences. Attempts to grasp 'our self' reflexively are broken-backed; we can only grasp it, be conscious of it, by distancing from it. We thereby subtly reconfigure it, as image, in the very act whereby we grasp it through doubling it, in alienation from it. It is like taking a photo; it is part of the sense in which modern culture is 'photographic'. And this 'doubling' is related to the constitution of identity in this interior darkroom, wherein reflexive experience mediates presence into presences, into doubles and other figures. In this process of self-constitution and self-projection, the self as problematically reflexive, seeking self-knowledge, and the self as charismatic creator, come together in their inevitable separation. And one symptom of this is a heightened possibility that these recalcitrant experiences of separation and doubling will be coded as 'unconscious'; that the unconscious, indeed, is a category that presupposes this revolution in consciousness.

Castle writes that 'For as long as the external world is populated by spirits ... the mind remains unconscious of itself, focused elsewhere, and unable to assert either its autonomy or its creative claims on the world'. From having been unconscious of itself, it becomes conscious of its unconscious, as it were, even as it engages with its own disturbingly paradoxical spirit-producing powers, which make it capable of going beyond its own 'appropriate' limits, into madness itself, in 'the compulsive image-making of the reverie-prone individual' that results in 'the unleashing of spectres'.[80] One might say that going from being 'unconscious' of the mind's workings to attempting a reflexive understanding of them merely and necessarily displaces the darkness, relocates an unconscious 'inside', and constitutes mind as a perpetual struggle to grasp and discipline the recalcitrant images and fantasies that are themselves the results, the projections, of its own activities. The doubling of the self as image, and its inscrutability as 'unconscious', go hand in hand, while our ability to construct the 'master narrative' of coherent selfhood out of the play of unruly images and fantasies is forever inadequate, just as the imperative to make the attempt, in the name of the 'rational self', is constantly there. Thus, the unconscious is the uncanny in the self, reflecting its obscurity to itself, its reflexive inability to coincide with itself, even perhaps the self as it questions its own location, and that of its spectral products.

The spectre, the phantasm, can thus be seen to have two coinciding sources in this ontology of the modern experience. Both mind and camera operate as mechanisms for the production of the image, as a surrogate for presence, the means whereby presence is reconfigured into presences. Firstly, in the context of mind, the double, as image of the embodied self, seems to 'lift off' from the surface of the world, take on its own reality, known in its difference by its appearance in places it should not be, or would not be expected (yet related to its place and time of origin ...). In the second case, it is as though the image floats free of the technological apparatus of its production, in photography and film. The result is the same: the phantasm can become the uncanny double of the image, even to the point of becoming visually identical with it. Spirits and spirit photos emerge as manifestly products of the same universe. The prevalence of phrases such as 'modern necromancy' in early discussions of the photo[81] seems hardly surprising, and Gunning has explored the conjunction of the scientific and the uncanny in the world of spirit photography, presenting 'a uniquely modern conception of the spirit world as caught up in the endless play of image making and reproduction'.[82]

Shadowing the modern

In trying to know itself *as* itself, the self engages in this uncanny game of doubling and haunting, reflexively unable to capture the experience of selfhood, experience as such, in its immediacy and plenitude: there is always a remainder, a residue, a shadow, represented, in displaced form, through the vagaries of 'representation' itself. This in turn runs parallel to the impossibility of project as realisation, the Enlightenment project of the modern, whether as a social dynamic or refracted through the projects of our lives: it must always be haunted by its own darkness. These two, together, constitute the uncanny structure of the modern, with its implications for our inability to theorise it adequately as experience. In elaborating both these dimensions, as we move towards a conclusion, we can further suggest that this approach, in turn, both presupposes and implies a perspective on 'figuration' itself.

We are told that Kant defines enlightenment as 'the freeing of the individual from his fear of shadows'.[83] But perhaps enlightenment is productive of shadows in the first place: to reveal, to cast light, is to constitute the background as dark, hence to take away with one move the knowledge one acquires with the other. In this respect, the Enlightenment would embody the paradox inherent in the Freudian uncanny, the twinfold process whereby hidden becomes unhidden as familiar becomes unfamiliar. Conversely, then, if enlightenment is the goal, and the project aspires to its *total* realisation, it points towards the 'paranoid city of absolute transparency',[84] in which the lightness of being emerges as the darkness of the project involved in bringing it about, in which power emerges as, paradoxically, the power to render obscure in the very obsession with surveillance and revelation. In such a world, shadows would indeed be potentially ever-present, and objects of fear. And what is radical in Benjamin is his recasting of enlightenment in the language of the everyday cycle of night and day, with 'awakening' as the key that subverts the awake/asleep dichotomy of Enlightenment as project. To awaken is to inhabit a strange twilight realm, half-clarity, half-dream. And the dream faces both ways: it is the aspiration to a better future – as emphasised in the rhetoric of enlightenment – but it is also life in/as penumbra, day as inseparable from shadow, night spilling over into day. For Benjamin, the *Jetztzeit*, the 'now of recognizability', is the point at which things put on their true (Surrealist) face, a moment in which 'awakening' is as much dream as lucid consciousness. This conjunction of sleeping and waking provides the twilight state of modern consciousness.

The Enlightenment, on this reinterpretation, *needs* its darkness: that is both its point of departure, what makes it possible – and necessary – and its horizon, its limit. But *this* darkness is a darkness it can live with, rather than a threat. Darkness reminds us that to *realise* the project would be darkness indeed, the darkness of tyranny. Enlightenment reminds us that, after the light, there comes again the night; and this darkness, from which we awake – though perhaps never fully – is the darkness inherent in life itself. For Rancière, modernity thus entails 'the thinking of emancipation in terms of unfulfillment'.[85] Always one has to live – and one has to write about – modernity in the relative absence of enlightenment; hence the inevitability of twilight and ghosts. This absence is the horizon of the modern, the dual face of its dream, stretching the infinity of its promise over the repetitive return of its night-time visions; the very condition, perhaps, of living the experience that constitutes it.

And this is just as true of the 'reflexive' aspect of modernity: either the reflexive move itself *takes time*, hence becoming or remaining recalcitrant to its own grasp of itself; or it fractures time into a multiplicity of mini-times; or its reflexive grasp remains formal, abstract – and both of the latter imply that 'time' as linear and continuous escapes altogether. Modernity as time is thus constantly producing and reproducing the conditions of uncanny figuration, aspects that return as potentially familiar yet misrecognised. Producing the time that it is comfortable with – ordering it in terms of progress and/or decadence, utopianism and/or nostalgia – modern culture endlessly reproduces a figural past that haunts it, a past in which the past *as* past, and the dead *as* dead, are forever 'unplaced'. The apparently small, even trivial, voice of the uncanny can thus reverberate powerfully through the whole structure of modern civilisation. It suggests not only that no closure could ever be possible, no state of self-sufficient transparency beyond darkness, beyond the penumbra, but that the 'reflexive' aspect of the project itself contributes significantly to the recalcitrant unease and obscurity that is continually reproduced at its heart.

We can move towards the figural by remembering that the project of modernity presupposes a model of the integrated, 'rational' subject with a necessary degree of 'self-awareness', and there are two categories of limitations to the latter: firstly, the inscrutability of motives, the possibility of systematically engendered self-misunderstanding, producing theories of the 'recalcitrant subject', both suffering from, yet also complicit in, its own mystification (Marx, Nietzsche, Freud); secondly, reflexively inadequate understanding, the impossibility of getting a grasp of the total picture when inside it, a perspective latent in structuralist and post-structuralist positionings of the subject in language and culture but not as often given explicit formulation. Both of these involve not just the subject but its relation to the object, and, crucially, to the object as 'context', as that which 'surrounds' the subject, ultimately something it participates in, not something it can simply distance itself from, but this comes to the fore particularly in the second perspective, which is indeed led to interrogate self/other and subject/object distinctions themselves, in the light of this 'reflexive inadequacy' of self-understanding.

A theory of figuration characterises the way aspects of the reality of which we are a part necessarily escape our grasp but are still 'present' to it, in a change of register whereby the penumbra around what is overt, available as representation, becomes *figured*, or 'figures' in the representation, as a distortion in its contours. One of the implications of this is that we can no longer refer *simply* to 'representation', since the distinction between 'reality' and 'thought' is *itself* necessarily questioned by this reflexive figuration, the products of which are neither simply aspects of reality nor merely metaphorical substitutions *within* the world of thought. Rather, 'grasp' or representation thereby slides into projection, a bodying-forth, in specific 'concrete' form, of the penumbra. And such 'projections' are not necessarily or exclusively projections of those aspects of the subject that may, at the time or generally, be most readily seen as 'subjective'; they can also be projections as embedded or embodied in the world, and may indeed be *experienced* as more to do with the world than with the subject. They may be experienced as obdurate, obscure, intense aspects or presences of the world itself. This figuration becomes 'uncanny' when our fundamental sense of the 'proper', of space, time and identity, along with our ability to grasp these, are challenged, hence involving both subject and object in this disturbance of the experience/representation/reality boundaries. A feature of the latter can be, as we have seen, that 'representation' can seem to float free of its 'proper' moorings, revealing the way that the modern development of 'mediated' representation, in conjunction with modern notions of the self, grasped or projected as image, are both interlinked and central to this sense of the uncanny.

We can get closer to this if we recall that these 'figures' have effects. In *this* sense, it is unimportant whether a reader is startled, frightened, or shocked, by reading an uncanny narrative, or by having a more direct, less mediated, uncanny experience. What matters is that whether in fiction or everyday life, something has to *feel* real if it is to be experienced as 'uncanny', just as that feeling coincides with acute ontological doubt around precisely that reality/fiction, truth/illusion boundary itself, and 'where' the experience is 'placed', relative to it. Figuration itself begins in this uncertain area, just as it only forms itself through an appearance – and an apparel – that moves across these boundaries, reproducing ambiguity, uncertainty and otherness. Thus 'presence' comes costumed in borrowed vestments, as the play of figure,[86] opening up possibilities of displacement and dissociation whereby the 'otherness' (of the self, the body, the social, etc.) becomes alienated, unrecognised, whether in ordinary life or the phantasms of popular culture.

To pursue this, we can return to the language of shadow and penumbra, and take up some suggestive comments from Marina Warner, who reminds us that photography was seen as 'shadow play', with the camera able to convey ghostly images suggesting the 'shade' (Latin *penumbra*) that thereby also evoked the person after death. She adds that 'Those who are neither living nor dead cannot project an image, either as mirror reflection or as shadow': spectres and images, shadowy presences that are also non-presences, are *already* shadows, one might say, and shadows that figure figuration itself. Claiming that shadows 'can help summon the insubstantial character of spirit and the emergence of ideas',[87] one can add that this also engenders the figural *as* this very relation between 'self' and reflection on experience.

Referring to the power of black and white photos, and silhouette images, as emerging from the light that played over the subjects, she writes: 'They are emanations, captured and stilled. Is that a figure of speech? They are copies of the originals, and in that sense, their character ceases to be metaphorical. It is here, on this edge where the figurative touches the actual and the image becomes reality, that shadow eerily communicates individual presence', and this effect grows as shadow becomes shade or reflection. Then, 'the projected image of a person brushes the condition of spirit'.[88] This passage vividly *refuses* the conventional distinctions, the constitutive distinctions of modern consciousness – metaphorical/literal, figurative/actual, image/reality – in order to focus on the impossible point between them, where figuration itself is bodied forth, as that which both makes these distinctions possible, grounds them, and yet cannot be formulated from within these terms, through them. And this is where modernity both opens up the possibility of experiences that reveal disturbances or uncertainties across these boundaries, while making them necessarily unresolvable within thought, closing off the possibility of making sense of them.

The 'impossible point' – this void, this absence in the real that indicates my impossible self-presence – it is this that constitutes the ultimate condition for uncanny figuration. Thus Elkins refers to an abyss, suggesting that 'An abyss is literally a cleft in the world, and figuratively a fissure in meaning ... you can stare at it forever without hope of understanding it'. He reminds us, for example, that paintings can have 'empty centers, voids where something should be', just as 'We can feel an uncanny residue, an inexplicable supplement, an aura, a presence that is indisputably there even if no one can see it'.[89] And we have an intriguing brief comment by Žižek, where he suggests that a scene in *Vertigo* where Scottie is shown observing an image of Madeleine in a mirror, through a barely open door, in effect shows him observing her from 'a crack in our reality', or a 'pre-ontological shadowy realm',[90] a crack that fissures two worlds, reveals them as disjointed, a displacement into the film of our own real disjunction from ourselves. And one might add that death seems to be inseparable from this cleft in the world, this uncanny presence, as was implied in the previous discussion of the Poe story; hence doppelgängers, doubles, shadows and reflections become displaced figurations of this impossible self-presence.

The figural is produced from within, yet cannot be articulated from within; it has a potential for haunting. It is never fully present, yet not absent either; it embodies indeterminate efficacy, the efficacy of the imagination; it can relate form to content, space and time. It is always potentially able to float free, as spectral. Hence the uncanny as 'possible experience', taking place *in* space and time, even as it dislocates them, involving a sense of diffuse unease, along with more specific 'figures' which challenge the boundary and identity assumptions of modern culture. Suggesting that 'phantasm' and 'phantom' cannot be clearly distinguished, Wolfreys adds that the phantasm 'is not itself nor a representation of itself, but rather a figure, one amongst many, which spaces and haunts my identity',[91] a formulation which appropriately links 'figure' to the theme of selfhood discussed previously.

As we have seen, uncanny experiences are disturbing because they suggest the *possibility* of the cataclysm: they provoke doubt, uncertainty, a *frisson* of fear, about the adequacy of our grasp of the whole structure of experience. The boundaries waver; uneasy borderlands loom up, in the penumbra, around the fringes, of thought and consciousness. This is well expressed by Rodley, who suggests that the attributes of the uncanny are 'those of dread rather than actual terror, of the haunting rather than the apparition'.[92] The uncanny is the zone of intersection between the known and the felt, and the familiar and the strange – the place of 'haunting', whether or not a ghost is involved. Spectres haunt, but haunting – always uncanny – can occur without the spectral; haunting indicates the potential manifestation of figure in more determinate form. The spectral can be *haunting* precisely because the figure is, *in itself*, fundamentally shadowy, indeterminate, uncanny. The ghost is a most appropriate figure, *the* most appropriate figure perhaps, for figure itself. In this sense, Derrida is right to suggest that 'it is perhaps the hidden figure of all figures'.[93] And this fits with Richardson's study of ghost experiences in the Hudson Valley: 'actual' ghosts are more specific 'manifestations', figurations, of this 'sense of troubling uncanniness', so that 'a sense of hauntedness is not necessarily reliant on actual apparitions'; there can simply be 'assertions of eerie imaginative and emotional connection to the past at specific sites'.[94]

Let us stay with the ghost itself, for a moment, in the light of this perspective on figuration. We can recall the intriguing theory of Balzac, that each body 'consists of a series of ghosts, in an infinity of superimposed layers', and that each photo detaches one of these.[95] These spectral layers, floating through the air (or ether), seem uncannily similar to the images we would construct of ghosts in our minds anyway, as Scarry suggests when she asks why a good ghost story can be so *believable* when most of us would claim no actual experience of ghosts; she argues, in response, that 'the story instructs its hearers to create an image whose own properties are second nature to the imagination: it instructs its hearers to depict in the mind something thin, dry, filmy, two-dimensional, and without solidity'. Thus 'we at once recognize ... precisely the thing described'.[96] And accounts of alleged ghost experiences fit this quite well. Richardson shows how ghosts are described in terms of 'vagueness, colorlessness, wispiness, incompleteness', manifesting 'lack of definition or identifiers'; they are 'inchoate or faded'.[97] They are presences rather than identities, as it were.[98]

The uncanny, then, as 'unformed feeling', in the gap between perception and cognition, is interesting because it is suggestive of the foundation of experience as it is grasped, figured, in *aesthetic* terms. The uncanny is feeling as it is available to be shaped, projected by the imagination, rather than appropriated conceptually in knowledge. So the 'uncanny feeling' points to the necessity of a more proactive imagination to give us a sense of the 'something other in' cognition that is also beyond it, the aesthetic shading that blurs the boundaries of our endeavours to represent experience and thereby situates itself – obscurely – in these very borders. And it is *this* that makes possible the figuration of experience, its potential to disrupt the smooth representational economy of cognition and literary or artistic appropriation.

There is a sense of power or force that fractures meaning, even as we try to grasp it *as* meaning. Just as the disruptive figures of film or text can evoke mysterious 'powers' or a sense of the supernatural, so our very (in)ability to grasp this maps that very same process, whereby we figure the experience as uncanny in a way that reproduces that power *in* our experience, in aesthetic mode, reflecting the excess of experience in or over any attempt to know it. The uncanny, then, points us towards a grasp of these dynamics of figuration that suggest an irreducible dimension or condition of modern experience: both an *aspect* of this, and a particular 'structure of feeling' within it. This affects our very ability to *categorise* experience, make judgements about particular kinds of experience, the relations between them, and the sense we can make of them. Disturbing our feelings simultaneously disturbs our ability to 'sort' these feelings. Clearly this is in some sense 'aesthetic', but it is aesthetics as the disturbing home that endeavours to find a place for the ultimate in the unhomely.

The uncanny is an experience that calls into being our reflexivity, reminds us of it, of our inability to switch off our minds when 'experiencing' an experience, even as it emphasises the impossibility of grasping presence as such. The uncanny exists in and through these specific experiences, even as it shows them to be penetrated by broader reflexive concerns that in turn throw us back into specifics, into figuration, through their very status as unresolvable. The only promise the uncanny can offer, then, is the promise of irresolution. In raising these worries about experience from within it, the uncanny questions the nature of the fundamental, taken for granted categories that serve to constitute these experiences as intelligible for us. And it necessarily questions the whole reflexive project of modernity itself, the idea that we could ever be sufficiently 'present' to ourselves. What we encounter is the world of secular allegories of fragmentation that both feed on and reinforce the uncanny, the sense of the uncertain in experience, the reflexive gap, the sense that experience is inflected with a reflexive consciousness that it can never escape and never resolve. Hence this unhomely modern world, strange even in its familiarity, in which we can be strangely at home – at home to the very strangers who are ourselves.

Notes

1. C. Baudelaire, 'The Painter of Modern Life', in *Selected Writings on Art and Literature* (Harmondsworth: Penguin Books, 1992 [1863]), p. 408 (trans. P. Charvet, slightly amended). Baudelaire's poems are replete with spectres. In '*Les Sept Vieillards*' (1859), an old man passes by, followed by another, *identical*, then another, forming a '*cortège infernal*'. The very way the old man only *becomes* spectral when doubled, multiplied, serves as a vivid figure for the doublings of self and images to be discussed later in this chapter.
2. E. Bronfen, *Over Her Dead Body: Death, femininity and the aesthetic* (Manchester: Manchester University Press, 1992), p. 113.
3. A limited reaction against the emphasis on discourse and textuality found in post-structuralist and deconstructive approaches is evident in hints at a theory of figuration that draw significantly on theorists who at least partially resisted this emphasis, notably Lyotard and Deleuze. For discussions and applications of these, and other approaches, see D. N. Rodowick, *Reading the Figural, or, Philosophy after the New Media* (Durham, NC: Duke University Press, 2001); R. Bogue, *Deleuze on Music, Painting and the Arts* (London: Routledge, 2003), ch. 5; J. Elkins, *On Pictures and the Words That Fail Them* (Cambridge: Cambridge University Press, 1998), ch. 3; and S. Lash, *Sociology of Postmodernism* (London: Routledge, 1990), ch. 7. Influenced by a 'corporeal turn' in cultural studies, linking affect, the uncanny, and figures of the social, see also J. Elmer, *Reading at the Social Limit: Affect, Mass Culture, and Edgar Allan Poe* (Stanford: Stanford University Press, 1995).
4. B. Howells, *Baudelaire: Individualism, Dandyism and the Philosphy of History* (Oxford: Legenda, 1996) p. 18.

5. J. Rancière, 'The Archaeomodern Turn', in M. P. Steinberg (ed.), *Walter Benjamin and the Demands of History* (Ithaca, NY: Cornell University Press, 1996), p. 28.
6. S. Freud, 'The "Uncanny", in *Art and Literature*, The Pelican Freud Library, vol. 14 (Harmondsworth: Penguin Books, 1985 [1919]), p. 340.
7. N. Royle, *The Uncanny* (Manchester: Manchester University Press, 2003), p. 18.
8. E. A. Poe, 'The Oval Portrait', in *Tales of Mystery and Imagination* (London: J. M. Dent, 1990 [1842]), pp. 202–5.
9. E. Cadava, *Words of Light: Theses on the Photography of History* (Princeton: Princeton University Press, 1997), p. 110.
10. Bronfen, p. 115.
11. J. Baudrillard, *Symbolic Exchange and Death* (London: Sage, 1993), p. 142. One can add that Freud, logically enough, points out that the double can also be seen as indicating the opposite, immortality ('Uncanny', pp. 356–7).
12. Bronfen, p. 116.
13. H. Cixous, 'Fiction and Its Phantoms: A Reading of Freud's *Das Unheimliche*', *New Literary History* (1976), 7: 3, pp. 542, 543.
14. Royle, p. 2.
15. Cadava, pp. 107–15.
16. C. Asendorf, *Batteries of Life: On the History of Things and Their Perception in Modernity* (Berkeley: California University Press, 1993), pp. 126, 129, 130.
17. On Vivien and the sapphism/decadence nexus, see J. DeJean, *Fictions of Sappho 1546–1937* (Chicago: Chicago University Press, 1989), pp. 245–85, and B. Elliott and J. -A. Wallace, *Women Artists and Writers: Modernist (Im)positionings* (London: Routledge, 1994), ch. 2.
18. On decadence, see B. Spackman, *Decadent Genealogies: The Rhetoric of Sickness from Baudelaire to D'Annunzio* (Ithaca, NY: Cornell University Press, 1989).
19. M. de Certeau, *The Practice of Everyday Life* (Berkeley: California University Press, 1984), p. 108.
20. Asendorf, p. 133.
21. Cadava, p. 113.
22. W. Benjamin, 'The Work of Art in the Age of Mass Reproduction', *Illuminations* (London: Fontana, 1992), p. 216.
23. Cadava, p. 80.
24. W. Benjamin, 'Surrealism', *Reflections* (New York: Schocken Books, 1986), p. 182.
25. S. Stewart, *On Longing: Narratives of the Miniature, the Gigantic, the Souvenir, the Collection* (Durham, NC: Duke University Press, 1993), p. 61.
26. On dolls, see also E. -M. Simms, 'Uncanny Dolls: Images of Death in Rilke and Freud', *New Literary History* (1996), 27.
27. D. Barnes, *Nightwood* (London: Faber, 1985 [1936]), pp. 209, 209–10, 28.
28. Stewart, p. 124.
29. S. Benstock, *Women of the Left Bank: Paris, 1900–1940* (London: Virago, 1987), p. 257.
30. E. G. Carlston, *Thinking Fascism: Sapphic Modernism and Fascist Modernity* (Stanford: Stanford University Press, 1998), p. 72. (Exploring the controversial area indicated in the title, the author treats Barnes's anti-fascist propensities fairly.)
31. Royle, pp. 36, 183, 184.

32. L. Marcus, 'Laughing at Leviticus: *Nightwood* as Woman's Circus Epic', in M. L. Broe (ed.), *Silence and Power: A Reevaluation of Djuna Barnes* (Carbondale: Southern Illinois University Press, 1991), p. 240.
33. Barnes, p. 194.
34. Barnes, p. 56.
35. Barnes, pp. 206, 65, 60.
36. S. Gilbert and S. Gubar, *Sexchanges*, vol. 2 of *No Man's Land: The Place of the Woman Writer in the Twentieth Century* (New Haven: Yale University Press, 1989), p. 361.
37. Barnes, pp. 64, 73.
38. Barnes, p. 59.
39. Barnes, pp. 17, 21.
40. Barnes, pp. 80, 80, 136.
41. Barnes, p. 91.
42. Barnes, pp. 94, 96.
43. Barnes, pp. 94–6.
44. Barnes, p. 221.
45. See P. Herring, 'Zadel Barnes: Journalist', *Review of Contemporary Fiction* (1993), 13: 3, pp. 107–16, for discussion of Barnes's complex family background (and the sexual abuse allegations); or see the same author's biography, *Djuna: The Life and Work of Djuna Barnes* (New York: Viking, 1995).
46. Barnes, p. 169.
47. Marcus, p. 244.
48. Barnes, p. 60.
49. In her insightful, Freud-inflected account, Bronfen (pp. 339–46) particularly explores this fascination with death and the complexity of motives in this scene of the film.
50. T. Castle, *The Female Thermometer: Eighteenth-Century Culture and the Invention of the Uncanny* (Oxford: Oxford University Press, 1995), p. 37, and ch. 2, *passim*.
51. A. Bresnick, 'Prosopoetic Compulsion: Reading the Uncanny in Freud and Hoffmann', *Germanic Review* (1996), 71: 2, p. 125.
52. K. Marx, *Capital*, vol. 1 (Harmondsworth: Penguin, 1976), p. 165.
53. J. Derrida, *Specters of Marx* (London: Routledge Classics, 2006), pp. 186–99, 207–9 (or Routledge, 1994, pp. 148–58, 165–6).
54. A. Gordon, *Ghostly Matters: Haunting and the Sociological Imagination* (Minneapolis: Minnesota University Press, 1997), p. 202.
55. See for example D. Spoto, *The Art of Alfred Hitchcock* (New York: Doubleday, 1976). And Hitchcock himself is known to have been influenced, in his imaging of the uncanny, by the paintings of Edward Hopper, whose haunting pictures of spaces that are as claustrophobic when depicting the outside as the inside can stand as prime figurations of 'uncanny presence'. See M. Iversen, 'In the Blind Field: Hopper and the Uncanny', *Art History* (1998) 21: 3, pp. 409–29.
56. C. Barr, *Vertigo* (London: British Film Institute, 2002), pp. 34, 34, 77.
57. E. T. A. Hoffmann, 'The Sandman', from *The Golden Pot and Other Tales* (Oxford: Oxford Unversity Press, 1992 [1816]), p. 90.
58. Implications of the term are explored in R. Williams, *Notes on the Underground: An Essay on Technology, Society, and the Imagination* (Cambridge, MA: MIT Press, 1990).

59. Bronfen (p. 345) points out that the end of the film could be seen as a re-staging of the initial trauma, rather than its resolution.
60. M. -H. Huet, *Monstrous Imagination* (Cambridge, MA: Harvard University Press, 1993), pp. 234, 235.
61. S. White, 'Allegory and Referentiality: *Vertigo* and Feminist Criticism', *Modern Language Notes* (1991), 106: 5, p. 924.
62. L. Møller, *The Freudian Reading: Analytical and Fictional Constructions* (Philadelphia: Pennsylvania University Press, 1991), pp. 118, 120.
63. Bresnick, p. 129.
64. Hoffmann, p. 100.
65. Presenting this conflict between them as a choice between 'ethical stability and aesthetic artifice', Ellison's recent interpretation is broadly compatible but not identical: see D. Ellison, *Ethics and Aesthetics in European Modernist Literature: From the Sublime to the Uncanny* (Cambridge: Cambridge University Press, 2001), p. 70 and ch. 3, *passim*.
66. Hoffmann, pp. 94–5.
67. Castle, ch. 9.
68. Hoffmann, pp. 95, 101.
69. Hoffmann, p. 102.
70. R. J. Pudaloff, 'Witchcraft at Salem: (Mis)representing the subject', *Semiotica* (1991) 83: 3/4, pp. 344–5.
71. Castle, p. 17.
72. See M. Dolar, '"I Shall Be with You on Your Wedding-night": Lacan and the Uncanny', *October* (1991) 58, p. 7. But Benjamin is of course the key source for thinking modernity as allegory: for an account that emphasises this dimension, see C. Buci-Glucksmann, *Baroque Reason: The Aesthetics of Modernity* (London: Sage, 1994). See also S. Buck-Morss, *The Dialectics of Seeing: Walter Benjamin and the Arcades Project* (Cambridge, MA: MIT Press, 1989), esp. ch. 6. Within literary theory, Paul de Man's essay 'The Rhetoric of Temporality', sec. 1, in *Blindness and Insight: Essays in the Rhetoric of Contemporary Criticism* (London: Methuen, 1983), remains vital.
73. Castle, pp. 8, 174.
74. Cited in Castle, p. 181. One can add that the *Shorter Oxford Dictionary* lists 'an object or source of dread or terror, imagined as an apparition', and 'an image or phantom produced by reflection' as meanings of 'spectre': these nicely encapsulate the subject/object, experience/representation tensions inherent in this model.
75. Pudaloff, p. 345.
76. G. Batchen, *Burning with Desire: The Conception of Photography* (Cambridge, MA: MIT Press, 1997), pp. 69, 77, 76.
77. Cadava, p. 76.
78. W. Benjamin, 'Surrealism'.
79. Batchen, pp. 91, 93.
80. Castle, pp. 143, 183.
81. Batchen, p. 92.
82. T. Gunning, 'Phantom Images and Modern Manifestations: Spirit Photography, Magic Theater, Trick Films, and Photography's Uncanny', in P. Petro (ed.), *Fugitive Images: From Photography to Video* (Bloomington: Indiana University Press, 1995), p. 67.

83. D. Morgan, *Kant Trouble: The obscurites of the enlightened* (London: Routledge, 2000), p. 56.
84. J. Donald, *Imagining the Modern City* (London: Athlone Press, 1999), p. 84.
85. Rancière, p. 28.
86. Hence Derrida on 'Figures of Borrowing, Borrowed Figures, Figurality as the Figure of Borrowing', *Specters*, p. 136 (109).
87. M. Warner, *Phantasmagoria: Spirit Visions, Metaphors, and Media into the Twenty-first Century* (Oxford: Oxford University press, 2006), pp. 15, 177, 91.
88. Warner, pp. 165–6.
89. J. Elkins, *Pictures and Tears* (London: Routledge, 2001), pp. 201, 190, 181.
90. S. Žižek, *The Fright of Real Tears: Krzysztof Kieślowski between Theory and Post-Theory* (London: British Film Institute, 2001), p. 131.
91. J. Wolfreys, *Victorian Hauntings: Spectrality, Gothic, the Uncanny and Literature* (London: Palgrave Macmillan, 2002), p. 151, fn. 12.
92. C. Rodley (ed.) *Lynch on Lynch* (London: Faber, 1997), Introduction, p. x.
93. Derrida, *Specters*, p. 150 (120).
94. J. Richardson, *Possessions: The History and Uses of Haunting in the Hudson Valley* (Princeton: Harvard University Press, 2003), pp. 24, 5, 5.
95. Cit. Q. Bajac, *The Invention of Photography* (London: Thames and Hudson, 2002), p. 143.
96. E. Scarry, 'On vivacity', *Representations* (1995) 52, p. 13.
97. Richardson, pp. 26, 26, 27.
98. Two other recent accounts, those of Gordon and Derrida, put more emphasis on the political and moral dimensions, ghosts as insistent voices demanding justice. In her account, often moving, Gordon presents ghosts as 'the unhallowed dead of the modern project' who force us to confront 'the violence of the force that made them' (p. 22). This emphasis is valuable, but there are problems: ghosts do not generally make demands or articulate grievances, though they can do so. (See Richardson, pp. 27, 160–72; and R. C. Finucane, *Ghosts: Appearances of the Dead and Cultural Transformations* New York: Prometheus Books, 1996.) Of course, Derrida's account goes well beyond 'ghosts', as it were; but there is a tension in *Specters* between the emphasis on the specificity, the identity and the demands of the ghost, and Derrida's own recognition that 'ghostliness', or the uncanny sense of 'haunting', somehow points to this sense of *irresolution*, this disturbingly timeless sense of the uncanny as 'other' to the time of modernity, questioning it. The ghost itself seems to swing uneasily between the two – at times, in the process, seeming to become a rather empty trope – and his 'hauntology', elaborating the abstract and potentially metaphysical pole of the contrast, seems to take us away from the task of elaborating a theory of figuration to link them more closely.

2
Night and the Uncanny

Elisabeth Bronfen

The night is a double of the day, a comment on its activities, a countersite. In most cultures, the setting of the sun has always been connected with the advent of a different way of thinking and behaving. As our sight diminishes, other senses – notably our faculties of hearing and of the imagination – come to be increased. Our sense of distance and measure changes, the contours of the persons or objects we meet become blurred, we encounter a sense of disorientation, which can be either fascinating or threatening. In contrast to its appearance in daylight, the world surrounding us is harder to characterize; it shifts between the familiar and the unfamiliar. The danger potentially lurking in the night has, furthermore, always inspired tales of superstitious powers beyond those ruled by diurnal reason. Apart from thieves, arsonists and conspirators, ghosts, vampires and the devil himself seek the protection of darkness to pursue their unholy goals. At the same time, precisely because the night requires a higher degree of vigilance than the day, its darkness affords revelations. The night is the right time for the divine visions of early Christian mystics, for encountering the spirits of one's departed loved ones, for telling ghost stories around a fire or for seeing in one's dreams things one's conscious mind would censor during the day.

The uncanny (*unheimlich*), according to Freud, is something which is secretly familiar (*heimlich-heimisch*), but because it pertains to knowledge one would prefer to forget, has undergone repression, only to return in a transformed shape, rendering it strange and terrifying. Some of the most prominent examples Freud lists touch upon gothic motives usually connected with the night, notably involuntary repetition compulsion, the omnipotence of thought, the double, the uncertainty whether something is animate or inanimate, real or fantasy. Curiously, although Freud describes the uncanny as 'something which ought to have remained hidden but has come to light',[1] he doesn't include any discussion of the night as a stage for its articulation. Yet most mythopoetic narratives conceive the night as a primordial place of origin, be it the chaos of antiquity or the darkness into which, in Genesis, God's word brings light. In that these cosmogonies define the everyday, marked by an incessant alternation between night and day, in relation to an earlier state of uninterrupted night (which can, however, only be conceived belatedly), they trace a similar trajectory to the one Freud offers for psychic development. We can speak of a primordial night only from our position within a world of the everyday, from which it has been irrevocably repressed, as we can only conceive of the state before originary repression within the terms of our consciousness and its unconscious symptoms. The ordinary night is, thus, uncanny in the sense that it allows us to conceive this irretrievable point of origin precisely through those after-effects, which render the time between dusk and dawn strange, dangerous as well as compelling.

If one considers further that antiquity imaged the night as the maternal goddess Nyx, who gives birth to sleep, death, fate as well as all emanations of fantasy, another correspondence to Freud's uncanny emerges. Whenever a dreamer says to himself, 'this place is familiar to me, I've been here before', Freud claims, 'we may interpret the place as being his mother's genitals or her body'.[2] Like the maternal womb, one might speculate, the night is what was once *heimisch*, familiar, even while we need to repress a longing for this primordial home so as to remain in a day, ruled by paternal laws, because returning to this home is tantamount to death. Indeed, the demonisation of the night, as site of pagan spirits and Christian demons, indicates precisely the repression at stake for Freud in his discussion of the uncanny. A primordial night is both repressed and remembered as an originary home, enticing or terrifying, unequivocally ungraspable within the logic and language of our conscious, everyday existence, except when transcoded into images marked by defamiliarization.

At the same time, mythopoetics has always acknowledged that because it recalls the darkness before earthly existence, the ordinary night allows for intimations of the eternal. The most important point for Freud's own theoretization of a universal collective unconscious comes from romantic psychology, notably Schelling's notion of a world soul and Schubert's discussion of a nocturnal side of the natural sciences (*Nachtseite der Naturwissenschaft*); more precisely the notion that we are part of an all-encompassing, groundless and endless spiritual field, which connects the present to its past and its future.[3] If Freud claims that death is unknown to the unconscious, he does so because he takes from these romantic psychologists the notion of a psychic space in which everything remains preserved. This site is rendered accessible when one screens out conscious rationality by following that *other* vision, which the night side of the psyche affords. It reveals itself when one allows one's unconscious to speak through the repression imposed upon it by diurnal reason, and the uncanny is the privileged mode for doing so. The wager subtending the following discussion of aesthetic depictions of the night as site for the articulation of psychic uncanniness is the following. While philosophy makes the claim that its *theoria* – based as it is on the premise of bringing light – is of the day, literature and the other arts perform precisely the nocturnal side of knowledge which philosophy disclaims. Literature as the uncanny double of philosophy does so by self-consciously choosing the night as the chronotopos for narratives of self-discovery, be they psychological *rite-de-passage* or passages that lead to the transition into an immaterial world of pure signs, which modern aesthetics affords.

There are, of course, many scenarios where the night is both a stage and a state of mind: pastoral summer nights with their romantic moonlight, gothic nights with their fantastic hauntings, nights in foreign places with their exoticism or nights of seclusion that serve as portals to discoveries of an erotic, a spiritual or a contemplative kind. For my discussion I have chosen one specific nocturnal landscape, namely the modern city, and more specifically one particular type of nightwalker, namely the nocturnal *flâneur*, who penetrates into the night so as to resolve psychic issues that not only bother him during the day, but can also not be resolved there. His experiences are 'extimate' (the intimate, which is also external) in the sense that he goes through an external night to find an intimacy that has been repressed in the dark interiority of his psyche, the unconscious. The uncanny night I am concerned with is thus not an anthropological reality but rather an imaginary cityscape, textually constructed. As the precondition for psychic change, it emerges as the double of the day in a very precise sense. In the night we prepare for the coming of dawn by experiencing that which is both familiar and strange, and which, having been faced, allows us to move into a new day. Its uncanny difference to what is considered the ordinary everyday is what talks to us, compels us, even while this imaginary night comes into existence precisely because we address it and talk about it. There is, however, another wager subtending the cross-mapping of Arthur Schnitzler's *Dream Novella* (1925) and Martin Scorsese's *Taxi*

Driver (1976), which I am proposing in this essay; one in which I follow Stanley Cavell's claim that Hollywood rewrites philosophy.[4] By reading a modernist novella together with a post-modern film, what is brought into focus is the way both rewrite a critical trope Hegel develops in his *Jenaer Realphilosophie.* For it is precisely in this romantic philosopher's discussion of articulations of psychic dislocation, which he calls 'night of the world', that we find one of the most resilient precursors of Freud's notion of the uncanny.[5]

* * *

At the beginning of Schnitzler's *Dream Novella,* a married couple finds itself embroiled in a quarrel about 'hidden desires, which can obscure even the clearest soul and plunge it into confusion'.[6] The wife Albertine confesses that she was ready last summer to leave her family for a young sailor she met during their holidays and her husband Fridolin confesses his adulterous desires for a fifteen-year-old girl. The discussion is interrupted when the husband is called away on a visit to a dying patient. What follows are two separate journeys through nocturnal uncanniness. Driven by the sexual fantasies their discussion has unleashed, the doctor wanders into the unfamiliar nightlife of Vienna while his wife stays at home. Having gone to bed without him, she encounters in her dream scenes of sexual humiliation and death that uncannily resonate with those Fridolin finds himself compulsively drawn toward. While Schnitzler's doctor actively goes into the night, he seems to do so without a will of his own; as though he were following a repetition compulsion to re-enact what he has heard from his wife without having any mastery over his wanderings. Albertine, in turn, cannot roam the nocturnal streets of Vienna the way her husband does, but also doesn't have to. While Fridolin must consciously experience his familiar world turned strange before he can confront the sexual desires that have broken through the shield of repression, Albertine is closer to the nocturnal side of her desires. Schnitzler's gender politics are such that the visions the *Nachtseite* of her psyche afford her in her dreams may be uncanny, but they don't threaten her certainty of self. Her husband, in turn, needs to embark on a hallucinatory journey, at the end of which he will come to lose all certainty of self, before he can wake up into a viable day.

This gender difference is particularly noteworthy once Schnitzler's novella is read in conjunction with Hegel's discussion of the nothingness subtending the psychic formation of the subject. In a passage of the *Jenaer Realphilosophie* entitled 'Night of the World', he claims: 'The human being is this night, this empty nothing, that contains everything in its simplicity, a wealth of endless representations, images ... This is the night, the interiority of nature, pure self ... One catches sight of this night when one looks another human being in the eye – and there gazes upon a night that becomes awful.'[7] Along the lines of Freud's unconscious, Hegel posits a dark kernel of nothingness at the centre of the subject, which contains all conceivable images of itself, albeit in a state of possibility, before any actual emergence. For this reason he conceives of pure subjectivity as a night, from which a plethora of manifestations of the self can ceaselessly be brought forth. At the same time, all phantasmagoric representations can only emerge in a nocturnal mental state. It is *at* night, and *in* the night that one can encounter and experience the abyss, the pure nothing, from which all ordinary images of the self emerge. This is the critical trope Schnitzler explores in his *Dream Novella*, aligning Hegel's 'night of the world' with Freud's unconscious as the 'night side of the psyche'. Indeed, what he unfolds is how the uncanny, refracting everyday experiences, is perceived by both Fridolin and his wife in the phantasmagoric enactments their nocturnal wanderings afford them. The difference in Schnitzler's literary reiteration of both Hegel and Freud's philosophical tropes is one of gender. Albertine comes to experience the nothingness at the kernel of her subjectivity in a dream scene her unconscious enacts for her, while her husband Fridolin needs to be led through his hallucinations by others. At the same time, although they journey separately, Fridolin and Albertine come together at the end of the second night, so as to negotiate how to return back into the day.

But significantly, Schnitzler's dream novella doesn't begin with two adults talking at night about sexual transgressions. The point of departure is instead Albertine's child, reading aloud an exotic goodnight story, in which twenty-four brown slaves are rowing Prince Amgiad to the palace of the caliph; 'The prince is lying on deck, wrapped in his purple cloak, under the nocturnal sky and his gaze ... '.[8] At this point in the story the little girl's eyes fall shut and she falls asleep. If, then, Schnitzler's novella sets in with someone falling into a dream state after having read about a nocturnal scene in an imaginary world, equally important is the fact that the child closes her eyes as she is about to tell her parents what the prince is gazing at. One might fruitfully call this ellipsis in Schnitzler's narrative a rhetorical gesture of the uncanny, given that it sustains a state of suspension between dreaming with eyes wide open in the act of reading and reading with shut eyes. After all, the nocturnal vision dreams afford is such that the sleeping subject comes to read its unconscious. What the parents, in turn, will embark upon after the child has fallen asleep entails an enactment of spectrality Stanley Kubrick, in his cinematic adaptation of the novella, aptly called seeing forbidden desires with 'eyes wide shut'. The dreams they will encounter, in bed and on the streets of Vienna, in turn rewrite not only the story the child has been reading. They also uncannily repeat events of the masked ball they were both happy to leave the evening before, to spend a night of erotic passion, only to wake to a 'grey morning'.[9]

Fridolin and Albertine's discussion about clandestine fantasies, both intimate and strange, which this ball and the goodnight story awoke in them, thus has as a further point of reference the ordinary events of their daily life. As such their nocturnal revelations are marked by precisely the belatedness so central to Freud's notion of the uncanny. Schnitzler is quite explicit on this point. As his narrator explains, 'only now that the day's work was completed and the child asleep, and from nowhere a disturbance to be expected', can the carnivalesque figures of the prior evening return. He goes on to note, the 'delusory appearance of lost opportunities envelops these figures magically and painfully'. The initially light-hearted recollection of the masked ball soon turns into a serious conversation about 'secret realms, for which they hardly entertain a desire, even while an ungraspable wind of fate could, if only in a dream, find them drifting there'. There is a disturbance, after all, but not from without. The figures that have taken hold of Fridolin and Albertine's imagination are not only nocturnal figures, because our protagonists encountered them at a masked ball, but also because in analogy to Hegel's notion of a night of the world they are of spectral fabric. They appear as phantasmagoria in the night, when all is dark and still, so as to give body to what Schnitzler's couple call 'lost opportunities, missed chances – both magical and painful'.[10]

At the same time, it is night when phantasmagoria appear, because the serious conversation Albertine and Fridolin move into, though allegedly a rational discourse, is itself not free from spectrality. After all, the fantasies they confess to each other are speculations. The adultery they speak of didn't happen, but it might have, and by virtue of being mentioned, these opportunities, though not acted upon, point to the fragility underlying this marriage. The intangibility of the fantasies they confess to each other, when it is dark all around them, is precisely what makes them such a potent disturbance. Kept in the dark these *potential* psychic representations will bear fruit. Ultimately it is, however, an external event which will interrupt this serious conversation. Fridolin is asked to visit a patient, who has just had a heart attack. Though he leaves his home without his wife, the adventures both will embark upon separately re-encode, in the language of nocturnal phantasmagoria, the clandestine zones of erotic transgressions they touched upon together in their conversation. But because the point of departure for their separate adventures is a narrative, Schnitzler also foregrounds that these adventures are textual from the start. Fridolin's journey to the end of his night of the world, which begins at the deathbed of the Hofrat and will lead him, one night later, to a beautiful dead woman in a morgue, uncannily repeats this serious conversation, itself prompted by a child reading her goodnight story, even while producing a narrative entitled *Dream Novella*.

The first strange event that occurs involves the daughter of his patient, the Hofrat. Marianne suddenly throws herself at the doctor, unabashedly confessing her erotic desire for him. Although he is able to disentangle himself from this embarrassing moment of hysteric histrionics, Fridolin finds he is annoyed with his wife and decides not to return home quite yet. But as he wanders through the streets of Vienna, the ground of certainty recedes further and further, because the people he meets seem increasingly spectral: a student he meets evokes the image of a fatal dual, a prostitute he follows to her room raises the spectre of syphilis. Finally even Albertine, whom he imagines to be sleeping at home, suddenly appears to him as a ghost. While this thought contains something disturbing, he notes that it also comforts him, because it liberates him from all responsibility. Indeed, he has entered into the uncanniness of detached nothingness which recalls Hegel's 'night of the world'. Fridolin explicitly claims that he feels homeless (*heimatlos*), 'thrown out of the known district of his Dasein into a different, foreign and far away world'.[11] In his psychic reality his home has become *unheimlich*, his wife strange, and he fancies himself no longer master of his own house. Instead he begins to enjoy the nocturnal cityscape of Vienna as stage and state of mind doubling his ordinary self, as the night doubles the day.

Ultimately he will accompany his old friend, the pianist Nachtigall, to a clandestine party in a mysterious villa on the outskirts of the city. Recognizing the danger involved in entering, he invokes the women he might return to, as though they were the only points of orientation left to him in this defamiliarized nocturnal world. 'What if I had better turn back?', he asks himself. 'But where to? To Pierrette in the costume shop, to the prostitute in the Buchfeldgasse? Or to Marianne, the daughter of the deceased? Or home.' Significantly, all the women are conceived in relation *to* and in contestation *of* his wife. At the same time, the one certainty

Fridolin has at this point is that he can't return to Albertine, even if, 'it means my death'. This uncanny alignment of the night and femininity finds its acme in the black-veiled woman who, as he enters, whispers to him that his presence might have fatal consequences. She will claim to sacrifice herself so as to allow him to escape, though Fridolin can only conjecture what this entails, since he is forced to leave the villa before he actually sees what she is willing to do for him. However, precisely because everything remains obscure, Fridolin has gained one certainty. As he finally returns home, he assures himself that he will seek a 'clarification for this adventure' the next day.[12]

What he finds in his marital bed is that during his absence his home has truly become *unheimlich*. After he wakes Albertine, she relates a dream to him that makes her utterly strange in his eyes, even while confirming his suspicion that he is no longer master in his own house. She confesses that in her own nocturnal vision she humiliated her husband, tortured him and ultimately had him executed, laughing over his dead body. Her dream narrative explicitly picks up where her daughter fell asleep, only now a slave is rowing Fridolin to her under a moonlit sky. Then, moving into the day, she exchanges her husband for the sailor of her confession, using her dream to work through psychic material from the previous evening, even while using her nocturnal vision to fulfil the chance she had missed in reality. At this point, however, a significant shift occurs, because as she describes how Fridolin is captured, tied up and executed, she reiterates the scene he experienced in the forbidden villa, but does so as an inversion. In her nocturnal vision he, and not a black-veiled woman, is naked, even while in contrast to his own fantasies of infidelity, Albertine casts him as staunchly faithful to her. He is to be executed because he refuses to become the lover of the Queen of the land, who resembles the girl Fridolin had confessed a desire for. As they begin to nail him to the cross Albertine finds herself overcome with laughter, because she wanted to ridicule her husband for his stupid willingness to sacrifice his life for her, and it is this laugh that forces her to awaken. If we recall Freud's claim that you wake up from your dream only once the representations it affords have become unbearable, Schnitzler calls upon us to ask: What is so unbearable about this laugh?

Indeed, the recognition this confession affords – far more perturbing than the serious conversation that initiated their nocturnal journeys – is complex. Schnitzler's *flâneur* is outraged and wants to punish his wife for the cruelty of her dream, even while feeling an inexplicable tenderness for her. At the same time, confronted with two nocturnal mysteries – the alleged sacrifice of the black-veiled woman and his wife's cruel fantasies – he finds himself in a double hermeneutic impasse. He decides to give up on the thought of finding an interpretation for his wife's dream and instead wanders through Vienna the next day in search of an explanation for the clandestine events that took place in the villa. In the grey light of day he revisits the places he had been the night before. The Hofrat's daughter is preparing to leave the city, the prostitute Mitzi is in a hospital, his friend Nachtigall has mysteriously disappeared, and at the villa, a letter awaits him, warning him not to pursue his investigation any further. Everything is, indeed, different, but nevertheless still uncanny; the ordinary equally tainted by nocturnal phantasmagoria. Even Albertine appears to be a mimicry of domesticity, her smile recalling the grimace of a revengeful femme fatale.

The omnipotence of thought that has taken hold of him forces Fridolin to put his entire world into doubt. He chooses to go out again after dinner and ultimately finds himself at midnight in the morgue. He had read about a Baroness in the newspaper, who had committed suicide, and now wants to believe that this is the mysterious woman from the villa. But Fridolin is also perfectly aware that what he is compulsively repeating is actually his wife's dream. He admits that 'since he read the notice in the paper, he had given to the dead woman, whose face he doesn't know, the face of Albertine, that indeed, as he only now uncannily comes to recognize, it had been his wife all along, whom he had been in search of'.[13] In this revelation, the night, feminine bodies of dangerous desire and his wife merge into a composite double image, recalling the antique goddess Nyx, bearing sleep and death in her arms. For as Fridolin looks at the beautiful corpse in the morgue, he juxtaposes onto her the image he had the prior night of a spectral Albertine, sleeping in their marital bed.

As Hegel's discussion of the night of the world suggests, looking into the face of the dead woman is horrible, because it offers no explanation. Instead it is a 'complete void, nothing', a dead face Fridolin can know nothing about, and thus a signifier for the nothingness at the heart of all the phantasmagoria the night has revealed to him. Yet for one last moment he wants to hold onto the uncanny emanation his mind produces. Convinced that the corpse has begun to move, he leans forward to kiss it, and is stopped just in time by the anatomist who has silently been watching him. Only then does Fridolin wake as from a trance. The corpse no longer holds any attraction for him, even though she embodies uncanniness *par excellence*, given that she enmeshes several components Freud ascribes to this psychic affect.

Over her body, the feminine and death double each other in such a manner as to blur the distinction between the animate and the inanimate. At the same time this unknown feminine corpse both is and isn't a living woman; it conjoins a body with its after-image. Finally, as a moment of the real, outside and beyond all narcissistic desires, this strange body double also signifies a second death, namely the demise of all the phantasmagoria Fridolin has encountered in the past two nights. As he leaves the morgue, he says of the dead woman, who was always nothing more than a screen-image of his wife, 'she could mean nothing other to him, destined for an irrevocable decomposition, than the pale corpse of the past night'.[14] The choice of trope is significant, because by attaching all the uncanniness of the past two nights to the corpse of a stranger, he can disengage the woman of his forbidden erotic fantasies from the wife she always stood in for; which means, he can finally return home to Albertine.

At the end of Fridolin's nocturnal wanderings, Schnitzler offers a third and final confession, in the course of which it becomes dawn. Albertine listens intently without interrupting her husband. After he asks her in despair what they are now to do, she responds, 'We must be grateful to fate that we have emerged unscathed from all adventures – real and dreamed.' She has overcome any doubt the uncanny events may have raised in her, precisely because she knows that nothing is certain. While Fridolin wants to be assured that they have awoken for ever, she knows that while the reality of one night isn't all there is to say about the innermost truth of a person, the phantasmagoria it has allowed to emerge can also not be banished from psychic reality. 'Never the future', she warns him.[15] The uncanny night of the world is that domain upon which the ordinary feeds. The truth it holds can neither be fully known nor fully jettisoned, even while stepping into the dawn of morning is a necessity. But there is an important formal stringency to Schnitzler's text. It ends precisely where it began, namely with the voice of the child. After having resolved the serious conversation that began two nights earlier, Albertine and Fridolin lie next to each other, neither sleeping nor talking. They have achieved a reprieve from their dangerous desires, which is what, according to Freud, a successful encounter with the uncanny is ultimately about. Then, at seven in the morning, 'and with the familiar noise from the street, with the triumphant light streaming through the crack in the curtain and the light child's laughter in the room next door, a new day began'. I am tempted to say, perhaps it was all the child's dream, recalling the ellipsis at the very beginning of the novella. At the end of the novella, the three dots marking the falling away of her voice can be read belatedly as the point of departure for a rhetorical gesture of uncanniness. Not only the difference between dream and reality has been rendered undecidable but also its point of origin.

* * *

Maurice Blanchot reformulates Freud's notion of the uncanny by foregrounding the loss of the familiar, and with it the intimation of death, which a return of the repressed can entail. *Autre nuit* is the term he coined to distinguish between a first, phenomenological night, in which we approach absence, and the other night. 'When everything has disappeared in the night', he explains, '"everything that has disappeared" appears'. What returns in this other night is all that has been brought to disappear. While one can be in the first night, repose there in sleep or in death, this other night does not open itself to us: 'in it, one is always outside'.[16] Engaging with this uncanny *autre nuit* entails the suspension of mimetic perception in an attempt to experience the imaginary as pure immateriality of signs. Picking up on both Hegel's notion of a night of the world, in which phantasmagoria appear, and Freud's uncanny, as a return of repressed fantasies, Blanchot's *autre nuit*, however, foregrounds the issue of aesthetic mediality in a manner particularly fruitful for a reading of *Taxi Driver* as a cinematic dream novella, because the uncanniness at stake in the film results from the equation of going into the night and going to the movies. My claim is that Martin Scorsese produces a narrative about film as a nocturnal medium, at whose navel we find pure nothingness emerging. While the phenomenological night, which serves as the stage and state of mind of the hero Travis (Robert de Niro), blurs the boundaries, the *l'autre nuit* has no bottom, and it is this performance of the dissolution of representation which *Taxi Driver* takes as its point of departure. Furthermore, like Schnitzler's novella, Scorsese's film also ends where it begins, namely on the level of pure language, only in this case not with a narrative ellipsis but rather the glow of bright lights blurring into each other in the dark.

During the title sequence of *Taxi Driver* a white cloud of smoke emerges from a black background until it almost fully fills the screen, only to unfold an ominous yellow checker cab, framed as a low shot. The cab passes in front of the camera from right to left, and as it exits the frame it leaves behind, as a trail, the title of the film 'Taxi Driver', written in red letters and juxtaposed onto the white cloud. The taxi, thus Scorsese visually argues, produces the title, which metonymically stands for the film we are about to see. Once it has left the frame, Scorsese cuts to an extreme close-up of the eyes of the man driving the cab. As his face is first lit and then falls into shadow, his eyes track from right to left. With a classic shot-reverse shot Scorsese moves to the nocturnal world unfolding before his gaze; the colourful, blurred red, blue and white lights in front of the windowpane of his car. The way in which the nocturnal cityscape is introduced in *Taxi Driver* is significant for two reasons. While the world when seen at night in general loses its contours, Scorsese's choice of *mise-en-scène* also highlights that what his taxi driver sees is not a mimetic world, but rather a representation, refracted through his subjective gaze. For a moment we see juxtaposed the lights behind the windowpane and Travis's eyes reflected on it, before we have only a view of the street through a rain-covered glass.

Only then does the windshield wiper begin to clean the window, as though to give us a sharper vision of this nightscape. Yet what Scorsese next unfolds is a visual bleeding out of the world outside the cab. Even while the car itself glides smoothly through the night, he shows us only blurred contours, becoming increasingly indistinct, and thus abstract, until out of this uncanny *autre nuit* finally emerges the first mimetically recognizable representation of a nocturnal scene, namely pedestrians crossing a sidewalk. Scorsese ends his credit sequence by returning chiasmically to where he began, first an extreme close-up of the eyes of his taxi-driver and then a cloud of smoke. The story of Travis Bickle's heroism, in the course of which he will save the girl Iris (Jodie Foster) from prostitution and kill the men she has been working for, emerges, like the title of the film, from this smoke. The New York nights about to set in serve as a stage where he can unleash his violent desires. At the same time, Travis is moving through a night that unfolds before his eyes like a film on a screen. The taxi, after all, is his private cinema. Like Schnitzler's *Dream Novella*, Scorsese's film thus self-reflexively engages with to its own mediality from the start; the aesthetic night it produces is an uncanny site that emerges from the dark to take phantasmagoric shape for his hero and for us, his spectators.

As Scorsese has explained, 'Much of *Taxi Driver* arose from my feeling that movies are really a kind of dream-state ... And the shock of walking out of the theatre into broad daylight can be terrifying. I watch movies all the time and I am also very bad at waking up. The film was like that for me – that sense of being almost awake.'[17] In the first sequence of the film we discover that Travis is a Vietnam veteran, who wants to drive a taxi at night because he is suffering from insomnia. In contrast to Schnitzler's Vienna of the *Dream Novella*, Scorsese's New York City of the mid-1970s is both gendered and racial. As Travis passes a theatre around

Time Square called 'Fascination', his voice-over explains, 'All the animals come out at night, whores, skunk pussies, buggers, queens, fairies, dopers, junkies. Sick venal', while Scorsese stages him watching these creatures of the night through his back-mirror and the windows of his car. He adds what has become the most memorable line of the film, 'Someday a real rain will come and wash this scum off the streets', while the camera pans along the rain-covered tarmac of Broadway; reflecting, as in the credit sequence, the lights from the nocturnal cityscape. Like Fridolin he will stray on these streets rendered uncanny by a night which corresponds to his psychic dislocation, because he, too, has no home he is master of. In contrast to Schnitzler's *flâneur*, however, he has neither a wife nor a child, and thus nothing to curb the phantasmagoria that renders his ordinary life ever more strange. He will become obsessed with Betsy (Cybill Shepherd), a young woman, working for Sen. Charles Palantine, and initially believe her to be his saving angel until, because of a disastrous visit to a porno theatre, she will reject him, and he will lose all hold on the world of diurnal familiarity.

Scorsese's depiction of a Vietnam veteran's embrace of radical uncanniness can fruitfully be read in relation to the night as the last frontier.[18] In their conversations, the other night drivers discuss the violence they encounter by driving to those parts of New York City where, in the mid-1970s, the uncanny darkness of the night was conflated with racial alterity. To highlight the conjunction between the urban night and the frontier, Scorsese has Travis follow Iris to the Lower East Side and talk to her pimp, who, after initially taking him for an undercover agent, calls him a 'real cowboy'. 'Sport' Matthew (Harvey Keitel) not only dresses like a Hollywood Indian, with his ponytail, his black-feathered hat and turquoise jewels on his hands; the final confrontation between the two also recalls the one between John Ford's Ethan and Chief Scar at the acme of *The Searchers*. Scorsese explicitly conceives his film as a refiguration of John Ford's Western, in which a veteran from the Civil War rescues a girl who had been in captivity for most of her adult life. The twist he introduces into his post-Vietnam version, however, is that his 'real cowboy' turns himself into an uncanny double on several scores. Travis not only blurs the boundary between reality and dream by recasting himself as the cliché of the lone ranger, who takes the law into his own hands, but by transforming his body into a killing machine, he also destabilizes the difference between the human body and prosthetic weapons. In the famous mirror scene, he will look at his own image, repeatedly holding a gun to this double, and finally shoot at himself, explaining to his self-reflection, 'you're dead'. This is Scorsese's cinematic rendition of what Freud calls a doubling, dividing and interchanging of the self, owing to which the subject 'identifies himself with someone else, so that he is in doubt as to which his self is, or substitutes the extraneous self for his own'.[19]

Travis will ultimately shave his head so as to look like an urban Mohawk Indian, and in so doing double the pimp he goes after, once his attempt to assassinate Sen. Charles Palantine fails. He will survive the brutal slaughter he unleashes in the East Village house Iris works in, become a local hero and, after returning from the hospital, continue driving his cab at night. As Amy Taubin has noted, the politics of *Taxi Driver* are ambivalent, leaving us to decide whether the film aligns itself with Travis's racism or whether Scorsese deconstructs Travis's paranoid re-encoding of nocturnal New York into a violated feminine body, which must be saved from its polluting aggressors.[20]

Yet one might fruitfully highlight a different uncanny interface, namely the one between the cinematic gaze and the violence it entails. During one of his rides, Travis picks up a man who asks him to drive over to the curb in front of a particular building. Played by Scorsese himself, this uncanny stranger insists that Travis put the meter back on, while they simply sit and watch. For the first time in the film we see Travis's head from the back, while in what follows, Scorsese stages himself and de Niro as two movie-goers sitting one behind the other, discussing what they are seeing on a screen in front of them. Slowly, the stranger begins to direct Travis's gaze to the light on the second floor, closest to the edge of the building, and then to the woman, whose silhouette can be seen in the window. Laughing demonically he explains that she is his wife, visiting her black lover, and that he is going to kill her. The irony of the scene is such that the stranger is directing Travis in the same manner that Scorsese is directing Robert de Niro. In so doing, he draws our attention to what his camera does, namely focus our gaze, by shifting from a long shot to the close up of a detail. This gaze, so self-reflexively produced by a man who is both a stranger and the director of the film, uncannily blurs the diegesis of the film with its extradiegetic component, fuses the hero Travis with the actor de Niro, as well as with us, the implied spectator.

The body, furthermore, at which this gaze is self-consciously directed, is the shadow of a woman behind a white screen – cinema, within cinema, within cinema. The rhetorical superlative contained within this *mise-en-scène* is significant for the ethics of *Taxi Driver*. By forcing Travis to recognize what he has been doing all along, namely seeing the world as the projection of his internal demons, the stranger sitting behind him produces a visual self-reflexivity, where the viewed phantasmagoria ricochets back onto the nocturnal *flâneur*, whose demonic eyes have been the locus of the film narrative. As the two men continue to wait in front of the building, the stranger finally unfolds a violent fantasy of his own, describing how he will shoot his wife's face and pussy with a .44 Magnum pistol. Cutting away from the woman in the window, Scorsese presents us instead with a series of shot-reverse shots. These splice together the back of Travis's head and not the man sitting behind him, but rather the image of him that he sees in his back mirror.

The *mise-en scène* rhetorically highlights two things. For one, the stranger emerges as the uncanny double of the taxi-driver, existing primarily as refracted representation in his back mirror. For another he functions as a manifestation of the real (much like the corpse in Schnitzler's *Dream Novella*). Forced not simply to share the violent fantasy of another man, but to recognize that he is in a 'night of the world' of his own, Travis finds himself confronted with a self-reflection that renders him unfamiliar to himself. In the space of the mirror where he normally saw his own eye, he is now looking into the eye of another, and this insight is as horrible as Fridolin's gaze at the dead eyes of the strange woman in the morgue. But Scorsese ends on yet another turn of the screw. The acme of the stranger's diatribe, functioning as an uncanny repetition of Travis's desire for rain to wash away the scum off the streets, is a curious invocation of sight: 'Did you ever see what a .44 Magnum can do to a woman's pussy? That you should see.' At this point in the conversation we see Travis readjusting his rear window so as to get a new, and perhaps and a clearer view of this stranger, who voices his most intimate desires, while the latter, laughing, keeps repeating 'you must think I'm pretty sick'. By turning once more to the woman in the window, Scorsese cuts to a new scene. Travis hasn't answered the question posed by the man who both doubles and directs him, and in so doing forces him to recognize the paranoid fantasy his mind has rendered real, as images perceived through glass, back-lit curtains and mirrors.

As Martin Scorsese has noted about his nocturnal *flâneur*, 'Although at the end of the film he seems to be in control again, we give the impression that any second the time bomb might go off again.'[21] Indeed, in the very last sequence of the film, Betsy, whom Travis hasn't seen since their disastrous date at the porno theatre, gets into his cab. He takes her home, refuses her money, and instead drives back into the night. As he glides through the neon-lit streets, his gaze suddenly catches hold of something and Scorsese shows us a demonic flicker in Travis's eyes, before he readjusts his mirror. At this moment the screen splits in two, so that as the final credits role, we once more see a non-mimetic representation of the nocturnal cityscape. It is blurred, but not as in the credit sequence, owing to the rain. Rather it has lost its contours, because what Travis sees through the glass and what is reflected on the glass have come visually to be enmeshed into the uncanny site Blanchot calls *autre nuit*. The representation of the night that ensues is one that ricochets back on itself to a point of nothingness, from which a plethora of images emerge. We are at the navel not only of the phantasmagoria produced by Travis's insomnia, but also of those produced by Scorsese's cinematic dream. We have the sense of seeing a film of the night, both outside and inside the windowpane, static and in motion, doubled and juxtaposed. Then, seamlessly, one of the two layers slowly fades away and we are outside, on the street, watching the black silhouettes of pedestrians trying to hail a cab, until the screen falls into complete darkness.

Without us noticing it, Travis has moved out of our frame of vision, faded into the artificial lights and the dark shadows of Scorsese's New York night. This final shot is, of course, an explicit tribute to the famous ending of *The Searchers*, in which John Wayne hovers for several seconds on the threshold of the home into which his niece Debbie, whom he has saved from captivity, has already entered, only to turn away and walk back into the prairie. Like John Wayne's Ethan, de Niro's Travis remains in his nocturnal prairie, which is to say, he is still out there in the uncanny dark, into which all cinema falls when its narrative is over and the lights go on. He remains in a night from which, according to Hegel, all images emerge, and from which, according to Freud, repressed representations return. We, in turn, have seamlessly fallen out of this night, are now outside, but Scorsese has deftly moved us into the *autre nuit* of pure aesthetic representation. In contrast to Schnitzler's 'Dream Novella' with its laughter of a child, who has woken up from her dream to signal the beginning of a new day, there is no dawn at the end of *Taxi Driver*. But there is a different awakening. If Travis remains in a night that has receded from our grasp, then he does so in order for us to wake up, gently, not abruptly to the light of day outside the cinema, but simply to a stage and state of mind – outside. This is cinema's rhetoric of the uncanny.

Notes

1. Sigmund Freud, 'The "Uncanny"', The Standard Edition vol. XVII (London: Hogarth Press, 1955), p. 241. All references are from this edition.
2. Freud, p. 245.
3. For a discussion of romantic psychology, see Henri F. Ellenberger, *The Discovery of the Unconscious. The History and Evolution of Dynamic Psychiatry* (New York: Basic Books, 1970).

4. See Stanley Cavell, *Cities of Words. Pedagogical Letters on a Register of the Moral Life* (Cambridge: Harvard University Press, 2004).
5. Georg Wilhelm Friedrich Hegel, *Jenaer Realphilosophie* in *Frühe philosophische Systeme* (Frankfurt am Main: Ullstein, 1974). All citations are from this edition, translations are by the author. For a discussion of the interlinkage between Freud and romantic philosophy, see also Slavoj Zizek's introduction, 'The Abyss of Freedom' to F.W.J. Schelling, *Ages of the World* (Ann Arbor: The University of Michigan Press, 1997), pp. 1–104.
6. Arthur Schnitzler, 'Traumnovelle', *Traumnovelle und andere Erzählungen* (Frankfurt am Main: S. Fischer, 1979), p. 60. All citations are from this edition, the translations are by the author.
7. Hegel, p. 181.
8. Schnitzler, p. 59.
9. Schnitzler, p. 60.
10. Schnitzler, pp. 60, 61, 60.
11. Schnitzler, p. 76.
12. Schnitzler, pp. 87, 96.
13. Schnitzler, p. 122.
14. Schnitzler, p. 127.
15. Schnitzler, pp. 128, 129.
16. Maurice Blanchot, 'Le Dehors, la Nuit', in *L'espace Littéraire* (Paris: Gallimard, 1955), translation of the cited passages is by the author, pp. 215–16.
17. Cited in Ian Christie and David Thompson, *Scorsese on Scorsese* (London: Faber and Faber, 2003), p. 54.
18. See Murray Melbin, *Night as Frontier* (New York: The Free Press, 1987) as well as Mark Caldwell, *New York Night: The Mystique and its History* (New York: Scribner, 2005).
19. Freud, p. 234.
20. See Amy Taubin, *Taxi Driver* (London: BFI, 2000).
21. Christie and Thompson, *Scorsese*, p. 62.

3

Uncanny Reflections, Modern Illusions: Sighting the Modern Optical Uncanny

Tom Gunning

The uncanny: Modern? Optical?

> Reluctantly I picked up the binoculars, for it was a distasteful task to me. Ever since I could remember, I had felt a revulsion for all optical instruments. Somehow they seemed wicked to me – binoculars which could make objects seem either small and distant or else uncannily close. Or a microscope which could magnify a small worm into the dimensions of a monster.
>
> Edogawa Rampo[1]

Is there a specifically *modern* uncanny? Freud's famous essay relates the uncanny to the timeless processes of the unconscious, and even refers back to archaic modes of thought – animism, magical powers of consciousness, the return of the dead, the existence of doubles.[2] But while I would never claim that the uncanny is exclusively a modern phenomenon, I would certainly claim there is a modern uncanny. Much of what we think of as uncanny entails the emergence of a modern world: the struggle that an enlightened scientific worldview undertook with what it understood as superstition and illusion. The uncanny can arise when certain beliefs, taken for granted in traditional cultures, become unsettling and strange (yet, as Freud indicates, also hauntingly familiar) to modern experience. Likewise radical new technologies on first appearance can seem somehow magical and uncanny, recalling the wish fulfillments that magical thought projected into fairy tales and rituals of magic.

The uncanny refers to the unsettling and contradictory. In Freud's philological treatment of the German term translated as uncanny, *unheimlich*, the word embodies a sort of coincidence of opposites, since *heimlich* (homely, familiar) and its apparent lexical opposite *unheimlich* (uncanny, but literally 'un-home-like') can sometimes be used interchangeably. *Heimlich* in certain contexts indicates something hidden, mysterious, or unconscious. As Freud puts it, 'Thus *heimlich* is a word the meaning of which develops in the direction of ambivalence, until it finally coincides with its opposite, *unheimlich*.'[3] (Although I am not sure we should press the analogy, the English word 'canny' and 'uncanny' can also be used interchangeably in certain circumstance. The phrases 'he has a canny ability to throw a knife' and 'he has an uncanny ability to throw a knife' mean more or less the same thing – in fact, the latter may be seen as an intensification of the former, rather than its opposite). Freud defines the uncanny as 'that class of the frightening that leads back to what is known of old and long familiar'.[4] 'An unsettling uncertainty that evokes an odd familiarity in the midst of strangeness' provides my working definition of the uncanny. I acknowledge the problem that this definition depends partly on an affective response (the uncanny shudder that would seem to generate the phenomenon) that is hard to generalize. However, since I will trace the uncanny as embodied in practices (both texts and performances), I believe that there is enough structural consistency to allow a description of this experience phenomenologically, even if, by definition, it eludes precise verbal description or logical analysis.

Freud indicated that Ernst Jentsch's slightly earlier description of the uncanny remained inadequate, because the intellectual uncertainty with which Jentsch identified the term offered too broad a territory and could not explain the affective quality of the experience of the uncanny, which Freud, in his classic essay, tried to do.[5] My ambition comes closer to Jentsch's descriptive task than Freud's explanatory one, but I acknowledge Freud's great insight that the uncanny is more than a logical uncertainty. As a psychological phenomenon the uncanny points us not simply to confusion, but to the dynamic effect this uncertainty causes, not only in the reader/viewer, but in texts themselves, as fixed categories of experience – such as dream/reality or supernatural/everyday – become ambivalent. This essay attempts to probe how the unsettling effect of the uncanny plays a key role in the history and the pre-history of cinema, as indicated by a discussion of texts, apparatuses, and a phenomenological discussion of the viewer's experience.

The second part of my topic also deserves some discussion. Why – or how – is the uncanny *optical*? I should state categorically that I do not believe that all uncanny experiences are optical. Not only could uncanny experience derive from any of the senses (or their confluence), it need not be especially rooted in a specific sensual representation.

Indeed, uncanny experiences (such as my favorite example, *déjà vu*) may even seem to evade the senses, overwhelming them with a seemingly more primal experience linked perhaps to dreams or memories. Nor would I claim all optical uncanny experience is modern, as visions and dreams make up a considerable part of archaic religious experience. But in modernity not only does the optical uncanny become crucial and dramatic (as evident in the development of Fantastic literature), but the modern scientific and technological exploration of vision and optics (such as the proliferation of new optical devices) multiply and articulate the possibilities of the optical uncanny.

My essay approaches visual and optical culture broadly. Although I focus on visual experiences of unsettling uncertainty, these are often described in verbal rather than visual texts. Literary and filmic stories therefore play a key role in my investigation. Narratives literally explicate the uncanny, unfolding its implications. However, I would also maintain that the uncanny does not demand a narrative, as we usually understand it – a form involving actions motivated by characters, leading to some sort of resolution. Critics have examined the structure and history of Fantastic literature and their relation to the uncanny, but the less narrativized forms of the optical uncanny offered by magic shows or the visual devices of cinema, whether special effects or animation, have received relatively little attention. The scenography of magic tricks relies more on display than on diegesis (or attractions rather than narrative). Such magic acts can be integrated into a narrative, or they can operate in various degrees of independence from storytelling. Thus this essay deals with both the narrative and the display aspects of the optical uncanny in cinema, as well as in the visual and literary forms that preceded and accompanied the development of motion pictures.

The optical uncanny within Fantastic narratives

> And, wishing to describe the inner pictures in all their vivid colors, with their lights and their shades, you struggled in vain to find words with which to express yourself. But you felt you must gather up all the events that had happened, wonderful, splendid, terrible, jocose and awful, in the very first word, so that the whole might be revealed by a single electric discharge, so to speak.
>
> E. T. A. Hoffmann, 'The Sandman'[6]

The narrative form of the uncanny seems to me best understood in relation to the literary genre known as the Fantastic. The analysis given to this genre by Tzvetan Todorov provides a model of clarity and precision.[7] Since his analysis is well known and has been widely discussed, I will restrict myself to a brief summary. In Todorov's schema, the Fantastic exists between two closely related genres. The first he calls the strange (*l'etrange*).[8] Unfortunately, the English translation by the redoubtable Richard Howard (cued, it must be admitted, by certain comments by Todorov, who seems to endorse this identification) translates this term by 'uncanny'.[9] However, I think it can be demonstrated that the genre of the Fantastic is closer to the uncanny as understood by Freud and Jentsch and the critics who have followed in their wake. Therefore I will translate Todorov's term as 'strange'. Strange stories recount unusual but quite explainable circumstances, extremes of violence or grotesque situations that strike the reader as uncommon, but not impossible. On the other side of the Fantastic lies the genre Todorov calls the Marvelous, a fictional world in which the magical and mythological constitute part of the nature of things, such as the Tales of the Arabian Nights or fairytales, or the romances of Tolkien.[10] The Fantastic as a genre not only lies between these two genres, but represents their destabilization and contamination.

According to Todorov, the Fantastic takes place within a world in which the supernatural is not taken for granted, creating a hesitation for characters or readers (or both) about the proper interpretation of events.[11] While some films or literary texts (such as Jacques Tourneur's *Cat People* or Henry James's *The Turn of the Screw*) maintain uncertainty about the supernatural status of events until, or even beyond, the end of the story, many more narratives evoke uncertainty more briefly. Characters initially doubt the existence of the supernatural but eventually either uncover natural explanations (a genre Todorov dubs the Fantastic/Strange, typified for literary historians by the Gothic novels of Ann Radcliffe – and by their students by the animated cartoon *Scooby-Doo*), or finally must acknowledge the existence of a supernatural event (a genre Todorov calls The Fantastic/Marvelous, found in most nineteenth-century ghost stories and contemporary horror films).[12]

Less an affect (such as fear or horror) than a reading position founded on a prolonged uncertainty about the nature of the fictional world, this fantastic hesitation defines the genre. While the uncanny cannot be restricted to the Fantastic genre, I think we can identify the uncanny with this hesitation, since the Fantastic as a genre depends on an experience of unsettling uncertainty. Although his structuralist method excludes a detailed exploration of context, Todorov understands that the Fantastic appears as a historical and culturally determined genre.[13] I would point out that the Fantastic can only occur in an era or culture in which an attitude of skepticism has become available. Thus, when Todorov speaks of 'our world, the one we know, a world without devils, sylphides, or vampires',[14] the 'our' implicitly excludes both pre-Enlightenment eras or traditional cultures which admit the possibility of supernatural factors. The rationalist and scientific orientation implied in Todorov's understanding of 'our' world can only portray the Marvelous with either a certain irony, or an explicit suspension of realist expectations. Doubting the supernatural would seem to be a default mode within a rational and realistically portrayed modern world.

The Fantastic genre develops an uncanny experience into a story. But how does the specifically 'optical' uncanny relate to this narrative genre? While not all Fantastic stories deal with the optical uncanny, in his discussion of Fantastic themes in literature Todorov highlighted the role played by perception and especially vision.[15] Many Fantastic narratives turn on issues of ambiguous vision, since doubting one's perception supplies a major motivation for the Fantastic hesitation. Literary Fantastic tales, while expressed in language, often make visual perception the hinge upon which the Fantastic hesitation pivots. But as a Fantastic theme, vision implies more than ordinary perception. In his treatment of the theme of vision within the German Romantic stories of E. T. A. Hoffmann, Todorov stresses, 'it is not vision itself that is linked to the world of the marvelous, but rather eyeglasses and mirrors, those symbols of indirect, distorted, subverted vision.'[16] Todorov adds, 'These objects are, in a sense, vision materialized or rendered opaque, a quintessence of sight.'[17] Visual devices such as telescopes, spectacles and especially mirrors serve as figures of vision, providing an optical rhetoric parallel to verbal tropes. Optical rhetoric contributes to Fantastic narrative in both verbal and visual form (such as the use of shadows and off-screen space in *Cat People*, or supernatural parallels established by crosscutting in *Nosferatu*) by unsettling our confidence in vision and raising the possibility that supernatural forces are determining events.

The optical uncanny and the rhetoric of visual display

> Thus when I indulged in some amusing paradox, to draw public attention away from the side where the trick was to be performed, you alone escaped the snare, and fixed your eyes on the right spot.[18]
>
> Jean-Eugène Robert-Houdin (describing a conversation with his first magical mentor Torrini)

As I stated at the outset, I do not restrict the optical uncanny to narrative forms, whether verbal or visual. Optical displays, such as magic tricks, are also designed to provoke uncanny effects. In magic illusions, uncanny optics play with the perception of the viewer, without necessarily creating an imagined diegetic world. Fiction insulates its depicted events from the reality testing common to daily life and thus allows the Marvelous literary genres of fairytale and fantasy to exist. But if we turn to the non-narrative aspects of the optical uncanny, such as the magic trick, the possibility arises of seeming to breach this separation between the fictional and the real, which can provide a new dimension of uncanny experience. As Freud put it, 'a great deal that is not uncanny in fiction would be so if it happened in real life.'[19] Seeing an event – such as an elephant apparently vanishing before our very eyes, or a woman floating in midair – that contradicts rational expectations generates a different, perhaps more powerful, hesitation than reading an account of such an event.

As powerful as the fact that a magical illusion takes place before our very eyes may be, nonetheless magical illusions should not be identified simply with paranormal experiences that we take for real. Magic shows occur within a realm of artifice – as opposed, say, to an uncanny event that seems to occur in the middle of everyday life, such as a bizarre coincidence or the apparent vision of an apparition, or the experience of *déjà vu*. Magic tricks play with an appearance of an actual event, much as Fantastic stories play with the appearance of realism, but they remain within the realm of play. Magicians, as I have discussed in other essays[20] (and will discuss further on in this essay) generally do not claim to cause a supernatural event, merely its appearance. The scenography of magic illusions assumes modern skepticism, and, like the Fantastic tale, makes the viewer oscillate between doubt and belief, through the illusionist's manipulation of our perception.

Thus the magic trick depends on a hesitation that recalls the Fantastic hesitation, but which instead of coming from a fictional world is enacted before the viewer, invoking not so much our imagination as it plays with our perception. A magical illusion causes us to doubt our ordinary vision, whether by sleight of hand ('the hand is quicker than the eye') or through elaborate visual illusions achieved by concealed technology (for instance, the false bottom of a prop, or the wires and balance apparatus which makes a woman appear to float in the air).

Magical illusions, therefore, can operate independently of narrative and outside of the arts of language. Of course, magical illusions can embed themselves in a narrative spoken by the magician, and language plays a curious role in the form of magical spells. But while the narrative can appropriate the magical illusion (as in *féerique* performances in France in the nineteenth century, or Hollywood films using special effects), illusions can equally well maintain varying degrees of independence. Likewise magical words immediately assert their difference from ordinary language not only through their apparent supernatural efficacy, but their lack of translatability (Abracadabra, Sim sala Bim, and Hocus Pocus are in fact corruptions of foreign phrases prized precisely for their exotic incomprehensibility).

In the non-narrative optical uncanny (and my purpose is differentiation, not mutual exclusion, since the forms often combine in specific texts) of the magical illusion, the magician or artificer controls the visual perception of the viewer, much as the narrator of a Fantastic tale controls the reader through the devices of narration. While magician's handbooks emphasize the manual skill of the prestidigitator or the complexity of their props, these techniques are ultimately aimed at controlling the perceptions of the audience. Manual dexterity or technical ingenuity provides means of creating a deceptive yet persuasive visual appearance, which conceals actual processes from the viewer. The most influential of French magicians, Jean-Eugène Robert-Houdin (whose name was later parodied – and reputation sullied – by Harry Houdini), indicated that even the most basic of all magic tricks, the cup and balls, involves not only control of the hand, but just as fundamentally, fooling the eye:

> It is well known that the trick with the balls wonderfully improves the touch, but does it not improve the vision at the same time? In fact, when a juggler throws into the air four balls crossing each other in various directions, he requires an extraordinary power of sight to follow the direction his hands have given to each of the balls.[21]

The magician's visual acuity contrasts with the ordinary viewer's undisciplined eye, which the magician counts on misleading, whether by speed of manipulation, strategies of misdirection, or the aid of technological devices. Magic illusions, from prestidigitation to highly technological illusions, such as cinema, involve a manipulation of sight and control of vision, producing not simply an intellectual doubt, but a profound uncertainty about the nature of perception that can open the confused viewer to the possibility of the supernatural.

Impossible to believe my own eyes! Perception and skeptical hesitation

> It was like a photograph, but moved as a real dog moved, its tongue lolling, its ears pricked, its tail wagging. Then the dog turned its profile to the audience, raised one of its back legs, and began to piss. The gentlemen in the room rushed for the door to avoid getting drenched.
>
> Eduardo Mendoza, *The City of Miracles*[22]

Rather than pure persuasion, modern magic incorporates a hesitation similar to that of the Fantastic tale as described by Todorov. The magician does not seek to convince, but to entertain. In previous essays I have described the particular contradiction of the magic performance in the modern era in which fantastic illusions are created, yet no supernatural powers are claimed by the magician.[23] In contrast to the wondrous performances of shamans in traditional cultures designed to cause cures or cast spells, the modern magician seeks to entertain rather than inspire belief. The complex and deeply dialectical nature of the modern conjurer is nicely summarized in a statement made by the mysterious but influential magician Philippe Philipsthal (probable inventor of the Phantasmagoria), a German showman who performed in France during the era of the Revolution under the name Paul Philidor.[24] Philidor would introduce his late eighteenth-century ghost shows with this preamble:

> I will not show you ghosts, because there are no such things; but I will produce before you enactments and images, which are imagined to be ghosts, in the dreams of the imagination or in the falsehoods of charlatans. I am neither priest nor magician. I do not wish to deceive you; but I will astonish you.[25]

In the magic show the optical uncanny plays a role parallel to hesitation in the Fantastic tale, articulating the somewhat uncertain hold that modern man has on a rational and scientific view of things. As Freud claims, the modern rational and scientific view of things, while confident in its apodictic claims, also encounters psychological resistance, both from repressed unconscious content and from the inertia of primitive modes of thought that have supposedly been superceded.[26] In the modern enlightened era, we doubt the existence of the supernatural, but nonetheless we are also drawn to it, even seduced by it.

Modern magic shows operate within the context of post-Enlightenment skepticism: inherently doubting the existence of the supernatural, but also delighting playfully in the illusion of such events. The magic show assumes the questioning of sensual perception that Descartes made essential to the process of systematic doubt. The magic trick does not launch an argument or demonstration aimed at toppling the modern view of things, but rather presents a trick, an artificial and created illusion entered into in a spirit of play. The opposition between the nineteenth-century Spiritualists who did seek to demonstrate the existence of a supernatural spirit world and the stage magicians – from Maskelyne, to Robert-Houdin, to Méliès, to Houdini – who parodied and mocked their claims marks this difference, as I have discussed elsewhere.[27] Rather than an anxious and credulous spectator, the viewer of modern magic becomes fascinated and entertained by a contradiction between what they see and what they know in fact to be the nature of things. The optical uncanny occurs precisely within this split between vision and belief, triggering the experience of not believing one's own eyes. An early nineteenth-century attendee of the Phantasmagoria (the elaborate display of optical illusions based in the magic lantern that E. G. Robertson developed from the spectacle offered earlier by Philipsthal) described the effect of the show in this manner:

> It is certain the illusion is complete. The total darkness of the place, the choice of images, the astonishing magic of their truly terrifying growth, the conjuring that accompanies them, everything combines to strike your imagination and to seize exclusively all your observational senses. Reason has told you well that these things are mere phantoms, catoptric tricks devised with artistry, carried out with skill, presented with intelligence, your weakened brain can only believe what it is made to see, and we believe ourselves to be transported into another world and another century.[28]

The optical uncanny as evoked by the magic illusion questions the existence of the supernatural, yet playfully (and usually temporarily) circumvents the hold of logic and reason in order to revel in the way the senses, and vision especially, can be deceived into an appearance of the impossible.

Skepticism toward the data given by the senses appears in various cultures and eras, including Buddhist and Hindu doctrines, as well as the Greek philosophical tradition and even the religious practices of the Jesuits or Protestant puritans. But the modern era in the West, marked by the systematic doubt of the senses formulated by Descartes, brought the questioning of visual perception into particular focus. In the eighteenth century the demonstration of the principles of optics, which had been essential to the Enlightenment project as embodied in the work on optics by Descartes and Newton in the seventeenth century, moved from the practitioners of Natural Magic to the pioneers of experimental science. While earlier natural magicians such as Giambattista della Porta or Athanasius Kircher had displayed the wonders of nature as marvels of God's creation, Enlightenment scientists sought regularity and predictable rules beneath the marvelous appearances.[29] Optical illusions were explicable, and the effects of lenses and mirrors, as well as the physiology of the human eye could be scientifically explained.

Furthermore, the new sciences introduced and developed new optical devices, such as the telescope and microscope, which greatly expanded the power of sight, but also denaturalized it, making vision partly a function of new scientific instruments.[30] The optical uncanny often offered a reflection and occasionally a caprice based on the instrumental nature of modern visual experience. This new preoccupation with visual devices can be found both in fiction, as in Todorov's discussion of the tales of E. T. A. Hoffmann, or in the use of various optical devices in the Phantasmagoria or the increasingly careful control of the spectator's perception through light and mirrors found in later nineteenth-century magic shows. Demonstrations of scientific instruments and their effects intertwine with magic shows, from the *salon de physique* displays of electricity and distorting mirrors that Robertson offered as a prologue to his more gothic and sinister magical illusions, to the American television show from my childhood which demonstrated science to children, *Mr. Wizard*.[31] In the nineteenth century public demonstrations of scientific instruments and experiments became a form of urban entertainment. The Polytechnic Institute in London and Barnum's Museum in the US were only the best known of many such demonstration halls in which the line between education and entertainment, demonstration and magical illusion often became quite blurred.[32] As the nineteenth century progressed, both scientific demonstrations and magical illusion continued to develop as forms of popular entertainment, although the two tended increasingly to diverge in terms of techniques and institutions.[33]

Optical devices: Uncanny technologies of science and magic

> With the aid of a fine Kuff solar microscope we projected her image and neatly detached the reflection from the white wall, smoothly and without any damage. As soon as the reflection floated free it shot like a lightning flash into the lens, which was shattered in a thousand pieces. Before us stood the princess, fresh and full of life.
>
> E. T. A. Hoffmann, 'Master Flea'[34]

During the nineteenth century, the optical uncanny nourished the domains of both literature and spectacle, from German and French Romanticism to the modern magic theater represented by Maskelyne and Cook's Egyptian Hall or the Parisian Théâtre Robert-Houdin and ultimately the early magic films of Georges Méliès. As French scholar of Romanticism, Max Milner, has put it in his study *La fantasmagorie*:

> At the same moment that in France the deployment of optical devices gave birth to a spectacle, the Phantasmagoria (a term which, along with the adjective it spawns, will come to signify an important aspect of the active imagination), the German Romantics, reflecting on the powers of the imagination, would constantly use the same optical techniques as metaphors for creative activities that appeared to them in a new light. The fantastic genre, especially as it developed in Germany and France demonstrated this basic convergence between the imaginary and the optical.[35]

Like Todorov, Milner details how the tales of Hoffmann (as well as Tieck, Chamisso, Jean Paul, and other German Romantics) employed optical devices as figures for the creative imagination. The telescope Nathaniel buys from Coppelius in 'The Sandman'; the mirror and its reflections in 'The Deserted House' and 'A New Year's Eve Adventure'; the magically transforming spectacles, the mirrored coach and the magical reflecting pool in the novella 'Princess Brambilla'; and perhaps most complex of all the panoply of microscopes and clairvoyant lenses found in 'the Master Flea'.[36]

In this delightful novella Hoffmann stages a battle between two seventeenth-century pioneers of the use of the microscope, Leeuwenhoek and Swammerdam, over the possession of a Master Flea who enlists the aid of a middle-aged bachelor Peregrinus Tyss and places a microscopic lens in his eye, which enables him to read other people's thoughts. Leeuwenhoek had made the Master Flea perform in his flea circus, using a projecting telescope to reveal the miniature spectacle to his audience. Swammerdam and Leeuwenhoek fight a duel with collapsing telescopes. Hoffmann renders the relation the German Romantics forged between the optical and the psychological explicit in the microscopic lens placed in Tyss's eye, which like the actual ophthalmoscope allows Tyss to penetrate the inner eye: 'Behind the cornea of Swammer's eye he perceived curious nerves and filaments whose wondrously tangled course he was able to follow far into the brain and to discern Swammer's thoughts.'[37]

Scientific optical devices could be retooled in Fantastic tales to provide new forms of perception that envisioned marvelous realms. Hoffmann and a number of writers of Fantastic fiction (including Théophile Gautier, Jules Verne, and the extraordinary Japanese writer Edgowara Rampo) all explored the ambiguities of mediated vision not only to introduce optical marvels, but to create hesitation about the veracity of perception, all questioning in some way whether the visions that new technology offered could be trusted. This apparently paradoxical dovetailing of scientific instruments and archaic modes of thought reflects the transitional role the uncanny can play, exploring unaccustomed aspects of new technology, rehearsing both anxieties and desires which envision technology in terms of modern magic.

But if Fantastic narratives ambiguously envision the new science and technology in terms of magic and wonder, stage magicians throughout the nineteenth century employed modern optical devices that allowed a new control over visual experience. In the late eighteenth century, the Phantasmagoria used refinements to the magic lantern, involving a brighter and mobile lantern, back projection and a new focusing device to create phantoms that seemed to charge the audience. Robert-Houdin used a powerful electromagnet to create his 'heavy coffer' illusion in which strong men seemed unable to lift a metal box from the stage when the magnet concealed beneath the flooring was operating, while even a child could lift it when the magnet was switched off. (The electromagnet explained the illusion, but the act of concealing it from view reveals again the control of vision required by magic illusions, even when optical devices are not used.)

The golden age of optical magic occurred later in the nineteenth century, ushered in by an illusion that premiered at London's primary show place of scientific demonstration, the Polytechnic Institute. Historian of magic Jim Steinmeyer claims, 'Pepper's Ghost represented a new category of illusion: optical conjuring.'[38] The Phantasmagoria offered an earlier example of optical magic, but whereas the Phantasmagoria relied on images projected from painted lantern glass slides, Pepper's Ghost and the illusions that followed in its wake involved various manipulations of mirror reflections. Invented by Henry Dircks and refined by Royal Polytechnic entrepreneur John Henry Pepper who premiered it in 1862, the illusion relied on simple optics. A pane of transparent glass emerged from slots in the stage, appearing in front of a playing space, but angled so that it caught a reflection of a highly illuminated figure (usually an actor) from an area not visible to the audience. From the audience's point of view (and in the optical magic theater the control of audience sightlines played an essential role) the transparent glass itself remained invisible, and only the reflection appeared, a transparent figure superimposed on the stage scene behind the glass. Historian of magic Sidney W. Clark claimed that this illusion, 'first brought home the immense possibilities of glass, plain or silvered, in the production of magic illusions'.[39]

Mirrors played an important part in the history of magic and witchcraft. Reginald Scot's *The Discoverie of Witchcraft* from 1584 devoted several pages to their properties, claming magic mirrors can show images, not by ordinary reflection, but through supernatural powers:

> what image or favour soever you shall print in your imagination, you shall think you see the same therein. Others are so framed, as therein you may see what others doo in places far distant; others whereby you shall see men hanging in the aire; others whereby you may see men flieng in the aire; others wherein you may see one coming & another going; others where one image shall seem to be a hundred &c. There be glasses also wherein one man may see another man's image, and not his own; others to make manie similitudes; others to make none at all ... others that represent not the image received within them but cast them off in the aire, appearing like airie images ... There be clear glasses that make thing seem little, things farre off to be at hand, and that which is neer, to be farre off.[40]

Natural magicians such as Giambattista della Porta discussed the virtues of mirrors and lenses in a manner that blended their optical qualities with supernatural ones.[41] In a more rationalist spirit, Sir David Brewster's treatment of Natural Magic in the early nineteenth century claimed to explain the apparent supernatural powers of traditional mages and sorcerers through their manipulations of mirror images.[42] But even in the sixteenth century, for Scot the magical properties of mirrors reflected their illusionistic properties: 'But the wondrous devises, and miraculous sights and concepts made and contained in glass doo fare exceed all other; wherein the art of perspective is verie necessarie.'[43] That mirror reflections and the 'art of perspective' could be classed with magic reveals how technologies once thought to be uncanny later became an essential part of the techniques and skills of realistic representational arts.

Both Fantastic tales and magical displays made use of mirrors in the later nineteenth century, but in somewhat opposed manners. The theme of the mirror as a site of supernatural visitation is a common topos in the Fantastic, perhaps most beautifully worked out in

Théophile Gautier's 1866 novella *Spirite*.[44] Gautier's Fantastic tales, such as 'La Morte amoureuse', a key text for Todorov's analysis of the genre, or his masterful exploration of the peril and seduction of voyeurism in 'Omphale', based themselves in the ambiguities of visual experience.[45] In *Spirite* this theme of vision becomes embodied in a Venetian mirror, the device whereby the spirit visitor appears and obsesses the narrator. Gautier describes the process by which the spirit becomes visible with detailed, almost scientific, optical description, which not only exemplifies the realistic treatment in which the Fantastic genre embeds their supernatural events, but also a modern awareness of the physiology of sight (e.g. the bluish effect of low light on vision, known as the Purkinje effect), and the science of optics:

> At the center of this glistening surround, the mirror, whose dimensions were small, like Venetian mirrors, seemed to be a bluish black, indefinitely profound and like an opening made onto a void full of perfect darkness [...]
> Finally he thought that within this darkness he could make out a kind of vague milky whiteness, a kind of distant flickering glow which seemed to be getting nearer.[46]

The blending of the optical and the psychological that particularly marks nineteenth-century fantasy (so that, as Terry Castle has detailed,[47] the term phantasmagoria becomes increasingly applied to psychological states of reverie rather than an optical magic show) characterizes Gautier's use of the optical uncanny, as well that of Gérard de Nerval, Edgar Poe, and other late Romantics.

The visible and the invisible: The vanishing act of the optical uncanny

> But whereas all who gazed into it used to feel a special pleasure, there now were many who showed irritation and anger when they saw all Nature and themselves reflected in it, because it was against all dignity, indeed against all human reason and all arduously gained wisdom, to behold things upside down, especially one's own Self.
>
> E. T. A. Hoffmann, 'Princess Brambilla'[48]

Late nineteenth-century optical magic shows, far from displaying the uncanny powers of mirrors, employed newly available large sheet of flawless glass as a technology of concealment. One does not see the glass in 'Pepper's Ghost', but rather its reflections, appearing as an apparition floating on air. Magic's long tradition of concealing the actual process of transformation or disappearance (which can also be accomplished by concealed trap doors or seemingly invisible wires) becomes enriched through the ability of glass to be seen through, or to reflect – nothing. As Steinmeyer has brilliantly pointed out, the optical illusions that followed upon 'Pepper's Ghost' primarily arranged mirrors in order to conceal people or parts of bodies. By reflecting neutral backgrounds while seeming to allow the viewer to peer into the depths of a cabinet on between the legs of a table, such illusions as 'Proteus' caused a man to disappear, while 'The Sphinx' displayed a speaking head on a table seemingly detached from a body. Carefully angled mirrors provided what Steinmeyer aptly calls, 'an optical formula for invisibility'.[49] While the optical uncanny appeared in fantastic tales as spectacular magical optical devices that endowed those who look into it with miraculous powers of vision, optical conjuring used real (rather than imaginary) optical devices invisibly in order to create a magical illusion. These illusions employed the laws of optics and ordinary mirrors, lenses, and projected light to create illusions of the supernatural.

Thus we encounter a central paradox of modern optical magic. It can be simultaneously rational in its method and seemingly supernatural in its effect. It carefully displays certain aspects of its spectacle in order to create a managed illusion, while concealing other aspects. Illusions such as 'Pepper's Ghost', while fascinating in themselves, can be (and immediately were) integrated into fantastic narratives, such as stage productions of Dickens's 'The Haunted Man'.[50] Indeed – and here the paradoxes of the optical uncanny begin to undo themselves – similar optical devices can be used to create realistic rather than uncanny effects. Although electronic rather than optical, video techniques, such as the blue screen that allows maps to appear behind weathermen or characters to be placed in distant environments, have become the everyday techniques of television and cinema. While we think of special effects primarily in terms of the optical uncanny, most CGI effects in contemporary films do not present us with tornados, Gollum, or flying superheroes, but pass unnoticed as they render environments or figures intended to appear ordinary. The most common trick performed by optical special effects today is literally causing themselves to become invisible, unnoticed, – to disappear.

For Freud the uncanny is not only unsettling, but untimely. Combining in an unsettling manner the sensation of the familiar and the unfamiliar, the *Unheimlich*, according to Freud, brings back something that has been forgotten, or more properly speaking, repressed from conscious memory. Freud derives the uncanny from two possible sources, repressed material in the unconscious (such as the castration complex which he finds lurking within Hoffmann's story 'The Sandman') or primitive beliefs that have been surmounted by advances in rational thought, but which still exert a pull on the psyche. The return of the repressed and the residue of surmounted beliefs both refer to past experience, although a past that has been made difficult to access using conscious or historical memory. The uncanny not only finds one of its clearest examples in the experience of *déjà vu*, but this paradoxical experience also reflects its contradictory relation to the past. The uncanny strikes us as somehow returning us to a past moment, but a past moment, which, while almost overwhelmingly (and certainly unsettlingly) familiar, nonetheless cannot be grasped or represented by conscious memory. But just as *déjà vu* tends to fade, I would claim that the uncanny has also an unstable temporality. Although some experiences may always provoke uncanny associations for certain people, more often common familiarity seems to undo uncanny effects.

Elsewhere I have claimed that while wonder tends to fade with familiarity, uncanny effects may arise when wondrous or disturbing affects that have been dulled with familiarity suddenly are re-ignited through an unexpected encounter.[51] We might approach a variety of technologies in this way, especially those whose effects when novel were strongly associated with magical processes, such as the telephone's ability to carry a voice to great distances, the photograph's ability to fashion a visual double, or the cinema's ability to preserve a moment in time. Daily use and familiarity with these devices may destroy their uncanny nature, but Fantastic fiction has often created uncanny scenarios by restoring their initial supernatural associations: telephone calls from the dead, photographs that seem to change in relation to their subjects, or films that affect hearers like wraiths. At its origins cinema generated its own uncanny optical fantasies in its first audiences. For many of these early spectators the medium itself appeared like a magic trick, bringing pictures to life – 'Animated pictures'.[52] The extraordinary novel by Eduardo Mendoza, *The City of Marvels*, embroiders this fantasy of cinema's first reception:

> The first viewers did not confuse what they were seeing on the screen with real life (as the legend invented a *posterior* would have us believe); rather they believed they were seeing photographs in

> motion. This led them to think that via the movie projector any image could be set in motion. 'Soon before our astonished gaze the Venus de Milo and the Sistine chapel, to mention only two examples, will come to life,' we read in an 1899 scientific journal.[53]

Mendoza's 1986 novel engages here in hyperbole and, as a historian of early cinema I am fairly confident this scientific journal exists only in his fantastic imagination. However, Mendoza accurately reflects an uncanny possibility spawned by the appearance of animated pictures. The sudden animation of a still image formed a common attraction of many early film projections, as the film image was first projected frozen and then endowed with animation by cranking the projector up to speed, which created wonder and, for many viewers, an uncanny experience.[54] As brilliant recent works by Laura Mulvey and Garrett Stewart have shown us,[55] the moving image still recurrently entails its contrary, the still: its resolution into the conditions of its production, the zone of cinema's death, and resurrection. Thus we can understand the recent claim that all cinema exists as a subclass of animation less as a triumph of new media over the old, but as a return to the original conditions of the filmic process.[56]

Animation: the illusion of motion given to individual still images constitutes the core illusion of cinema, its ultimate magic trick. At the point of origin the illusion of motion provided an attraction in itself, as the early cinema showmen displayed the cinematic apparatus as the ultimate conjuring device within Steinmeyer's long tradition of optical conjuring. But following the process by which an initially magical device becomes simply a medium, cinema became a means of showing the world in motion, of projecting familiar and exotic views. Georges Méliès was one of a number of early stage magicians who recognized the invention of motion pictures as a new form of optical conjuring and acquired a projector and camera in order to present films at the Théâtre Robert-Houdin (as the Egyptian Hall, the premier showplace for theatrical magic in Great Britain, also showed motion pictures managed by such conjurers as Felicien Trewey and David Devant).[57] Like most of the films first shown in magic showplaces, Méliès's earliest films presented views of ordinary occurrences, and consisted of scenes of trains arriving at stations and men playing cards. However, Méliès and others soon realized the possibilities the motion picture camera offered magicians for the control of viewer vision.

Most stage illusions control vision spatially by hiding the apparatus that creates the illusion; an essential aspect of working the trick remains concealed from the audience's view, left off-stage or camouflaged. Méliès and the pioneers of trick films realized that the cinema, by its presentation of a seemingly continuous run of time, could conceal essential aspects of an illusion (the aspects which actually *caused* the transformation or disappearance) in another way – not only spatially, but temporally – by literally cutting some part of the time taken in production out of the film while creating an illusion of continuity during the film's projection. Méliès combined stop motion (stopping the camera, while carefully maintaining the same framing in order to preserve continuity, and altering some part of the scene, such as removing a prop or actor) with cutting the film (to eliminate telltale bits of the work of transformation). Thus he cinematically caused figures or objects to magically disappear or transform into something else entirely. The cinema created magical displays that, rather than recording a familiar world, created impossible magical happenings on the screen. Such tricks could stand on their own as attractions for the audience, but Méliès and others also integrated them into more extended stories or scenarios of action.

The optical uncanny has a long history that could include the visual displays recorded in ancient accounts of magic and wonders (such as the revelations that ended the Mysteries of Eleusis). But modern skepticism about supernatural causes and mastering of the principles of optics through modern science and mechanics gave birth to a modern uncanny in Freud's sense: an encounter with a mode of thought seemingly surmounted whose apparent recrudescence causes an unsettling yet fascinating sensation. The uncanny gazes across an abyss at something left behind, and yet suddenly recalled. With the modern science of optics the possibility of generating such sensations directly and intentionally gave birth to a modern optical conjuring, which dates back at least to the seventeenth-century catoptric mirror tricks of Kircher and Della Porta and gains impetus in the next century with the technical perfection of projected and reflected images. By the nineteenth century, the literary genre of the Fantastic and optical conjuring introduced a highly developed technology and rhetoric of the modern optical uncanny. The uncanny does not imply simply succumbing to an illusion, but rather being thrown into a state of uncertainty triggered by a sudden renewal of repressed or seemingly surmounted ways of thinking – without entirely removing their strangeness. For reasons that I believe are cultural and historical as much as psychological, this uncertainty fascinates us, and the fantastic tale and the magic trick are designed to provoke this uncanny pleasure.

There is no question that the nineteenth century saw the most intense period of modern uncanny optics, the flowering of the fantastic tale and of optical conjuring and magic theater, as well as increasingly complex optical entertainment devices (stereoscopes, multi-lens dissolving view magic lanterns, instantaneous photography) that ultimately included motion pictures. But does the modern uncanny survive into the twentieth and twenty-first century? Todorov claims the literature of the fantastic undergoes both a transformation and a decline in the twentieth century. The Fantastic, Todorov argues, is not replaced by realism (which acts more as a complement of the Fantastic than its exclusion), but by a modernist literature typified by Kafka in which the uncanny is no longer doubted, but rather taken for granted ('In Kafka, the supernatural event no longer provokes hesitation, for the world described is entirely bizarre'[58]).

But of course the Fantastic is only one way of processing the uncanny, and if the narrative structure of the Fantastic declines in the twentieth century, the uncanny becomes pervasive. The work of Kafka, or contemporary filmmakers, such as David Lynch, Elias Merhige, the Quay Brothers, Kurosawa Kiyoshi, Chan Wook Park, or Guillermo del Toro, represent less the attenuation of the uncanny than its colonization of the realistic world. As opposed to the continuous progress of enlightenment that Freud assumed, such works call into question the stability of the ordinary world, as if modern experience routinely anticipates the onslaught of the unfamiliar. Within these contemporary works modern technology generates uncanny situations rather than explaining them rationally. Cinema's obsession with special effects aspires to create a technological optical simulacrum torn between realistic appearance and believability and uncanny effects.[59] The contemporary nature of the optical uncanny continues to be worked and played out on a plethora of screens that so immerse us with moving images that we hardly take them in consciously. But is our conscious perception the issue?

While he claims the unconscious exists outside of time, Freud's work also chronicles the transformations brought to civilization by modernity. Freud's 'The Uncanny' emerged from a welter of personal (see Neil Hertz's account of its relation to the suicide of Tausk[60]), historical (the context of the Germany's traumatic defeat in WWI), and technological change. 'The Uncanny' was partly sparked by Freud's reading of the essay by his disciple Otto Rank on *The Double*.[61] Freud discusses in a footnote to his essay the film *The Student of Prague*, mentioning that it served as the starting point for Rank's treatment of this uncanny theme.[62] While a fair amount of nonsense has been written claiming that Freud disliked the cinema, this essay indicates his openness to Rank's serious treatment of a film. I want to close this consideration of the optical uncanny with comments Rank wrote in reaction to the 1913 Paul Wegener-Hanns Heinz Ewers-Stellan Rye *The Student of Prague*, a profound work and one of the first feature length films dealing with the Fantastic, which launched the second great era (after the trick films that Wegener explicitly paid tribute to in this film) of Fantastic cinema in the silent German cinema:

> It may perhaps turn out that cinematography, which in numerous ways reminds us of the dream-work, can also express certain psychological facts and relationships – which the writer often is unable to describe with verbal clarity – in such clear and conspicuous imagery that it facilitates our understanding of them. [...] the uniqueness of cinematography in visibly portraying psychological events calls our attention, with exaggerated clarity, to the fact that the interesting and meaningful problems of man's relationship to himself – and the fateful disturbance of this relation – finds here an imaginative representation.[63]

Rank acknowledges cinema's power in representing psychological processes, and the homology he draws between cinema and the dream-work underscores the slumbering uncanny power of cinema, its ability to animate the inert, to make the impossible occur before our eyes and, like so many modern optical devices, to summon up fantasies of a mode of vision beyond ordinary sight.

Notes

1. Edogawa Rampo, 'The Traveler with the Painted Rag Picture', in *Japanese Tales of Mystery and Imagination*, trans. James B. Harris (Tokyo: Charles Tuttle and Co., 1956), p. 218.
2. Sigmund Freud, 'The "Uncanny"', Standard Edition of *The Complete Psychological Works of Sigmund Freud*, ed. and trans. James Strachey (London: The Hogarth Press, 1955), pp. 217–56.
3. Freud, p. 226.
4. Ibid., p. 220.
5. Ibid., p. 230; See also Ernst Jentsch, 'On the Psychology of the Uncanny', trans. Roy Sellars, in *Uncanny Modernity*, ed. Jo Collins and John Jervis, (Basingstoke: Palgrave Macmillan Ltd., 2008), pp. 216–28.
6. In Hoffmann, *The Best Tales of Hoffmann*, trans. J. T. Bealby (New York: Dover Publications), p. 195.
7. Tzvetan Todorov, *The Fantastic: A Structural Approach to a Literary Genre* (Ithaca, NY: Cornell University Press, 1975), trans. Richard Howard.

8. Todorov, pp. 41–51.
9. Ibid., p. 46.
10. Ibid., pp. 51–7.
11. Ibid., pp. 25–40.
12. Ibid., p. 44.
13. Ibid., p. 166.
14. Ibid., p. 25.
15. Ibid., pp. 120–3.
16. Ibid., p. 122.
17. Ibid., p. 123.
18. Jean-Eugène, Robert-Houdin, *Memoirs,* trans. R. Shelton Mackenzie (Minneapolis, MN: Carl W. Jones, 1944), p. 51.
19. Freud, p. 249.
20. Gunning, 'Phantasmagoria and the Manufacturing of Illusions and Wonder: Towards a Cultural Optics of the Cinematic Apparatus', *The Cinema, A New Technology for the 20th Century*, ed. Andre Gaudreault, Catherine Russell, and Pierre Veronneau (Editions Payot Lausanne, 2004), pp. 31–44; 'Animated Pictures: Tales of Cinema's Forgotten Future', *Michigan Quarterly Review*, 34: 4 (Fall 1995), pp. 465–85. See also, Simon During, *Modern Enchantments: The Cultural Power of Secular Magic* (Cambridge: Harvard University Press, 2002) for an important discussion of modern magic. A wonderfully expansive and imaginative treatment of visual ambiguities and uncanny effect also appear in Marina Warner, *Phantasmagoria: Spirit Visions, Metaphors and Media into the Twentieth First Century* (London: Oxford University Press, 2006).
21. Robert-Houdin, p. 32.
22. Eduardo Mendoza, *The City of Miracles* (New York: Pocket Books, 1988), trans. Bernard Molloy, p. 285.
23. Gunning, 'Phantasmagoria'; 'Animated Pictures'.
24. See the recent account of Philipsthal in Mervyn Heard, *Phantasmagoria: The Secret Life of the Magic Lantern* (Hastings; The Projection Box, 2006), pp. 57–84.
25. Quoted in Laurent Mannoni, *The Great Art of Light and Shadow* (Exeter: University of Exeter Press, 2000), p. 144.
26. Freud, p. 247.
27. Gunning, 'Phantom Images and Modern Manifestations: Spirit Photography, Magic Theater, Trick Films and Photography's Uncanny', in *Fugitive Images from Photography to Video,* ed. Patrice Petro (Bloomington: Indiana University Press, 1995).
28. Grimod de la Reynière, in the *Courrier des Spectacles,* March 7, 1800, quoted by Mannoni, p. 162.
29. An excellent account of Kircher and the methods of Natural Magic appears in Thomas L. Hanks and Robert J. Silverman, *Instruments and Imagination* (Princeton: Princeton University Press, 1995), esp. pp. 3–71. On the element of wonder in pre-Enlightenment culture, see Lorraine Daston and Katherine Park, *Wonders and the Order of Nature 1150–1750* (New York: Zone Books, 1998).
30. The effect especially of the microscope is treated in Catherine Wilson, *Early Modern Philosophy and the Invention of the Microscope* (Princeton: Princeton University Press, 1995).

31. On Robertson see Heard, and Françoise Levie, *Étienne-Gaspard Robertson: La vie d'un fantasmagore* (Brussels: Le Préambule, 1990).
32. Richard D. Altick, *The Shows of London* (Cambridge: Harvard University Press, 1978).
33. See Iwan Rhys Morus, *Frankenstein's Children: Electricity, Exhibition, and Experiment in Early-Nineteenth-Century London* (Princeton: Princeton University Press, 1998).
34. E. T. A Hoffmann, 'The Master Flea', in *Three Märchen of E. T. A. Hoffmann*, trans. Charles E. Passage (Columbia: University of South Carolina Press, 1971), p. 284.
35. Max Milner, *La fantasmagorie* (Paris: PUF, 1982), p. 38. My translation.
36. Ibid., pp. 43–93.
37. Hoffmann, 'The Master Flea', pp. 313–14.
38. Jim Steinmeyer, *Hiding the Elephant: How Magicians Invented the Impossible and Learned to Disappear* (New York: Carroll and Graf, 2003), p. 43.
39. Quoted in During, p. 143.
40. Reginald Scot, *The Discoverie of Witchcraft* (reprint, New York: Dover Publications, 1972), p. 179.
41. Giambattista della Porta, *Natural Magick* (reprint, New York: Basic Books, 1957).
42. Sir David Brewster, *Letters on Natural Magic addressed to Sir Walter Scott 1832* (reprint, London: Kensington Publications, 2002).
43. Scot, p. 179.
44. Théophile Gautier, *Spirite*, trans. Patrick Jenkins (Cambs: Dedalus, 1995).
45. Théophile Gautier, *One of Cleopatra's Nights*, trans. Lafcadio Hearn (reprint, Gillette: Wayside Press, 1999).
46. Gautier, *Spirite*, p. 69.
47. Terry Castle, *The Female Thermometer: Eighteenth Century Culture and the Invention of the Uncanny* (New York, Oxford University Press, 1995) pp. 140–67.
48. Hoffmann, 'Princess Brambilla', in *Three Märchen*, p. 201.
49. Steinmeyer, p. 43.
50. Altick, p. 505.
51. Gunning, 'Re-Newing Old Technologies: Astonishment, Second Nature, and the Uncanny in Technology from the Previous Turn-of -the-Century', in *Rethinking Media Change: The Aesthetics of Transition*, eds David Thorburn and Henry Jenkins (Cambridge: MIT Press, 2003), pp. 39–59.
52. See my discussion of this in both 'Animated Pictures', and 'Primitive Cinema, a Frame-up? or The Trick's on Us', *Cinema Journal*, 28: 2 (Winter 1989), pp. 3–12.
53. Mendoza, *The City of Marvels*, p. 286.
54. Gunning, 'An Aesthetic of Astonishment: Early Film and the [In]Credulous Spectator', *Art and Text*, 34 (Fall 1989), pp. 31–45.
55. Garrett Stewart, *Between Film and Screen: Modernism's Photosynthesis* (Chicago: University of Chicago Press, 1999); Laura Mulvey, *Death 24X a Second: Stillness and the Moving Image* (London: Reaktion Books, 2006).
56. Lev Manovich, *The Language of New Media* (Cambridge: MIT Press, 2002), p. 302.
57. See Erik Barnouw, *The Magician and the Cinema* (New York: Oxford University Press, 1981), for a survey of this relation.
58. Todorov, p. 173.

59. See my discussion of the effect of CGI in 'Gollum and Golem: Special Effects and the Technology of Artificial Bodies', in *From Hobbits to Hollywood: Essays on Peter Jackson's Lord of the Rings*, eds Ernest Mathijs and Murray Pomerance (Amsterdam and New York: Rodolphi, 2006), pp. 319–49.
60. Neil Hertz, 'Freud and the Sandman', in *The End of the Line: Essays on Psychoanalysis and the Sublime* (New York: Columbia University Press, 1985), pp. 114–18.
61. Otto Rank, *The Double, a Psychoanalytical Study*, trans. Harry Tucker jr. (New York: Meridian Press, 1979).
62. Freud, p. 236.
63. Rank, pp. 6–7.

4

As It Happened ... *Borderline*, the Uncanny and the Cosmopolitan

James Donald

The borderline has the air of a place where the uncanny belongs: an intermediate and uneasy zone between different states, a no-man's-land both politically and existentially. The spatial metaphor does not altogether fit, however, at least not in thinking about Freud's 1919 essay on 'The "Uncanny"'. In good Kantian fashion, Freud's aim there is to draw a conceptual borderline around what is specific and unique to the *Unheimlich*. The term, he acknowledges, has something to do with broader categories like fear, dread and horror, but that is too fuzzy for Freud: 'we may expect that a special core of feeling is present which justifies the use of a special conceptual term. One is curious to know what this common core is which allows us to distinguish as "uncanny" certain things which lie within the field of what is frightening.' The desire to fix the limits of the concept leads to Freud's opening digression into the etymology of *heimlich* and *unheimlich*. Although the opposition between the two makes it tempting 'to conclude that what is "uncanny" is frightening precisely because it is *not* known and familiar', Freud discovers, of course, that the relationship between the two is not one of a boundary or outer edge where the ontological security of the known and the familiar abuts the strangeness and danger of the unknown imagined as another space.[1]

Instead the *Unheimlich* turns out to be a kind of viral incursion within the *Heimlich*: '... *heimlich* is a word the meaning of which develops in the direction of ambivalence, until it finally coincides with its opposite, *unheimlich*. *Unheimlich* is in some way or other a sub-species of *Heimlich*'. The uncanny thus implies a convoluted yet constitutive dislocation in being rather than another place. For Freud, it is a *temporal* dislocation – a recurrence from the past – that disrupts the *spatial* metaphor of the home. He cross-refers the *heimlich/unheimlich* ambivalence to Schelling's definition: 'According to him, everything is *unheimlich* that ought to have remained secret and hidden but has come to light.' Typically of the movement of the essay, Freud later narrows down this recurrence to a dynamic of Oedipal repression:

> It often happens that neurotic men declare that they feel there is something uncanny about the female genital organs. This *unheimlich* place, however, is the entrance to the former *Heim* of all human beings, to the place where each one of us lived once upon a time and in the beginning. There is a joking saying that 'Love is home-sickness'; and whenever a man dreams of a place or a country and says to himself, while he is still dreaming: 'this place is familiar to me, I've been here before', we may interpret the place as being his mother's genitals or body. In this case too, then the *unheimlich* is what was once *heimisch*, familiar; the prefix '*un*' ['un-'] is the token of repression.[2]

Freud thus sees this ambivalence about belonging or feeling-at-home as one symptom (among others) that might lead to a diagnosis of neurosis, and specifically of masculine neurosis. But is he right to present it as a pathology? Writing about *Angst* in the second half of the 1920s, in *Being and Time*, Heidegger picked up on this theme of uncanny dislocation, or the origin that had become alien and discomfiting, but suggests instead that this is an insecurity that defines the nature and experience of being.[3]

> Anxiety (*Angst*) pulls Dasein back from its falling-away emergence in the 'world'. Everyday familiarity collapses. Dasein is isolated, but isolated *as* Being-in-the-world. Being-in enters into the existential 'mode' of the '*not-at-home*'. Nothing else is meant by our talk about 'uncanniness'.[4]

The scare-quoted 'world' to which Heidegger refers, and from which *Dasein* anxiously recoils is, according to James Phillips, 'the worldliness of chatter and curiosity'. But, as Phillips goes on to explain, this is only half the story.

> Dasein is thrown back upon itself in the uncanny and, in being thrown back upon itself, it is bereft of its familiarity with its environment. And yet it is world, now without quotation marks, that suddenly emerges from under the instrumentalization by which Dasein falls away from itself in falling toward the cosmopolitan realm of its inauthenticity. The world that emerges is Dasein's Being-in-the-world

> even as Dasein suffers on account of its intense strangeness: '*That in the face of which one has anxiety is Being-in-the-world as such.*' Dasein abruptly finds itself both within the world and not at home.[5]

'Within the world' and yet at the same time 'not at home': here Phillips captures the definitive uncanniness of subjectivity perceived by both Freud and Heidegger that I would argue (and whatever they thought) marks the modernity of their thinking. It is Heidegger who drew the more radical inference and offered the more fundamental explanation: '*From an existential-ontological point of view, the "not-at-home" must be conceived as the more primordial phenomenon.*'[6]

For Freud, the symptomatology of the uncanny leads to neurosis. For Heidegger, philosophically, the experience leads to an account of *Heimat* or homeland not as a secure and nourishing origin but as uncannily familiar in the sense of rendering the 'more primordial' insistence of the 'not-at-home' in *Dasein*'s own Being. In a sense, both conceptions might be seen as tragic interpretations of the unhomely, at least when set in contrast to the more joyous take on the 'not-at-homeness' of modern being to be found in *The Gay Science*. There Nietzsche sees not the alienation of an origin through *repression* but a principled *rejection* by the self-elected homeless of the peremptory claims of cultural and political belonging.

> We, who are homeless, are too manifold and mixed racially and in our descent being 'modern men,' and consequently do not feel tempted to participate in the mendacious racial self-admiration and racial indecency that parades in Germany today as a sign of a German way of thinking.

Nietzsche's ethical alternative to *Heimat* is neither Heidegger's banal 'world' nor an abstract humanitarianism, but rather self-creation through affective social relationships that are always experienced as an oscillation between belonging and disorientation. However bad such moderns may be at being good Germans, nonetheless Nietzsche insists that they have a place which is not an identity. 'We are ... good Europeans,' he proclaims, where *Europe* connotes less a geographical location or an historical imperialism than the universalism of Europe's philosophical discourse and the possibility of translating that both into a politics (human rights most notably in our time) and also into ways of being in the world.[7]

Here the borderline between *Heimat* and *Heimatlos*, like that between the *Heimlich* and the *Unheimlich*, evaporates as apparent opposites shade into one another: the uncanny and the cosmopolitan thus present themselves as two instances of a specifically modern experience of not-being-at-home as a mode of being-in-the-world.

Close Up

Borderline was, as it happened, the name of a film made in 1930 by an idiosyncratic bunch of cosmopolitan avant-garde intellectuals with a passion for cinema.[8] The group's nucleus consisted of three people. The expatriate American poet H.D., Hilda Doolittle, had been given her acronymic by Ezra Pound, to whom she had been briefly (and several times) engaged; later she would write about her analysis with Freud. The English novelist Annie Winifred Ellerman took the pen name of Bryher and was, not insignificantly, heiress to the fortune of the shipping magnate Sir John Ellerman. It was her money that supported the group and its creative projects. The third member was a talented if feckless young Scot, Kenneth Macpherson. This menagerie of three, as H.D.'s biographer Barbara Guest called it, were living together in an intricate minuet of sexual relationships and self-reflection on the depths of their emotions – they styled themselves collectively POOL – in the picturesque Swiss town of Territet. H.D. and Bryher were already in a life-long sexual relationship when H.D. met and embarked on an affair with Macpherson, sixteen years her junior, in 1926, the year in which her autobiographical novel *Palimpsest* was published. Macpherson in turn wrote his own novel about the relationship, which bordered on pastiche of his mistress's voice: *Poolreflection*.[9] Bryher married him and both women tried to give direction to his undoubted but largely undisciplined talents. In 1927, Bryher's expensive gift of a Debrie camera to Macpherson stimulated a collective enthusiasm for cinema that led not only to a number of POOL film experiments but also to the publication of the journal *Close Up*. This they announced, not without justification, as the first journal devoted to film as an art: they promised 'Theory and analysis: no gossip'.

The group's cosmopolitanism in this period was evident both in their interests, tastes and affiliations and in their restless shuttling around Europe and across the Atlantic. They would take the train not only to Paris but also to Berlin to dine with the director G.W. Pabst, who encouraged Macpherson's career and indulged the group's fantasy of H.D. as a potential rival to Louise Brooks, or to London in 1927 to see the musical *Show Boat* and the show-stopping performance of 'Ol' Man River' by Paul Robeson. They were introduced to Robeson and his wife

Eslanda by a fourth but non-resident member of the POOL group, the poet and journalist Robert Herring, who wrote about film for the literary monthly the *London Mercury*. Herring shared Macpherson's passion for jazz, and they sailed to Harlem to visit its jazz clubs and hear the music at its (supposed) source.

This restlessness meant that, at the same time as they attempted to create a specifically modernist art of film, the group's engagement in a primarily literary European avant-garde was mediated by participation in a different, distinctively American avant-garde: the literature and music of the Harlem Renaissance.[10] This gave their aesthetics a political edge, as they observed the interracial dynamics of Paris and London as well as New York. It also inflected their ethical self-creation as, in a Nietzschean sense, 'homeless'. The POOL group were without doubt 'modern men' and 'modern women'. Their lives were complicated and mobile enough to count as psychologically and morally *manifold* and they were certainly 'mixed' sexually if not racially. Apart from H.D. and Bryher's longstanding relationship, Herring was gay, and Macpherson's bisexuality increasingly consolidated into a pattern of pursuing young black men from around (as it happened) 1929 on. In such ways the POOL group became sensitive and alert to the imbrication and at least metaphorical portability of sexual and racial boundaries. This perception, which was also no doubt a desire, was then translated into the attempt to represent cinematically the vicissitudes of cosmopolitan being-in-the world: *Borderline*.

Before that, in August 1929, *Close Up* ran a special issue on 'The Negro in Film', prompted at least in part by that year's vogue for 'all talkie' feature musicals that were also 'all negro' – most notably Paul Sloane's *Hearts in Dixie* from Fox, featuring Stepin Fetchit, and King Vidor's first sound film *Hallelujah!* Reflecting the POOL group's interest in the culture of the Harlem Renaissance, the contributors included Walter White (leader of the National Association for the Advancement of Coloured People), Elmer Carter (editor of *Opportunity*, one of the key Renaissance journals) and Geraldyn Dismond (a journalist best known for her society – even gossip – columns). Their mostly quite brief contributions show a particular interest in the scope the films seemed to promise for African-American performers and African-American-owned production companies to flourish in the sound era.

Many of the journal's regular writers were more interested in the sound dimension of the films: a question at the heart of *Close Up*'s attempts to define a modernist aesthetic for film at this time. The 'Negro in Film' issue marks an important step in a gradual move from militant opposition to talkies and mourning for the lost universal visual language of silent cinema – 'the art that died' – to an accommodation with sound cinema's aesthetic and ethical potential. In his editorial, Macpherson acknowledges that, for all that it had destroyed, sound had at least had the virtue of allowing more intimate access to 'the Negro': 'Talking films took films from us but they have given us a glimpse of him.' Even the novelist Dorothy Richardson, the most obdurate of *Close Up*'s columnists in her resistance, admitted that the singing and the 'lush chorus of Negro-laughter' in *Hearts in Dixie* might be 'the noble acceptable twin of the silent film'– although she still dismissed the recorded speech as 'annihilating'.[11] The American Marxist Harry Potamkin sets the appearance of 'negro films' in the context of the Harlem Renaissance, but then attributes its timing explicitly to sound technology.

> The present vogue for negro films was inevitable. The film trails behind literature and stage for subject-matter. There has been a negro vogue since the spirituals were given their just place in popular attention. Many negro mediocrities have ridden to glory on this fad. Many white dabblers have attained fame by its exploitation. The new negro was suddenly born with it. [Countee] Cullen and [Langston] Hughes were crowned poets, but Jean Toomer, a great artist among the negroes, has not yet been publicly acclaimed. He first appeared before the hullabaloo was begun. The theatre took the negro up. First [the actor Charles] Gilpin and eventually came *Porgy*. Now the film, *Sound has made the negro the 'big-thing' of the film-moment.*[12]

What is not clear is whether Potamkin believed that sound somehow *caused* the wave of 'all negro' musicals, or that there was some affinity between African-American performers and sound cinema. And if the latter, what was the nature of that affinity?

One commonly accepted explanation at the time was a technical one. The quality of recording meant that voices on the screen did not sound great, and the timbre of 'negro' voices – their 'rich resonance ... in speech and song' as *Opportunity*'s Elmer Carter called it in his piece for *Close Up* – was widely supposed to make for more accurate and pleasing recordings.[13] Typical of this approach, but symptomatic also in revealing that more than sound quality was at stake, was a review of *Hearts in Dixie* that the *New Yorker*'s film critic Robert Benchley wrote in *Opportunity*. Black performers are seen as somehow solving a problem presented by talking pictures.

> Voices *can* be found which will register perfectly. Personalities *can* be found which are ideal for this medium. It may be that the talking-movies must be participated in exclusively by Negroes, but, if so, then so be it. In the Negro the sound-picture has found its ideal protagonist.[14]

The more fundamental question about sound to which 'the Negro' was supposedly the ideal and possibly only answer turned out to be this: why did audiences find the experience of mechanically reproduced speech difficult and disquieting?

This brings us back to the uncanny, as Mladen Dolar indicates in his discussion of a talking automaton at the beginning of his book *A Voice and Nothing More*.

> There is an uncanniness in the gap which enables a machine, by purely mechanical means, to produce something so uniquely human as voice and speech. It is as if the effect could emancipate itself from its mechanical origin, and start functioning as a surplus – indeed, as the ghost in the machine; as if there were an effect without a proper cause, an effect surpassing its explicable cause ...[15]

One specifically modern version of the uncanny – probably unique in Europe at least to the first three decades of the twentieth century – was the emergence of a subjectivity mediated through the mass-produced sounds and disembodied voices of gramophone, telephone, radio and talkies. This new soundscape was characterised by what Marcel Chion in his discussion of cinema sound calls the acousmatic: that is, sound one hears without seeing its originating cause or body.[16] It is this anxiety in the face of the uncanniness of the acousmatic – Marcel's first telephone conversation with his beloved grandmother in *The Guermantes Way* is perhaps the best-known literary example – that the presence of 'the Negro' on screen is somehow supposed to remedy or at least displace.

But, again, why 'the Negro'? In her perceptive article on 'race' and sound in the early Hollywood talkies, Alice Maurice sees two strategies at work. One was to use the bodies and voices of black performers and their 'inherent' or 'natural' talents to show off the power of the cinematic apparatus to capture and reproduce – to embody, almost – those talents and those performances. The other, which is especially pertinent here, was to emphasise what she calls the *hyperpresence* of black bodies to draw attention away from the apparatus and its artifice, and to compensate for its mimetic shortcomings – and also, I would add, to deflect the uncanniness produced by modern subjectivity's mediation through multiple technologies.[17] It is this hyperpresence that recurs in *Close Up* as the link between 'sound', 'the Negro' and the question of authenticity or being-in-the-world and hence the uncanny. Macpherson and his colleagues understood and rejected the condescending primitivism and cultural appropriation that had characterised much of the vogue for *l'art nègre* earlier in the decade. He was dismissive of films in which black characters were simply the projection of a white social conscience: 'the white man is always going to portray the negro as he likes to see him, no matter how benevolently.' Rather than representing difference within a white paradigm, he wanted 'the negro' to become 'his own historian' and 'his own agitator'.[18] But the limit to Macpherson's approach was an inability to think outside the paradigm of a kind of cultural eugenics, in which blackness uncannily recurs either as degenerative and malign or (for him) as benign and rejuvenating. That is why he still looked to a cinema that could present an authentic 'race mind' to counter the 'mendacious racial self-admiration and racial indecency' that Nietzsche had so tellingly predicted for Europe, a cinema that would embody difference from the inside out.

This constrained and compromised ideal is what Macpherson is getting at in his editorial when he asserts that attempts at 'universal cinema' have failed, and that the only hope lies in a 'strictly racial cinema'. This sounds startling, but the contrast he is drawing is between an inauthentic cosmopolitanism that he was already sheeting home to Hollywood and an embodied existential authenticity that he perceives in Stepin Fetchit's performance in *Hearts of Dixie*.

> There is more than promise in the jungle, lissom lankness that slams down something unanswerable in front of what we let go by as beauty ... Fetchit waves loose racial hands and they, like life, touch everything that the world contains. They are startling with what nobody meant to put into them, but which is all too there – histories, sagas, dynasties, Keatsian edges off things make a voiceless trouble back of the eye and the recording mind. Only afterwards you are really beset by them. They are not Fetchit's hands, they are the big step we have not yet taken. First of all these so utterly not incantationish gestures are unselfconsciousness, perfectly inherited greatness of race and race mind. It only begins there. We can scrap every trained toe waggle of a ballerina for the very least of these movements. Making this greatness articulate for the cinema is the fascinating pioneer work of somebody.[19]

Robert Herring reveals the rejuvenating eugenicism of the perspective more explicitly in his article 'Black Shadows'. In 'Negro Art', he claims, 'you will find a new life, very rich, very swift, intense, and dynamic, unlike ours, but full of things which we cannot help knowing we lack.' With a swipe at Carl van Vechten, the white doyen of the Harlem Renaissance, Herring insists that 'there should be Negro films made by and about them. Not black films passing for white, and not, please, white passing for black. We want no Van Vechtens of the movies.' Herring suggests that this potential authenticity of 'Negro art' can transcend even the mechanical artifice of sound: 'Now that it has been discovered that Negroes have voices, let it be found too that they have something to say.' He knows that it won't be found by way of way of Al Jolson in *The Jazz Singer*.

> And we don't get it by blacking our faces and wearing white gloves ... We want the real thing, always, the cinema demands the real thing, and heaven knows there is enough reality waiting there, if black shadows might move on our screens in their own patterns, and have their own screens, too, to do it on ... For surely they are as tired of all the as yet white, yellow, white – nothing but white – films; and heaven knows I am ...[20]

Harry Potamkin too wants blacker blackness, more authentic blackness – the trouble with authenticity, of course, being that it can never be authentic enough. He takes aim at King Vidor's casting of the light-skinned Nina Mae McKinney as the *femme fatale* in *Hallelujah!* and contrasts Vidor's fiction with Léon Poirier's pioneering ethnographic films (like his account of the Citroën expedition across Africa, *La Croisière noire*). Potamkin expresses his desire for an authenticating, unalienated origin as a brutal nostalgia: blackness in cinema, blackness and cinema, as *Heim*.

> And Vidor's *Hallelujah* with a good-looking yaller girl. As for me, I shall be assured of the white man's sincerity when he gives me a blue nigger. I want one as rich as the negroes in Poirier's documents of Africa. I am not interested primarily in verbal humour, in clowning nor in sociology. I want cinema and I want cinema at its source.[21]

Borderline

This not-quite-articulate sense of 'the negro' as the existential cure to the cultural wound represented by the *Unheimlich* recurs in the POOL group's 1930 film, *Borderline*. The ambition was to make a psychoanalytic film – or to make a film psychoanalytically, as Godard might have said – and, as in most POOL writings, the relationships explored were relationships between the members of the group. Bryher appears as a cigar-smoking manager of the bar that holds together the spatial organisation of the film and Herring is the jazz player who gazes adoringly at the photo of Robeson on his piano's music stand. But they act primarily as a kind of moral centre-cum-Greek chorus, commenting on the fictionalised relationship between Macpherson and H.D. that is centre stage. H.D. had aborted the child she was carrying by Macpherson in 1928.[22] The aftermath of that trauma may help to explain the fatal intensity of the spiral of dependency, jealousy and resentment in which the cerebral and over-civilised older woman Astrid (played by H.D. herself, using the Ibsenesque pseudonym Helga Doorn) and the alcoholic younger man, Thorne, played by Gavin Arthur, find themselves trapped. (The abortion may add another dimension to the otherwise heavy-handed Oedipal imagery of the knife with which Astrid taunts and nicks Thorne, and with which he then kills her.) The film's narration is deliberately fragmented, elliptical and even opaque. Rejecting the 'simplicity' of most films and the laziness of most audiences, Macpherson wanted *Borderline* to embody the 'complexity' of the issues and relationships that it was addressing. He was, he wrote, aiming at a quality of 'unexplainedness – like something seen through a window or key-hole'.[23] Hence the film starts *in medias res* and eschews establishing shots, a linear time structure or any clear demarcation between the representation of events, thoughts or memories. Its main structuring device is less a narrative sequence of events than the externalisation of the lethal relationship between the white couple into the social and psychological impact on the town of the presence of the initially estranged but soon reunited black couple played by Paul Robeson and Eslanda Goode Robeson.

The underlying story is in fact quite straightforward, as the 'libretto' that was issued to the audience at the film's first screening makes clear – even if the plot details in the film itself sometimes remain confusing after repeated viewings.

> In a small 'borderline' town, anywhere in Europe, Pete, a negro, is working in a cheap hotel café. His wife, Adah, who had left him some time previously, has arrived also in the same town, although neither is aware of the presence of the other.
>
> Adah is staying in rooms with Thorne and Astrid. Thorne is a young man whose life with Astrid has become a torment to them both.

> Both highly strung, their nerves are tense with continuous hostility evoked by Thorne's vague and destructive cravings. He has been involved in an affair with Adah, and the film opens with the quarrel which ends their relationship.

As a racially borderline figure, Adah (described in the libretto as a 'mulatto') crosses sexually from the black man to the white man and back to the black man. Her betrayal of Pete with Thorne provokes Astrid's jealousy and a self-loathing that erupts in a crude racism – 'They are niggers, my dear!' – that chimes all too easily with the proto-Nazi prejudices of the locals. When Thorne is acquitted for Astrid's murder, Pete is made a scapegoat and expelled from the town.

At the heart of the film's narrative and psychological strategy is the contrast between Thorne and Pete, or rather the subjective splitting and fantasy of wholeness that in combination they represent. There are only two occasions on which Thorne and Pete appear in frame together, but both are crucial to the racialised logic of the film. The first occurs at the end of a sequence when Thorne appears threateningly at the threshold of Adah's room after she and Pete have resumed a sexual relationship. For the most part, the sequence is structured as a series of shots and reverse shots that highlight the point of view of each man in turn, with the manager and the piano player who are holding Thorne back flicking their eyes between the two like spectators at a tennis match. Thorne, his forehead sheened with alcoholic sweat, appears dishevelled and impotently outraged, whereas Pete comes across as at first a little disconcerted, then quizzical, then self-assured, then (through Thorne's eyes) as sexually triumphant and insolently contemptuous. When the two are shown confronting each other in profile, it is very much as a tableau of black and white tonalities, with a brightly-lit patterned white curtain dividing the screen between them. The white-shirted Pete's face is wholly in shadow, whereas a dark-jacketed Thorne, being restrained by the manager whose face appears as a blob of white, has his downcast gaze lit in dramatic chiaroscuro. A closer shot shows only the profiles of the two men, Thorne at the extreme left of the frame brightly lit and humiliated against a dark wooden back, a smiling Pete at the right edge of the frame smiling, but still in shadow against the light fabric of the curtain. Towards the end of the film, a reconciliation between Thorne and Pete repeats the tableau shot. Both are now in the light, but with Thorne foregrounded against the white fabric and Pete against a dark flower-patterned wallpaper. In a close-up shot-reverse shot, each man's smiling face connotes a trans-racial masculine camaraderie that is emphasised by the extreme close up of their handshake.

Just before this reconciliation, Bryher's hotel manager passes on the letter of expulsion to Pete. Three intertitles play on the slippages of identifying pronouns in the process. In the first, Pete asks: 'What do you think?' In the second, the manager distances herself from the racism of the town but then acknowledges her own inescapable complicity in it: 'Sorry, Pete! What make it worse is that they think they're doing the right thing. We're like that!' In the third, expanding that *we* to embrace all humankind, a deflated Pete replies: 'Yes, we're like that.' As Pete leaves, Herring's forlorn piano player takes Pete's photograph from the piano, puts it in his wallet and pockets it. After the reconciliation, a quick shot of the piano's keys is followed by a head-and-shoulders 'portrait' of an overcoated Pete and then a comparatively long sequence of Pete waiting at the station for a train, the very sign of cosmopolitanism, with Pete counterposed elementally against the Alps. Intercut into the shots at the station are the piano's gesture of *bon voyage*, the return of the racist old woman to the bar as Bryher draws up the hotel's accounts, shots of Thorne sitting pensively in grassy mountainside meadows, and the barmaid wistfully rediscovering the now-dead rose that 'poor old Pete' had laughingly put behind his ear a few nights earlier. In the closing shot Bryher, pen in mouth, closes the ledger.

This conclusion resonates in an intriguing way with the resemblance between Heidegger's accounts of the uncanny and the call of conscience in *Being and Time*. The conscience that can be satisfied does not do the work that Heidegger wants conscience to do: by doing the right thing by such a conscience people come to feel at peace with themselves – at home – when Heidegger clearly wants the not-at-home to be acknowledged as more primordial. In the slippage between *they* and *we*, in the removal of Pete, and in the settling of accounts, it seems almost as though the POOL group are trying to distance themselves from their white background and its manifestation in the locals' pathological racism through the valorisation of blacks as the embodiment of authentic, neurosis-free humanity. At the same time, however, and in the same gesture, they might be read as trying to make amends (even if unconsciously) for white oppression and so to make peace – to square the ledger – with their own consciences and so to be at home with them.[24]

The cosmopolitan and uncanny connotations of the borderline are clearly discernable in the pamphlet that H.D. wrote about the film. Although she emphasises the neurosis of the white couple, using 'borderline' almost in a clinical sense, she points to the central ambiguity about being-at-home and not-feeling-at-home-in-the-world.

> There are in Europe, many just such little towns as this particular borderline town of some indefinite mid-European mountain district. There are trains coming and trains going. One of these trains has already deposited the half-world mondaine Astrid with Thorne, her lover. They have come here because of some specific nerve-problem, perhaps to rest, perhaps to recuperate, perhaps to economize, perhaps simply in hope of some emotional convalescence. They live as such people do the world over, in just such little borderline rooms as just such couples seek in Devonshire, in Cornwall, in the South of France, in Provincetown, United States. *They are borderline social cases, not out of life, not in life*; the woman is a sensitive neurotic, the man, a handsome, degenerate dipsomaniac. Thorne has not reached the end of his cravings, may step this side, that side of the border; Astrid, the white-cerebral is and is not outcast, is and is not a social alien, is and is not a normal human being, she is borderline.[25]

This existential and psychological instability is then both ascribed to and represented by a tangle of sexual and racial borderlines, and the complicated patterns of desire and hostility they engender. The neuroses and 'perversions' of the 'civilised' white couple are projected, both psychologically and narratively, onto their intimate relations with the black characters.

> These two are specifically chosen to offset another borderline couple of more dominant integrity. These last, Pete and his sweetheart Adah, have a less intensive problem, but border; they dwell on the cosmic racial borderline. They are black people among white people.[26]

H.D. argues that *Borderline* sees 'race' rightly as a boundary rather than an essence, and that in constructing the film Macpherson deliberately plays on the narrative displacements and dislocations between the semiotic, the psychic and sociological that 'race' as trope allows. In doing so, she implies, the film escapes both the stereotypical thinking and the condescending benevolence that characterised thinking about 'race' in the 1920s.

> Though in this specific mid-Europe, there is nothing intrinsically disharmonious in that, their situation is a sort rarely, if ever, touched on, in film art. Their problem is not dealt with as the everlasting black-white Problem with a capital. It remains however a motive to be counted on; though threads are woven in and

> through the fabric, white into black and black into white, Pete and Adah must inevitably remain 'borderline', whether by their own choice and psychic affiliation or through sheer crude brute causes.[27]

Later critics have been less kind, and many have insisted that even if H.D. and Macpherson may have been able to spot the limits and arbitrariness of other people's racial logics, they nonetheless unwittingly repeated the racialised pathology of alienation, fantasy and projection that they were trying to thematise and criticise. In its black and white cinematography and its narrative counterposing of hyperactive whites against Robeson in repose, Richard Dyer sees little more than another example of 'the white alienation versus blackfolks spirituality opposition that runs through discourses on blackness in the twenties and thirties'.[28] Hazel Carby complains that the effect of the film's 'modernist aesthetic' was 'to freeze Robeson into a modernist ideal of the Negro male, outside of history'.[29] And Jean Walton objects:

> Considering how race and sexuality intersect in *Borderline*, H.D. and the POOL group frequently and unthinkingly reproduce the distinction between the 'natural' and the 'civilized', with its apparently explanatory account of cultural attainment and neurosis, as a white/black binary: The film's black characters connote a 'natural' sexual morality that largely evades the repressive influence of 'civilized' (read white) moral codes.[30]

These critics, along with Macpherson himself, to a large extent restate Essie's own more light-hearted judgement as confided to her diary:

> Kenneth and H.D. used to make us so shriek with laughter with their naïve ideas of Negroes that Paul and I often completely ruined our make-up with tears of laughter, had to make up all over again. We never once felt we were colored with them.[31]

Although the film's inaccuracies or inadequacies in representing the experience of being-black-in-the-world have understandably dominated much of the critical discussion over recent decades, that focus can tend to overlook the question of what *Borderline* does actually tell us about the experience of being-a-white-cosmopolitan-in-the-world at the turn of the 1920s and 1930s. If 'that in the face of which one has anxiety is Being-in-the-world as such', as Heidegger asserted at that time, and this anxiety is the source of the uncanny sense of not-feeling-at-home, then again, as in the theoretical writings in the *Close Up* issue, the embodied – although still silent – presence of 'the negro' seems to be functioning as the sublime force that figures the forlorn desire for an unalienated or 'homely' being-in-the-world. In 1931, for example, in his chapter on cinema in Nancy Cunard's anthology *Negro*, Macpherson reflected somewhat ruefully on his editorial, the film and his response to Robeson:

> ... I had seen, perhaps I should say I had been haunted by, a sense of *virility or solidarity of being* which was at once discernible as imperatively Negroid.

Although in her pamphlet H.D. emphasises Robeson's stability and ethereality rather than his virility, the logic is the same.

> Mr. Robeson is obviously the ground under all their feet. He is stabilized, stable, the earth ... The giant negro is in the high clouds, white cumulous cloud banks in a higher heaven. Conversely, his white fellow-men are the shadows of white, are dark, neurotic ...

The makers of *Borderline* were under no illusions that the film was presenting a fully worked representation of Black subjectivity or even of the Black experience of racism. But in turning to 'the negro' as the cure for the unhomeliness and dis-ease of their lives, they did in fact rearticulate the inescapability of the uncanny. A psychoanalytic account might link 'the ground under all their feet' to mother earth and then to the maternal landscape and so (as Freud puts it) to that place, both *heimisch* and *unheimlich* 'where each one of us lived once upon a time and in the beginning'. But that would repeat the kind of over-neat explanation that mars the essay. Even though *Borderline* was made by Freudian true believers, and remains constrained within (as do we all) historically specific paradigms of racialised thinking, H.D. does see in Macpherson's vision a way of imagining the solaces and costs of cosmopolitanism as an alternative way of living homelessly. We may not like her answers, but her questions at least reveal an awareness of the scale of existential fluidity and self-reinvention needed to become cosmopolitan. In that sense, *Borderline* might be read as a variation on Nietzsche's theme of the ethical courage to be homeless:

> When is an African not an African? When obviously he is an earth-god. When is a woman not a woman? When obviously she is sleet and hail and a stuffed sea-gull. He says when is white not white and

> when is black white and when is white black? You may or may not like this sort of cinematography.[32]

Two Americans

Soon after the shooting of *Borderline* had been completed in April 1930, H.D. wrote a short story, *Two Americans*, that again picks over the film's themes, this time through the prism of the social interactions and psychodynamics between the POOL group and the Robesons. Here questions of exile, homelessness and nostalgia are worked through the erotic fascination with Robeson that H.D. shared with Macpherson and her anxious reaction to Robeson's easy friendship with Macpherson as two fellow artists, despite their racial difference; a camaraderie in which she feels that, as a woman, she cannot participate. The H.D.-figure Raymonde Ransome believes that her earlier affair with Macpherson/Daniel Kinoull is one reason for that exclusion, and she therefore now experiences the relationship as a wound: as a 'steel pin' or (perhaps with a nod to the Macpherson–Thorne character in *Borderline*) as a 'silver thorn' in her side.[33]

Materials such as steel and silver run through the story. 'Weather-worn marble, Raymonde Ransome, faced Saul Howard, seared bronze', H.D. writes.[34] This imagery seems to underline the felt materiality of symbolic differences, which are elsewhere articulated in terms of a racial masquerade.

> Their faces remained faces yet for all that, those faces had turned now forever into static symbols, they were mask on contrasting mask, the one white, the other, as it happened, black.[35]

That apparently bland interpolation 'as it happened' is less innocent or redundant than it might at first appear. The phrase gathers within itself much of the complexity of the issues around the uncanny that I have been discussing. It seems on the face of it to assert that this meeting is purely contingent, a singular event. This happened, and it happened to happen like this. Yet, at the same time, the phrase implies an awareness that *this* event, however apparently trivial and fortuitous, has been overdetermined by the full range of historical and cultural forces implicit in the lexicon of nation, cosmopolitanism, home and being-in-the-world. 'White' confronting 'black' is never just happenstance. And this is clear as H.D. goes on to portray Robeson–Howard as a mythical figure, as a pagan life force contrasting (perhaps again in an implicit reference to the abortion of Macpherson's child) with her own sterile

Puritanism, and again as the embodiment of that fullness which both reveals and promises to heal her own wounded, inadequate and inauthentic being.

> They met in a field of honour, herself entirely defeated, himself yet to be acclaimed for some king-ship the world is not ready to recognize. He was no black Christ. He was an earlier, less complicated symbol. He was the Dionysus as Nietzsche so valiantly struggled to define him; possibly she stood vaguely for counter balancing Nietzschean Apollo, though where he was complete, she was strikingly deficient. She was deficient, even, you might say, crippled in some psychic song-wing; his song flowed toward all the world, effortless, full of benign power, without intellectual gap or cross-purpose of hypercritical consciousness to blight it. There was no swerving from the beginning, the root, the entire deep in-rooted power of his gigantic Being. He was really no person at all. Seated opposite him, on the orange-lacquered low wooden seat that Gareth [*Bryher*] had had specially designed for just that fireside corner, Raymonde knew that. She let her own personality harden, 'fix' as it were; now she would be this forever.[36]

It is at this moment in the story that H.D. evokes the uncanniness of Robeson's voice: not just the extraordinary timbre and cadences of his *basso profundo*, but the whole logic of the acousmatic and the 'dis-acousmatization' when the source of the disembodied voice is revealed – a resolution of the uncanniness of the voice that Mladen Dolar insists is impossible. For Dolar, every supposed dissipation of the acousmatic uncanny reveals not the *integrity* of body, subject and voice, but, on the contrary, a still uncanny displacement or *ventriloquism*.[37] It is this ventriloquism that H.D. seems to disavow in the peculiar selection of the adverb *intrinsically* as, for the first time in the whole cycle of *Close Up*, *Borderline* and *Two Americans*, Robeson speaks. But at the same time, H.D. *enacts* Dolar's assertion. Far from being *intrinsic*, that is an integral feature of Robenson's body, the voice appears to be quite autonomous. It is not *he*, the man, who speaks, but rather *it*, the voice.

> For her, the 'voice' was speaking. It spoke to the world, every gramophone window displayed Saul Howard's records. The voice spoke on everyone's wireless. Howard himself was, in fact, on his way back to London, stopping off here from his concert in Vienna. The voice that spoke on everybody's wireless, spoke now to her intrinsically. It said, 'Daniel is a lovely fellow.'[38]

Once Saul Howard has spoken his agency becomes an issue. His presence in the world is perceived above all as an overwhelming physical grace, but there is more to him than that.

> His least movement was so gracious, he didn't have to think things out. Nevertheless, with an astonishing analytical power, he did think. That was the odd thing about Saul Howard, he did think. He had a mind, a steadfast sort of burning, a thing that glowed like a whole red sunset or like a coal mine, it was steady, a steady sort of warmth and heat, yet all the time intellectual; he thought not as a man thinks. Paula Howard, his wife, thought more as white folks, consistently, being more than half white.[39]

Here H.D. does slip into quite a crudely racialised contrast between elemental being and Essie-Paula's brittle civilisation. But what is driving this is again the craving for intensity of being or what Alice Maurice called 'hyperpresence' – *solidarity of being, the ground under all their feet* – that might cure the alienation, anxiety and uncanniness of modern being-in-the-world. The representation of Essie-Paula, and the narrator's identification with Robeson–Howard against her, reveals how this motivation then becomes bound up both with questions of envy and desire and with historically specific categories and taxonomies of 'race'. Paula's flaw – like Nina Mae McKinney's for Harry Potamkin – is that she is not black enough. Her compromising 'whiteness' makes her prey to the wound of civilisation.

> Paula was Paris, was striking, yet, all the time, she made it very clear that she was not to be confounded with the tribe who had given jazz to Europe. She had attained something for which something had been sacrificed. For the very valour of her achievement, someone should warn her just what it was she left out. Yet who was there now to warn her and what really had she lost? The tragedy of Paula was that Paula as herself would be so far more interesting than most of their white friends. The tragedy was that she showed up horribly her deficiencies beside Saul.[40]

The pivot of the story is then the overlaying of the existential investment in 'the negro' as *Heim* with a more mundane nostalgia which enables Raymonde to grasp both her rootedness in a certain relationship to America and also the necessity of her cosmopolitan exile if she – like Saul Howard – is to operate effectively as an artist. Their shared Americanness first becomes an issue as Raymonde discusses the Howards with Bennie (modelled on Robert Herring). The incident may well be taken from the biography that Eslanda had recently published about Paul, and which had caused a deep and never repaired healed rift in their marriage. It concerns Paula's account of her courtship of Saul.

> Bennie told them. 'She said the four most likely young bucks of Harlem wanted her. She said, then I saw Saul Howard strolling along Broadway with a Phi Kappi Nu key and a gold football trophy dangling from his watch-chain, and I said *now that's my man!*' Raymonde interpreted, 'it wasn't Broadway and it wasn't Phi Kappi Nu and Paula would never have said "now that's my man".' Bennie said, 'don't swank, Raymonde, just because' (he was being funny) 'you and Saul and Paula are Americans.'[41]

This prompts Raymonde to reflect on the first time they had seen Saul Howard, before Bennie introduced them, singing what she misrecognises as 'one of his incredible Spirituals in the middle of a shocking musical comedy'.

> Saul Howard on that particular stage, had come up almost Paula colour, the foot-lights bleached him, he looked and from the distance of the dress-circle, a light mulatto, as Gareth put it, 'one of those Harvard niggers who talk English.'
>
> They had dismissed Saul Howard as a high-brow sort of over-educated negro, who was descending, out of some superior idea of fashionable race loyalty, to singing spirituals of the moment. Saul Howard interpolated oddly into that London music-hall, was oddly not that. His heart that afternoon had not been in the thing that he did. Nevertheless, across that packed house, there was ripple of delicate blue grass, there was a flight of cardinal butterflies. Oddly and almost for the first time, in her tragically rooted London war-consciousness, Raymonde Ransome felt that America was her home.

At one level, Raymonde's 'tragically rooted London war-consciousness' refers to a number of personal traumas that H.D. had suffered during the War: the still-birth of a child, the death of her father and brother, the nervous collapse of her husband. Beyond that, it refers historically to the existential changes that came with the War and its aftermath, and the changes in the sensory as well as the psychological experience of the world analysed by people like Freud, Heidegger and Benjamin as well as novelists like Proust, Musil, Virginia Woolf and Dorothy Richardson. And it also underlines how central to this modern experience – this experience of modernity, of being modern – were the question of home and the sense of being not-at-home, of being out of kilter with one's environment. For H.D., this constitutive uncanniness was given an added twist through the contrast between the cosmopolitanism of London and the sudden pang of nostalgia for America as home.

The phrase 'as it happened', with all its resonances of contingency and inevitability, recurs at the conclusion of *Two Americans* as H.D. draws together the antinomies between white and black, female and male, and home and exile that are all symptoms of, and in an odd way act as psychic band-aids for, the anxiety and uncanniness of modern being-in-the-world.

> 'Mohammed and the mountain,' said Raymonde, facing, as it happened, the ridge of the French Grammont, 'did or didn't it come to him? It's come to me anyway. I mean,' she said, 'America.'[42]

Notes

I am grateful to Julian Murphet and James Phillips for their comments on a draft of this chapter. The research on which this article is based has been supported by Australian Research Council Discovery Grant DP0664990.

1. Sigmund Freud, 'The "Uncanny"', in *Art and Literature*, The Pelican Freud Library, vol. 14, ed. Albert Dickson, trans. James Strachey (Harmondsworth: Penguin, 1985), pp. 335–76; 339, 343.
2. Ibid., pp. 347, 345, 368.
3. My account of Heidegger is derived from James Phillips, *Heidegger's Volk: Between National Socialism and Poetry* (Stanford: Stanford University Press, 2005).
4. Heidegger, *Being and Time* (London: SCM Press, 1962), p. 233; cited in Phillips, *Heidegger's Volk* (in modified translation), p. 200.
5. Phillips, *Heidegger's Volk*, p. 200.
6. Heidegger, *Being and Time*, p. 231; cited in Phillips, *Heidegger's Volk*, p. 200.
7. Friedrich Nietzsche, *The Gay Science*, ed. Bernard Williams (Cambridge: Cambridge University Press, 2001), pp. 241–2. Here I follow the discussion of Nietzsche and cosmopolitanism in Andrew Benjamin, *Style and Time: Essays on the Politics of Appearance* (Evanston: Northwestern University Press, 2006), p. 120.
8. A high-quality DVD transfer of *Borderline* made by the British Film Institute is available of the Criterion Collection's compilation *Paul Robeson: Portraits of the Artist* (2007). In line with Macpherson's intentions, the film has been given a jazz score – in this instance by Courtney Pine.
9. See Susan Stanford Friedman, *Penelope's Web: Gender, Modernity, H.D.'s Fiction* (Cambridge: Cambridge University Press, 1990), p. 17.
10. Ibid., p. 13.
11. Richardson, *Close Up*, vol. 5, no. 3, September 1929, p. 214.
12. Potamkin, *Close Up*, August 1929, p. 108. Emphasis added.

13. Alice Maurice, '"Cinema at Its Source": Synchronizing Race and Sound in the Early Talkies', *camera obscura* 17.1 (2002), pp. 44–5. Elmer Carter, 'Of Negro Motion Pictures', *Close Up*, August 1929, p. 119.
14. Benchley, cited in Maurice, 'Cinema at Its Source', p. 32.
15. Mladen Dolar, *A Voice and Nothing More* (Cambridge, MA: MIT Press, 2006), p. 7.
16. Maurice Chion, *Audio-Vision: Sound on Screen* (New York: Columbia University Press, 1994).
17. Maurice, 'Cinema at its Source', p. 45.
18. Macpherson, *Close Up*, August 1929, p. 90.
19. Ibid., pp. 85, 87–8.
20. Herring, *Close Up*, August 1929, pp. 97, 101, 104.
21. Potamkin, *Close Up*, August 1929, p. 109.
22. See Donna Hollenberg, 'Abortion, Identity Formation, and the Expatriate Woman Writer: H.D. and Kay Boyle in the Twenties', *Twentieth Century Literature: A Scholarly and Critical Journal*, 40: 4 (Winter 1994), pp. 499–517.
23. Macpherson, *Close Up*, November 1930, p. 381.
24. My thanks to James Phillips for this insight.
25. H.D., '*Borderline*', in James Donald, Anne Friedberg and Laura Marcus (eds), *Close Up, 1927–1933: Cinema and Modernism* (Princeton: Princeton University Press, 1998), p. xxx. Emphasis added.
26. Donald, Friedberg and Marcus (eds), *Close Up, 1927–1933*, p. xxx.
27. Ibid., p. xxx.
28. Richard Dyer, *Heavenly Bodies* (Houndmills: Macmillan, 1987), pp. 131–2.
29. Hazel V. Carby, *Race Men* (Harvard: Harvard University Press, 2000), pp. 67–8.
30. Jean Walton, '"Nightmare of the Uncoordinated White-Folk": Race, Psychoanalysis, and H.D.'s *Borderline*', in Christopher Lane (ed.), *The Psychoanalysis of Race* (New York: Columbia University Press, 1998), pp. 400–1.
31. Martin Duberman, *Paul Robeson* (New York: Knopf, 1988), pp. 130ff.
32. Donald, Friedberg and Marcus (eds), *Close Up, 1927–1933*, p. 111.
33. H.D., 'Two Americans', with 'The Usual Star' (London: privately printed, 1928), p. 95.
34. H.D., 'Two Americans', p. 96.
35. Ibid., p. 93.
36. Ibid., pp. 93–4.
37. Dolar suggests: '... ultimately, *there is no such thing as disacousmatization*. The source of the voice can never be seen, it stems from an undisclosed and structurally concealed interior, it cannot possibly match what we can see. This conclusion may seem extraordinary, but it can be related even to banal everyday experience: there is always something totally incongruous in the relation between the appearance, the aspect, of a person and his or her voice, before we adapt to it. It is absurd, this voice cannot possibly stem from this body, it doesn't sound like this person at all, or this person doesn't look at all like his or her voice. Every emission of the voice is by its very essence *ventriloquism*' (p. 70).
38. H.D., 'Two Americans', pp. 94–5.
39. Ibid., pp. 97–8.
40. Ibid., pp. 101–2.
41. Ibid., pp. 105–6.
42. Ibid., p. 116.

5
Access Denied: Memory and Resistance in the Contemporary Ghost Film

Scott Brewster

To relive the past: that insistent impossibility of psychoanalysis and film. These forms of retelling invite, even demand, a distracted vision that flickers back and forth, scene by scene, repeating a past that is a present out of time. This essay examines the meditation on loss, frozen time and uncanny aftermaths in the contemporary ghost films *What Lies Beneath* (dir. Robert Zemeckis, 2000) and *The Others* (dir. Alejandro Amenábar, 2001) in the light of debates surrounding trauma, therapy and recovered memory over the last two decades. In these confessional cinematic tales, there is nothing to escape, no 'guilt' to confess, yet a traumatic event structures each film, and the very act of resistance to remembering irresistibly draws its 'survivor' back to that haunting moment. This model of restlessness, of unfinished business, is not readily assimilable to standard notions of repression, and stands as a counterpoint to the imperatives within contemporary therapy culture to reveal, recover and bring a closure to the traumatic past. *What Lies Beneath* and *The Others* refuse to offer such closure.

The protagonists in both films are lodged at once inside and outside trauma; in *The Others*, the dead mother and children impossibly live on after their trauma, and in *What Lies Beneath*, the traumatic forgetting of others (the husband's murdered lover) is performed. As such, their traumatic remembering is placeless and timeless. According to Ulrich Baer, in trauma there is a 'twofold structural disjunction between an experience and its integration into narrative memory'; such experiences are 'located somewhere outside memory yet within the psyche'.[1] Thus the trauma of the other cannot be fully determined or represented. Both films at once deny and grant a hearing to the returning dead, and their central protagonists live in the aftermath of some unspoken, unspeakable event. At one level, the unspeakable in *The Others* is the history of collaboration in Jersey during the Nazi occupation. According to Grace, the Germans kept cutting off the electricity supply, but in five years never managed to enter the house. She resists this unassimilable external force just as she eventually repels the current intruders, the Marlishes. Yet, when Charles 'returns' from the front, he is asked why he joined the war effort when 'we all surrendered', and became involved in a war that had no relevance to his family. *What Lies Beneath* is marked by two decades of judicial and legislative debates over the legitimacy of recovered memory and post-traumatic stress disorder (PTSD), which are debates about the very nature of the unsayable.

The films draw on a classic Gothic repertoire – isolated houses, enclosed or suffocating spaces, obscure depths, the returning dead, various forms of crypt, and the disturbance of the domestic sphere – and the countervailing demands to resist and access a past is figured in terms of rooms that are revisited, re-locked and re-opened, actions obsessively performed, mists that clear and envelop. Yet these are narratives that do not readily give up their secrets. Visually, each narrative deploys a limited colour palette, as if to suggest an environment voided of affect, or one that permits little illumination. In *What Lies Beneath*, truth is sought in reflective surfaces – mirrors, water – but 'the truth' cannot be glimpsed inside oneself: it is encountered only in another's unsettled account, and that encounter imposes obligation and responsibility on the one who witnesses. *The Others* also involves responsibility, and the recognition of wounds that do not heal: access to reparation and closure is denied. Despite appearances, the narrative's rituals of barring and enclosure do not shut up, or out, the truth of one's guilt, do not conceal or cover over a traumatic breach which the light of revelation will assuage. The light that eventually floods into the sombre interior does not provide restitution, but rather enables the subjects of trauma to live with (which is not the same as being enmeshed within) that trauma. As such, trauma underwrites the possibility of survival in *The Others*. In *What Lies Beneath*, the undertaking – the proper laying to rest – of the murdered girl is also an overtaking; trauma overtakes and underwrites, in the sense of guaranteeing a certain future, the present. Both films therefore conduct a laying to rest that comes after a reawakening.

Distracted vision

The unsettlement of these ghost films can be viewed in relation to Freud's anecdote about involuntary repetition in 'The Uncanny', in which he recalls his 'voyages of discovery' in a provincial Italian town, when he kept returning as if by design to a red-light district he was desperate (we presume) to escape:

> As I was walking, one hot summer afternoon, through the deserted streets of a provincial town in Italy which was unknown to me, I found myself in a quarter of whose character I could not long remain in doubt. Nothing but painted women were to be seen at the windows of the small houses, and I hastened to leave the narrow street at the next turning. But after having wandered about for a time without inquiring my way, I suddenly found myself back in the same street, where my presence was now beginning to excite attention. I hurried away once more, only to arrive by another *détour* at the same place yet a third time. Now, however, a feeling overcame me which I can only describe as uncanny, and I was glad enough to find myself back at the piazza I had left only a short while before, without any further voyages of discovery.[2]

In this picaresque adventure, Freud is seemingly unable to escape a labyrinth of temptation and anxiety. His account is confessional in character: he wants to tell his story, but is unsure about what the story tells. Freud succumbs to an uncanny feeling only when emerging from the apparently infinitely recesses of his enigmatic, disorientating experience, only when returning to the proper light of day. A sense of the uncanny emerges belatedly, and there is no attempt to account for the unconscious determinants that may have guided the sunstruck protagonist's repetitive steps. One can argue that Freud's anecdotal cataloguing of uncanny experiences such as this dwells on the aftermath of disturbing or unsettling events, rather than the pursuit of the uncanny moment back to its origin. The uncanny is treated as an event without origin, a remainder or survival. The feelings of helplessness and drift these distracted perambulations inspire locate the uncanny as a spatial and temporal resting-point which never allows us to advance, and yet which never allows us to stand comfortably still. As he wanders with increasing discomfort under the Italian sun, Freud's movements constitute a form of *restance*, a word that suggests re-instance, resistance and drift.[3]

In recounting the story, Freud occupies the roles of witness and of unwilling, unwitting participant. As participant, he cannot stop returning, and as witness he cannot ever return: in each case, however, the event 'lives on' and underwrites the present. This concern with involuntary repetition is shaped by his work on traumatic and war neuroses in *Beyond the Pleasure Principle*, published one year after 'The Uncanny'. Freud observes that patients suffering from traumatic neurosis are not 'occupied in their waking lives with memories of their accident' and may be more concerned with '*not* thinking of it'. Yet their dreams 'have the characteristic of repeatedly bringing the patient back into the situation of his accident, a situation from which he wakes up in another fright'.[4] Traumatic neurosis is thus puzzlingly resistant to the concept of wish fulfilment, since the traumatic event returns against the subject's wishes. In addition, traumatic neurosis, or what now can be defined as post-traumatic stress disorder, cannot be defined in relation to an originary event or its subsequent distortion by the unconscious mind. Those who live with trauma live with a past they cannot capture or dispense with. As Caruth comments, the pathology of trauma consists 'solely in the *structure of its experience* or reception: the event is not assimilated or experienced fully at the time, but only belatedly, in its repeated *possession* of the one who experiences it. To be traumatized is precisely to be possessed by an image or event.'[5]

Freud illustrates such possession by the image or the event by citing Tasso's tale of Tancred and Clorinda. Tancred, having unwittingly killed his beloved Clorinda in a duel, travels through a magic forest which terrifies his fellow Crusaders. When he slashes a tree with his sword, blood pours from the cut and Clorinda, whose soul has been imprisoned in the tree, is heard to lament that her lover has yet again inflicted a wound upon her. Caruth finds this example striking not just for 'the unconscious act of infliction of the injury and its inadvertent and unwished-for repetition, but the moving and sorrowful *voice* that cries out, a voice that is paradoxically released *through the wound*'. What we hear is 'the enigma of the otherness of a human voice that cries out from the wound'.[6] In the distracted visions of *The Others* and *What Lies Beneath*, the uncanny 'possession' of trauma transmits itself between victim and witness, and acts of repetition bear witness to this enigmatic voice. In *The Others*, the obsessive concern with sealing off, confining and obscuring re-enacts Grace's smothering of her children. Every time she shuts out light, or shuts in her children to protect them, she repeats the traumatic moment. Similarly, in *What Lies Beneath*, every time that Claire bathes or plunges into water, and then surfaces without knowing what lies beneath, she repeats the violence and deception that submerges the 'other' betrayed woman. It is only when Claire returns from the depths, having enabled the unquiet spirit to emerge, that she can bear witness to trauma.

Trauma and the talking ear

Since the late 1980s, ideas surrounding trauma, recovered memory, confession and closure have spilled out beyond clinics and consulting rooms to courts, legislative debating chambers and primetime television studios. In the US, medicine, trauma, law and politics have been closely interwoven since the Vietnam War. As Paul Antze and Michael Lambek observed a decade ago: 'Increasingly, memory worth talking about – worth remembering – is memory of trauma',[7] and Richard McNally remarks that by the end of the 1980s, the 'reluctance to disclose' of abuse survivors became 'inability to remember'.[8] A dual conviction drove therapy culture at this time: a conviction that there was a story that was not being told, and a conviction that therapy could uncover what could not be told. Peter Brooks argues that without confessional discourse, the modern notion of autonomous self would collapse: the talking cure 'has evolved into a generalized belief in the catharsis of confession, of the value of telling all, in public'.[9] Yet, does this confessional discourse reveal psychic truth or referential truth? It may be difficult to distinguish between these forms of truth, but in a court of law examining a case of child abuse such distinctions are crucial. As Freud acknowledges, however, analysis differs from confession; while both analyst and priest must elicit a 'confessional mode of discourse', analysis suspects confession and must supplement it. (It is of course striking that Freud-as-analyst cannot supplement his account of that uncanny experience in the provincial Italian town.) Confession is interested, marked by resistance and transference, and therefore resistance needs to be broken down, obstacles removed and a symptomatic narrative deciphered and reordered for therapeutic purposes. The work of analysis is thus performative in a way that confession cannot be. The analyst must simultaneously take up the place of the confessant, and act upon the secret, not just receive it passively. The true self that confession lays bare may not closely conform to the external world, and 'the confessional talk of psychoanalysis suggests that confession can be less a definition of the truth than a search for it, a posing of the question: who am I?'[10]

It is the non-verifiable status of confession that has provoked so much controversy in the last two decades, leading in one instance to the establishment of the False Memory Syndrome Foundation in US in 1992 to fight an alleged epidemic of compelling but false memories of abuse. Psychoanalysis is of course centrally implicated in what Todd Dufresne has termed the plague of contemporary therapy culture.[11] In the Freud Wars, critics levelled their sights in two ways: Freud was accused either of denying the reality of childhood abuse when he abandoned seduction theory, or of suggesting and producing the false memory of trauma in developing his theory of fantasy. In this account, Freud inaugurates psychoanalysis by falsifying his findings, and his therapeutic technique in turn produces further, damaging falsifications in the consulting room. As Dufresne argues, 'the myth of the unconscious is the direct result of a paranoid discourse bent on proving its own assumptions; a discourse, moreover, that not only provides a symptom language, but makes people sick because *of* it'. The theory of the unconscious encourages both analyst and patient to dredge deep until they find 'a dual consciousness that doesn't exist except as an outmoded theory of spirit possession'. Dufresne contends that a dose of repression, far from preventing a cure, actually aids recovery from trauma.[12] So much, as he says, for psychoanalysis as a therapeutic response to a traumatic past: survivors of abuse should actively resist the talking cure and soldier on.

Yet other forms of clinical diagnosis and classification have proved equally problematic. Cathy Caruth has observed how the recognition of PTSD in 1980 has complicated the understanding of pathology. The very symptomatology and uncanny repetitions of this condition disrupt conventional ideas of diagnosis and cure. If trauma has become an all-inclusive phenomenon, it is so because it 'brings us to the limits of our understanding; if psychoanalysis, psychiatry, sociology, and even literature are beginning to hear each other anew in the study of trauma, it is because they are listening through the radical disruption and gaps of traumatic experience'.[13] Trauma is presented here in terms of the difficulty and possibility of listening. Dori Laub has cast the response to trauma precisely in terms of listening and witnessing. For Laub, 'the victim's narrative – the very process of bearing witness to massive trauma – begins with someone who testifies to an absence'.[14] This testimony to trauma includes the hearer, who becomes the blank screen on which the event is inscribed for the first time. The listener is a witness to witness in both senses: she hears the one who experiences trauma, thus witnessing to that trauma, and also listens, or witnesses, to the act of witness. The listener must listen to and hear silence, speaking mutely in silence and in speech.[15] The act of witnessing also involves an uncanny repetition of events that duplicate or rehearse (in the sense that the past event is yet to come, or to happen in memory) the 'original' traumatic event.

To listen to the traumatic absences of film is to become a screen onto which its silent cuts can be projected. Film plays with revenants, eerie doubles and the sudden intrusion of past into present; in his study of the double, Otto Rank found early cinematography unique in 'visibly portraying psychological events'.[16] Nicholas Royle remarks that film is 'an affair of the ear, of the talking ear',[17] and can perhaps allow us to bear witness audibly and visibly to the traumatic wound or event, to make it 'live' again. As Joshua Hirsch has emphasised, through 'the indexical recording of images and sounds', cinema can bear witness to 'external' trauma in imitative fashion but, since it involves us so fundamentally in the imaginary, it also witnesses to psychological reality.[18] More problematically, it permits vicarious trauma, which can erase the different positions of victim, eyewitness and spectator. In an interesting twist, both films under discussion make available intratextually all three of these positions for its central protagonists. The central protagonists in *The Others* and *What Lies Beneath* are listeners and witness-victims, and the latter part of the discussion will explore Laub's sense of silent but participatory listening in the two films. But before that affair of the ear I want to return to Freud's understanding of the traumatic event.

When we dead awaken

As Cathy Caruth argues: 'Traumatic experience, beyond the psychological dimension of suffering, suggests a certain paradox: that the most direct seeing of a violent event may occur as an absolute inability to know it, that immediacy, paradoxically, may take the form of belatedness.'[19] This paradox is graphically illustrated for her in Freud's account of the 'model' dream of 'the Burning Child':

> A father had been watching beside his child's sick-bed for days and nights on end. After the child had died, he went into the next room to lie down, but left the door open so that he could see from his bedroom into the room in which his child's body was laid out, with tall candles standing round it. An old man had been engaged to keep watch over it, and sat beside the body murmuring prayers. After a few hours' sleep, the father had a dream that *his child was standing beside his bed, caught him by the arm and whispered to him reproachfully: 'Father, don't you see I'm burning?* He woke up, noticed a bright glare of light from the next room, hurried into it and found the old watchman had dropped off to sleep and that the wrappings and one of the arms of his beloved child's dead body had been burned by a lighted candle that had fallen on them.[20]

This dream reaches Freud through a series of acts of witnessing or listening: '[i]t was told to me by a woman patient who had herself heard it in a lecture on dreams; its actual source is still unknown to me'.[21] This is a dream without origin, both within the frame of the dream and in its transmission recalls. The dream's uncanny, 'sourceless' repetition recalls Freud's voyages in the Italian red-light area: the father does not wish to relive a moment that was missed in its first instance, yet he is compelled to return, even if that return is at once resisted and impossible. The father's dream-wish to keep the child alive is bound up with a more enigmatic wish to stay asleep, an instance of a fundamental desire of consciousness 'not to wake up'. The dream-wish is for a suspension of consciousness: a wish that consciousness be subject to a delay, and a wish that death will not catch up with life in the fantasy.

As Freud summarises, the dream 'was preferred to a waking reflection because it was able to show the child as once more alive'.[22] Lacan, however, notes that the wish to sleep is countermanded not just by external forces – the light of the fire – but is demanded from within the dream. It is the dream that wakes the sleeper, rather than prolonging itself. For Lacan, the dream is a function of awakening. The force of the trauma is not death alone, but the father's failure to witness the child's death:

> Is not the dream essentially, one might say, an act of homage to the missed reality – the reality that can no longer produce itself except by repeating endlessly in some never attained awakening? ... Only a rite, an endlessly repeated act, can commemorate this not very memorable encounter – for no one can say what the death of a child is, except the father qua father, that is to say, no conscious being.[23]

The traumatic event is 'knotted, unassimilated ... inaccessible to reflection, contemplation, or undoing'.[24] The father can only contemplate what the aftermath of the child's death means: the experience of trauma is *the experience of what comes after*. Awakening is thus the site of trauma, of the necessity and impossibility of responding to another's death. The bonding of the father with the child is tied up with the necessity and impossibility of confronting death. This bond is linked to missing the child's death, a temporal contradiction that repeats and misses the child's presence. It marks out an uncanny suspension of life and death, a repetition or enigmatic call that issues from no visible, discernible person or place. As Caruth observes, the father's survival can be understood as 'a mode of existence determined by the impossible structure of the response'. To live on after the missed encounter with death is our anguish and our responsibility. Death is always too soon, never at its proper time, never proper to us. The father's story of survival is ineluctably bound up with the child's words, and thus the story of the survivor is no longer the father's own, but a story that responds to the dead child's story. As Caruth, via Lacan, stresses, this is 'a story of urgent responsibility' and of an ethical relation to the real.[25]

The father's failure to witness, to respond to the child's call, is a failure to see both inside and outside: he does not see in time the negligence that allows the bed to catch fire, and did not see the child at the point of death. The child, however, does not call the father back to remain in his dream that will suspend the reality of death. Caruth emphasises that he tells his father to awaken, to testify: 'it is precisely the dead child, the child in its irreducible inaccessibility and otherness, who says to the father: *wake up, leave me, survive, survive to tell the story of my burning*'.[26] The father thus becomes one who can say 'what the death of a child is': this response is not about knowing, but the performance of speaking this carries with it the child's otherness.

Is awakening, then, in its inability to see, a true reception of an address? The address can be overheard as 'See me/I can't see/That is what you must tell you have seen.' Awakening is thus not an understanding but *a transmission*. Caruth argues that awakening is an act that repeats a departure and a difference: it is the departure of the survivor at the behest of the dead, and it is the intolerable difference between psychical afterlife and physical loss, or the difference between burning within and burning without.[27] Freud and Lacan's dream analyses are uncannily repeated in their own private losses: Freud's text is soon followed by the death of his daughter Sophie; and Lacan's reading is marked by the death of his daughter Caroline a few years after he delivered his seminar on the dream of the burning child. We discern here the structure of testimony: first, there is delayed testimony in the dream, then delayed testimony beyond the dream – testimony delayed twice over.

In keeping with this structure of delay, *The Others* and *What Lies Beneath* portray the time of the survivor, but in each case that survival is paradoxical. Both films witness to witness, and engage in the silent, implicated listening outlined by Laub. *The Others* is set in a wintry Jersey in 1945, and centres on Grace and her two children Nicholas and Anne. Grace's husband, Charles, is said to be serving at the front. They inhabit a gloomy house wreathed in thick fog. It opens with Grace in voiceover saying, 'Now, children, are you sitting comfortably?' and beginning to tell the story of Creation while we see a series of drawings of domestic scenes. Thus we start with an inductive narrative strongly informed by religious faith, and by the twin imperatives to testify and to listen. The 'truth' unfolds through multiple acts of participatory listening: Grace gradually believes her children's tales of intruders, and finally learns the reality of her situation from her servants: that they are all ghosts, 'survivors' of the house's often traumatic history.

The untimely awakening to the truth is prefigured in the film's opening scenes. From the title sequence, we cut to Grace screaming in her bed, as if waking from a nightmare. Three shadowy servants – Mrs Mills, Mr Tuttle and a mute young woman, Lydia – have knocked on the door, although Grace 'wasn't expecting them so soon'. We first encounter the children as they emerge from behind a locked door, having just been woken. They are said to be photosensitive, highly allergic to light, which were they to be exposed to it, would quickly suffocate them. As Grace says, the only thing in the house that moves is the light, but it 'changes everything'. Later, when Grace and the children acknowledge that Charles has 'moved on', the curtains are removed by the new occupants, and light floods in without malign effect. The children are only photosensitive 'before' the registering of the traumatic event. The children often allude to Mummy's madness, and to an unnamed event; Anne affirms 'it did happen', while Nicholas lives in denial. Grace maintains her defences through a process of splitting, separating out the one who suffers and the one who survives. Silence is 'prized very highly' in the house; and at times, as she admits, 'this house is not an ideal home'. She does not like 'fantasies' or 'strange ideas' and repeatedly uses Biblical maxims to stress the importance of truthfulness, but she punishes Anne harshly for her truthfulness in being able to identify the 'intruders'.

Mrs Mills is constantly on the point of telling all, but must instead listen silently and hear the story. She does not respond when Grace – correctly – speculates that Lydia has become mute due to some trauma. She is a strange counterpart of the blind medium that the 'intruders', the Marlish family, have employed to contact and exorcise the domestic ghosts. When the presence of ghosts or intruders can no longer be denied, Grace accepts that 'there is something which is not at rest' in the house. Mrs Mills comments that 'we've all heard stories of "beyond"', and that 'sometimes the world of the dead gets mixed up with the world of the living'. When Grace asserts that 'the Lord would never allow such an aberration', Mrs Mills replies that 'there isn't always an answer for everything'. Yet revelation or discovery remains subject to delay. As Grace leaves the house to seek answers from the village priest, Mr Tuttle is seen heaping dead leaves over gravestones to obscure them: Mrs Mills remarks that there is not yet a need to 'bring this out into the open'. Grace plunges into the fog, and meets Charles as he 'returns' from the front. When she says 'They said I should give you up for dead', he replies that 'They say a lot of things', alluding to voices that have encouraged Grace to move on, to relinquish the past. Yet the film's unsettled account with the dead is underscored by Charles's apparent status as missing in action. The past lives as the experience of aftershock: Grace cannot fully confess her 'crime' to Charles during his brief return, even though the children have told him 'what happened'. When Grace uncovers a Victorian Book of the Dead, in which corpses are arranged fully dressed for the camera, she cannot fathom the motivation behind such uncanny still lives. Yet the pictures, which stage the uncertainty between the living and dead body that marks the uncanny, figure precisely the suspended inanimation of the house's inhabitants.

At the same moment as Anne and Nicholas uncover the gravestones of the three servants, Grace discovers their portrait in the Book of the Dead. Neither Grace nor the children can hide any longer from spectrality; in listening to the servants, they are also obliged to listen to the intruders. The Marlishes are holding a séance to make contact with the restless ghosts of the house. It is during the séance that we learn the secret: that, on learning of her husband's death at the front, Grace smothered her children and shot herself. It is all-too tempting to read this traumatic confession in terms of exposure and closure, but the process of transmission and active listening does not exorcise or lay to rest the house's ghostly inhabitants. The medium, and all those gathered around the table, 'wake up' to bear witness to the story of 'burning', the missed encounter with death. If the survivors are able to move on, it is only in the sense that the Marlishes decide to leave the house the next morning. The recovered memory enables an opening to a kind of future for Grace and the children, a way of 'moving on' even as they remain in 'our house'. Domestic normality seems to have resumed when Mrs Mills offers a cup of tea, but the household must remain caught up in the aftershock of trauma. They have experienced the trauma of their sudden death belatedly, and must 'live on' in a perpetual recurrence of that belatedness. As an eavesdropper on the aftermath, the listener/spectator becomes a survivor too, obliged to listen to that 'original' moment of overwhelming pain and loss. Like the burning child, these ghosts demand an impossible response: they ask that the listener return from the missed encounter with death, and bear witness to the traumatic event that had no witness.

As in *The Others*, trauma is an intruder in *What Lies Beneath*, but this time it is another's trauma. The film involves Claire Spencer, a former classical musician who sacrificed her career for marriage to her husband Norman, a genetic scientist. Haunted by visions of a young woman, whom she eventually identifies as Madison Frank, a missing person, Claire uncovers first Norman's affair with Madison, then his murder of her. Claire is a survivor, and must bear witness to the traumatic event that she did not witness. The opening credits overlay the swirling, misty waters of a lake, before the shot dissolves into its weed-strewn depths. We then surface first in the form of a dead woman's face, which in turn blends into Claire's face in the bath. There are numerous scenes of such mirroring; in mirror images that force a double take, Claire glimpses Madison's ghostly form in a full bathtub, and in the lake adjacent to their house. At one point, as Claire is in the process of unravelling Norman's deception, there is an eerie scene of mimicry where Claire assumes, or is possessed by, the spirit of her dead counterpart.

Early in the narrative, we see Claire anxiously parting from her daughter who is leaving for college, a departure made more difficult by the fact that Claire is still recovering from a car accident that occurred the previous year. Her growing belief that the family home is haunted is attributed to a delayed reaction to this traumatic event. Sensing something wrong close to home, Claire spies on her new neighbours the Feurs, who have a passionate and violent relationship. Claire first misdiagnoses Mrs Feur's psychological distress across the garden fence, then wrongly believes that she has been killed by her husband. To exorcise the ghostly presence, she consults in turn an analyst, a book on demonology and witchcraft that proves extremely effective in conjuring Madison's spirit, and a ouija board. In a knowing allusion to the recovered memory controversy, the paraphernalia of satanic abuse is introduced to an elite New England home; Claire and Norman eventually burn a braid of the dead woman's hair to banish her from the house. Prompted by friends, and piecing together fragmentary evidence, Claire slowly 'remembers' that she had seen Norman with Madison at his professorial inauguration party, and had guessed their secret at the time. This explains the ghostly message in a misted bathroom mirror: 'You know'. Claire's car crash might thus have been a suicide attempt that she has repressed. As Madison's past becomes more tangible, however, the extent to which it is Claire's trauma, or buried memory, that is at stake in this tale of haunting is questionable. Yet when Norman confesses to his affair, he 'counsels' Claire in such a way that another's responsibility becomes her responsibility, even as he claims to be helping to relieve her of her burden. Norman speaks: he does not listen. In a brief, quasi-therapeutic encounter, Claire claims that there is a 'presence in the house' who is 'a young blond girl', and that she has unwittingly opened the door to this ghost. Norman's response positions

Claire as the victim of abuse or sexual violence: 'it's not your fault. Say it – it's not your fault'. She is at once asked to relinquish responsibility and obliged to account for her victimhood, turning her into the mirror image of the other blond woman who haunts their home. Yet this identification is not merely a passive reflection; Claire withdraws from Norman, clearly unconvinced by his reassuring tone. In this scene, Claire has moved from victim – a word that directs attention 'to perpetrators and to the damage they have inflicted on others'[28] – to *survivor*, one who emerges to listen, and breaks the dependency that victim status can perpetuate. As such, this is an active identification with Madison, who in her spectral visitations 'survives' the traumatic event.

Yet the responsibility to confess to a traumatic past – a past that is not Claire's alone – cannot easily be evaded. This responsibility is emphasised by Ellen Bass and Laura Davis in *The Courage to Heal*: 'If you don't remember your abuse, you're not alone. Many women don't have memories, and some never get memories. This doesn't mean they weren't abused.'[29] This injunction to remember evokes an originary traumatic trace, a moment anterior to consciousness, and is less an obligation to witness than an exhortation to take command of a shared past. This imposes on us a responsibility for and to others, but it is impelled by a diagnostic or hermeneutic zeal far removed from Laub's silent, participatory listening. Trauma *has* happened: it is the predicate of the future, and only awaits its exposure. It is precisely this sense of conviction, which often led to the conviction of others, that fuelled the controversies over recovered and false memory in the early 1990s.[30] It has also given way to the ubiquitous, often questionable and ultimately desensitising invocation of 'trauma', and its endless relaying through word and image. Under the therapeutic imperative outlined by Bass and Davis, there *will be* victims, abuses and secrets to find. Yet *What Lies Beneath* negotiates between two competing versions of witness. Claire is continually positioned as the self-policing subject obliged to acknowledge and account for her damage, and yet she increasingly assumes the role of a silent listener who opens up to the shock, the uncanny punctuation, of trauma. Claire is constantly encouraged to forget, move on and adjust, yet she refuses; she knows there *is something*, but it is not *in her*. It is the extension of the therapeutic imperative, and its overdetermined pursuit of abuse, that leads Claire to misconstrue her neighbours' intense marital relationship; her witnessing of apparent domestic violence initially obscures the trauma of another who *did* experience fatal violence. This seems to position Claire – and in turn the cinematic spectator – as a 'vicarious' witness. Hirsch discusses the way in which the witness's point of view can be transferred 'to a nonwitness through vicarious traumatization' in cinematic and documentary images, and also in the analytic encounter.[31] In *What Lies Beneath*, this relay of vicarious traumatization includes Claire, Norman, Claire's friend, her analyst and even the ghost of Madison, who returns to bear witness to what lies beyond witness.

So Claire is left in a position where she cannot avoid dredging the depths: she seeks closure by declaring that 'the girl must be brought up'. As Claire flees for her life from Norman's murderous rage, their truck careers off a bridge into a lake, and makes an uncanny descent to the very place Norman had entombed Madison in her car. Norman makes the last of several attempts to drown Claire, who is rescued by the intervention of the spectral Madison, leaving her husband to die and the young woman to rest at peace in the water. The corpse's face turns to a composite of Madison and Claire, and suggests an affinity between listener and victim. Yet can Claire move on, begin again? The closing scene depicts her standing mutely in a snowy landscape at Madison's grave, transmitting her encounter with the dead woman's otherness. The survivor can speak only of failure at the graveside, just as the father of the burning child can speak only from outside the experience of his son's pain. Trauma is experienced as delay or belatedness; as both films suggest, how can there be a final moment of reckoning, when irretrievable loss can be dealt with? Caruth characterises this 'open' response to trauma as a transformative awakening: 'awakening, in its very inability to see, is thus the true *reception of an address* that, precisely in its crossing from the burning within to the burning without, changes and reforms the addressee around the blindness of the imperative itself'.[32] For one who cannot protect or restore the life of the dead woman, the imperative in *What Lies Beneath* is to return from the depths of the lake as a living survivor who can bear witness to unbearable fact. Claire cannot 'see' Madison, but can testify to the gap between the living and the dead.

Conclusion

Caruth argues that the enigmatic core of trauma resides in 'the delay or incompletion in knowing, or even in seeing, an overwhelming occurrence'; there is an 'inherent latency' within the traumatic experience itself. This latency has implications for survivors and witnesses. For the survivor, 'trauma is a repeated suffering of the event, but it is also a continual leaving of its site'. For the witness, '[t]o listen to the crisis of a trauma ... is not only to listen for the event, but to hear in the testimony the survivor's departure from it; the challenge of the therapeutic listener, in other words, is *how to listen to departure*'.[33] Yet what is the nature of that departure in both films? It is not a final reckoning with the past. Grace's initial efforts as a 'survivor' in *The Others* revolve around the prevention of awakening, of letting light shine in: when illumination eventually arrives, it is less a matter of exposing a terrible secret than of enabling loss to be realised, to be lived with. Similarly, while Claire in *What Lies Beneath* seems intent on dredging up repressed depths, the emphasis is on coming up for air, surfacing from a state of suspension. Both films issue from the dead, from a paradoxical, impossible call to awaken and survive. If their testimony is a form of witnessing or disclosure, it is not in the service of restitution, retrieval or closure: it is about a sense of opening. Their survivors, who are not survivors and yet who live in and with the aftermath, must look to a future that is open to further punctuation, disruption and shock, where past and present collide. In an age of terror and absolutism overshadowed, like Nathaniel in Hoffmann's 'The Sandman', by 'the fear or dread of what may be to come',[34] we must leave the ruins, bearing pain and loss within us, listening to each other's departures, making the other's crisis our own.

Notes

1. Ulrich Baer, *Remnants of Song: Trauma and the Experience of Modernity in Charles Baudelaire and Paul Celan* (Stanford, CA: Stanford UP, 2000), p. 10.
2. Sigmund Freud, 'The "Uncanny"', in *Art and Literature*, The Pelican Freud Library, vol. 14, ed. Albert Dickson, trans. James Strachey (Harmondsworth: Penguin, 1985), pp. 335–76; 359.
3. Jacques Derrida deploys the term *restance* on a number of occasions. For the purposes of this essay, I am referring to Ian McLeod's translation note to Derrida's 'Speculations – on Freud' (Jacques Derrida, 'Speculations – on Freud,' trans. Ian McLeod, *Oxford Literary Review* 3: 2 (1978), pp. 78–97; 97).
4. Sigmund Freud, *Beyond the Pleasure Principle*, in *Metapsychology: the Theory of Psychoanalysis*, The Penguin Freud Library Vol. 11, ed. Angela Richards, trans. James Strachey (Harmondsworth: Penguin, 1991), pp. 269–338; 282.
5. Cathy Caruth, ed. *Trauma: Explorations in Memory* (Baltimore, ML: Johns Hopkins UP, 1995), pp. 4–5.
6. Cathy Caruth, *Unclaimed Experience: Trauma, Narrative, and History* (Baltimore and London; Johns Hopkins UP, 1996), p. 3.
7. Paul Antze and Michael Lambek, eds *Tense Past: Cultural Essays in Trauma and Memory* (New York: Routledge, 1996), p. xii.
8. Richard J. McNally, *Remembering Trauma* (Cambridge, MA: Harvard UP, 2003), p. 5.
9. Peter Brooks, *Troubling Confessions: Speaking Guilt in Law and Literature* (Chicago and London: University of Chicago Press, 2000), p. 140.
10. Ibid., pp. 116–7, 141.

11. Todd Dufresne, *Killing Freud: Twentieth Century Culture and the Death of Psychoanalysis* (New York: Continuum, 2003), p. viii.
12. Ibid., pp. 23, 24.
13. Caruth, *Trauma: Explorations in Memory*, pp. 3, 4.
14. Shoshana Felman and Dori Laub, *Testimony: Crises of Witnessing in Literature, Psychoanalysis and History* (New York and London: Routledge, 1992), p. 57.
15. Ibid., p. 58.
16. Otto Rank, *The Double: A Psychoanalytic Study*, trans. Harry Tucker Jr (Chapel Hill, NC: University of North Carolina Press, 1971 [1914]), p. 7.
17. Nicholas Royle, *The Uncanny* (Manchester: Manchester UP, 2003), p. 80.
18. Joshua Hirsch, *After Image: Film, Trauma and the Holocaust* (Philadelphia: Temple UP, 2004), pp. 6–7.
19. Cathy Caruth, 'Traumatic Awakenings', *Performativity and Performance*, ed. Andrew Parker and Eve Kosofsky Sedgewick (New York and London: Routledge, 1995), p. 89.
20. Sigmund Freud, *The Interpretation of Dreams*, in Pelican Freud Library Vol. 4, ed. Angela Richards, trans. James Strachey (Harmondsworth: Penguin, 1976), p. 652.
21. Freud, *The Interpretation of Dreams*, p. 652.
22. Ibid., p. 653.
23. Jacques Lacan, *The Four Fundamental Concepts of Psychoanalysis*, ed. Jacques-Alain Miller, trans. Alan Sheridan (Norton: New York, 1973) pp. 58, 59.
24. Ellie Ragland, 'Lacan, the Death Drive, and the Dream of the Burning Child', in *Death and Representation*, ed. Sarah Webster Goodwin and Elisabeth Bronfen (Baltimore, MA and London: Johns Hopkins University Press, 1993) pp. 80–102; 82–3.
25. Caruth, 'Traumatic Awakenings', pp. 97, 98.
26. Ibid., pp. 100–1.
27. Ibid., p. 102.
28. McNally, p. 2.
29. Ellen Bass and Laura Davis, *The Courage to Heal: A Guide for Women Survivors of Child Sexual Abuse* (New York: Harper and Row, 1988) p. 81.
30. McNally, pp. 14–15.
31. Hirsch, p. 22.
32. Caruth, 'Traumatic Awakenings', p. 101.
33. Caruth, *Trauma: Explorations in Memory*, pp. 5, 8, 10.
34. Royle, p. viii.

6

The Uncanny After Freud: The Contemporary Trauma Subject and the Fiction of Stephen King

Roger Luckhurst

I Trauma's returns

For about twenty years, Western culture has staged and restaged a particularly dramatic scene which tells us much about the nature of the contemporary subject. A distressed and disoriented individual is assailed by their own memory. He or she discovers, by involuntary flashbacks or perhaps by hypnotic regression, a whole tranche of memory that had been lying dormant, walled off or hidden away (somehow) in the psyche. The occluded memories always concern a devastating event or series of events, of such searing intensity that the conscious mind cannot bear it and so (somehow) propels it into the outer psychical darkness. The type of events that generate this defensive reaction are now generally brought under the umbrella category of 'trauma': the violence of war, familial abuse, rape, being a witness to an accident or disaster. There are complex arrays of symptoms that have been clustered under the clinical illness post-traumatic stress disorder (PTSD) since it entered official diagnostics in 1980, but this pattern of defence, period of latency and belated lifting of amnesia has most captured the wider cultural imagination.

This so-called 'recovered memory' was first popularised in self-help books and memoirs associated with therapists informed by feminism in the 1980s. Sylvia Fraser's *My Father's House* opened with a bewilderingly self-cancelling 'Author's Note': 'The story I have told in this book is autobiographical. As a result of amnesia, much of it was unknown to me until three years ago.'[1] The recovered details of her father's systematic abuse were inserted in menacing italicised retrospective asides into the recounting of an apparently ordinary childhood. The self-help guides told you: 'You may think you don't have memories, but often as you begin to talk about what you do remember, there emerges a constellation of feelings, reactions, and recollections that add up to substantial information ... If you think you were abused and your life shows the symptoms, then you were.'[2] These guides were overflowing with exemplary case studies, unwitting victims turned belated survivors. They were models to examine the nooks and crannies of one's own memory for symptomatic absences where hidden traumas might well lurk, since absence of evidence was not evidence of absence. The early 1990s saw an explosion of instances of recovered memory across different cultural locations. Law courts wrestled with several implications: what was the status of such recovered evidence if unsupported? Would the statute of limitations have to be suspended for memories of acts recovered from decades before? Psychological experts were ranged to support flatly contradictory assertions: either that trauma could induce blanket amnesia, or that such recoveries were likely confabulations of hypnotists or therapists, iatrogenic products of the very method of recovery. In popular culture, Oprah Winfrey's chat show hosted a series of celebrity confessions of recovered memories of childhood abuse, in a show made famous by Oprah's own confession in 1986. The show made figures like Trudi Chase, abused as a child and subsequently developing ninety-two multiple personalities, nationally famous. The *X Files* (1993–2002) popularised the work of Professor John Mack and other marginal psychologists and therapists who claimed that hypnotic recovery techniques were repeatedly uncovering scenes of alien abduction which had been suppressed from conscious recall by advanced extraterrestrial technologies.[3]

The subject of recovered memory was not restricted to the efflorescence of prime time TV, however. In 1991, Jane Smiley's novel *A Thousand Acres* was awarded the Pulitzer Prize. Its plot, a modern retelling of *King Lear*, centred on one of the patriarch's daughters recovering memories of paternal abuse in intrusive flashbacks that followed the precise trajectory outlined by trauma psychologists and self-help guides: 'I knew that he had been in there to me, that my father had lain with me in that bed, that I had looked at the top of his head, at his balding spot in the brown grizzled hair, while feeling him suck my breasts.'[4] Similarly, the last novel by W. G. Sebald, *Austerlitz*, was a sustained exercise in a retrospective reconstruction of a life marked by suppressed traumatic origins. Austerlitz's life had been full of dread and suspicion: in his childhood, 'I never shook off the feeling that something very obvious, very manifest was hidden from me.'[5] This hidden memory begins to obtrude on a symbolic site, Liverpool Street station in London, built on the old Bedlam asylum and where building work has turned up buried bodies from an ancient city graveyard. When Austerlitz enters an old section of the station his childhood memory floods back: his arrival in England from Prague, on one of the *Kindertransport*. These child transports had been an early Nazi method of depopulating German territory of Jews, before the decision to undertake full-scale extermination. Austerlitz had been fostered with Welsh Calvinists, renamed, and his Jewish past erased. His attempt to reconstruct his childhood and the fate of his parents only intensifies the agony of Austerlitz's unrelieved condition. Memory does not cure him; instead, history invades him, and he can exist only in traumatic timeless time: 'I feel more and more as if time did not exist at all, only various spaces ... between which the living and the dead can move back and forth as they like.'[6]

Recovered memory catastrophises the subject: Austerlitz is an exemplary figure of ruination, continually associated with collapsed buildings and failed defensive structures. At a stroke, recovered memory retrospectively rewrites a life narrative, altering the significance of every relationship and the motivation for every decision. Yet the catastrophic moment of recovery is usually only the first station on a path that leads to the prospect of a healing reunification of a fragmented and disadjusted mind. One emerges from this journey that most valued of contemporary identities: a survivor.

We are fascinated and appalled by the prospect of *resubjectivation* that the recovery of occluded traumatic memory seems to present. This, we might also say, is an uncanny experience, in both a loose and a strict sense.

Trauma psychology frequently resorts to loosely Gothic or supernatural tropes to articulate post-traumatic effects. Freud's close colleague Sandor Ferenczi believed in 'the sudden, surprising rise of new faculties after a trauma'.[7] Trauma 'makes the person in question ... more or less clairvoyant', Ferenczi argued, because the passage through trauma was a little death, and thus related to 'the supposition that the instant of dying ... is associated with that timeless and spaceless omniscience'.[8] The alarming consequence of this effect for the psychoanalyst was that his patients were able to read the analyst's mind, most particularly when his or her attention was adrift. Later psychologists have repeated this association of trauma with heightened powers. Large-scale traumatic events, such as Hiroshima, involve 'a permanent encounter with death', Robert Jay Lifton argued, leaving behind a host of 'homeless dead' that cannot easily be laid to rest.[9] Survivors of catastrophes are treated as liminal beings, exaggeratedly valued or feared for now possessing 'a quality of supernatural evil'.[10] Judith Herman's extremely influential *Trauma and Recovery* (a book that helped establish the currency of recovered memory in the early 1990s) proposes that

> the pathological environment of childhood abuse forces the development of extraordinary capacities, both creative and destructive. It fosters the development of abnormal states of consciousness in which the ordinary relations of body and mind, reality and imagination, knowledge and memory, no longer hold ... The language of the supernatural, banished for three hundred years from scientific discourse, still intrudes into the most sober attempts to describe the psychological manifestations of chronic childhood trauma.[11]

Janice Haaken noted that as the incest story took hold it was becoming overdetermined with all kinds of 'social symbolic loadings' by the late 1980s, including the 'clinical preoccupation with gothic scenes of sexual torture'.[12] Post-traumatic experience is intrinsically spooky, finding cultural expression in ghostly visitations, prophetic dread, weird coincidence or telepathic transfer: 'Traumatic anxiety *is* a ghost! It moves through the generations with the stealth and cunning of a most skilled spectre.'[13]

This scene of recovery might be regarded as more strictly uncanny, however. Freud defines some of the most intense experiences of the uncanny as those in which 'the frightening element can be shown to be something repressed which *recurs* ... for this uncanny is in reality nothing new or alien, but something which is familiar and old-established in the mind and which has become alienated from it only through a process of repression.'[14] Although Freud does his best to eliminate the rival associationist theory of the uncanny by Ernst Jentsch, Jentsch also grasped that the uncanny produced the greatest shivers when the illusion of 'psychical harmony' was disturbed: 'Then the dark knowledge dawns on the unschooled observer that mechanical processes are taking place in that which he was previously used to regarding as a unified psyche.'[15] The uncanny marks the moment when the psyche becomes aware of its own occlusions; perhaps, indeed, that the subject is *premised* on occlusion. The ghost or the double that comes back is the return of that portion of the self that does not promise completion, but a catastrophic rewriting of the self.

The uncanny has sometimes looked set to become not only the central concept for psychoanalysis, but to swallow much modern philosophical thought, and even to become a meta-concept for modernity itself. Nicholas Royle's work demonstrates this extension, but also simultaneous collapse. Since he only wants to use the conceptual framework of the uncanny as a template for all other thought (inevitably folding it back onto 'The Uncanny' itself), no wonder the uncanny is found everywhere, 'the key to understanding both modernity and post-modernity itself.'[16] Yet others have made more historically modest claims that the uncanny is related to the rise of modernity in the eighteenth century. Mladen Dolar argued that 'There is *a specific dimension of the uncanny that emerges with modernity*', related to the reserve of the 'sacred and untouchable' that the Enlightenment wishes to erase but leaves only displaced and haunting at the margins.[17] More plausibly still, Terry Castle has established that the secularisation of conceptions of subjectivity in the Enlightenment transposed 'ghostly' concepts into terms for psychic interiority, the uncanny produced 'like a kind of toxic side effect' for those psychic processes that could not be routinised by rationalism.[18]

Perhaps the uncanny is invoked so often in trauma theory because the concept of trauma is very similarly held to be 'responsive to and constitutive of "modernity"'.[19] The medico-legal concept of invisible, internal trauma to the nervous system was developed in relation to railway accidents in the 1860s, the site, as Wolfgang Schivelbusch has argued, of the 'first attempt to explain industrial traumata'.[20] The advances of technological modernity have, ever since, been accompanied by a discourse of trauma and catastrophe. 'Modernity has come to be understood under the sign of the wound', Mark Seltzer has claimed: 'the modern subject has become inseparable from the categories of shock and trauma.'[21] We could say that the wound acts uncannily, breaching boundaries, opening inside to outside, life to death, that the wound is a site of haunting.

But if modernity somehow ties together trauma and the uncanny, these loose metaphorical associations will not do. It is important to grasp that the contemporary trauma subject has not necessarily been theorised in relation to Freudian theory, but in the wake of a revolution in psychology in the 1970s that was either passively ignorant of psychoanalysis, or actively sought to displace it. The modern link between trauma and the uncanny is rarely routed through Freud's essay, and certainly not through its libidinal meta-psychology. This uncanny *after* Freud has in fact worked to recover psychological models of dissociation and splitting that existed *before* Freud. Late nineteenth-century fascination with trauma was eclipsed by psychoanalysis; the return of the trauma subject since 1980 suggests a resurgence of that Victorian theory. For a proper Freudian, with a sense of irony, this return might be considered truly uncanny, for it signals the return of 'modes of thought' securely believed by the psychoanalytic establishment to have surely been '*surmounted*'.[22]

The story of the appearance of PTSD in the third edition of the official *Diagnostic and Statistical Manual* (DSM) of the American Psychiatric Association, issued in 1980, has been told by several historians and is now relatively well known.[23] The initial impetus came from a group of psychiatric activists working with Vietnam Veterans Against the War from 1970. These therapists wanted a recognised 'combat syndrome' to enter official diagnostics, partly to allow for proper compensation of soldiers. When Robert Jay Lifton and his allies realised that this was unlikely, they worked comparatively with other groups to create a suite of symptoms that could encompass survivors of what was called 'concentration camp syndrome', as well as 'rape trauma', which had been developed in parallel to Vietnam by feminist activists, and also the traumatic symptoms psychiatrists saw as resulting from major natural or man-made disasters. From 1975, this group exerted pressure on the Task Force on Nomenclature to include a broadly defined trauma syndrome, which eventually became PTSD. Crucially, as Mitchell Wilson observes, the third edition of the *Diagnostic and Statistical Manual of Mental Disorders* (*DSM*) constituted a fundamental shift to medical, biological and quantitative models of the assessment of psychiatric illness, and an overthrow of the conflictual, psychodynamic models that had been associated with the dominant psychoanalytic framework of American psychiatry.[24] The organiser of the Task Force openly criticised psychoanalytic societies for non-participation, although this failure to cooperate was unsurprising given that the exercise was designed to displace them. As a new disease entity, PTSD conformed to the new medical model, incorporating quantitative study and biological evidence, particularly by claiming to relate trauma objectively to levels of the 'stress' hormone norepinephrine in the endocrine system.[25]

The *DSM* aimed only to taxonomise symptoms; it 'did not explicitly engage the issue of the nature of the disorders it named'.[26] When groups of researchers began to theorise the psychical mechanisms of traumatic reaction after PTSD had been officially recognised, they tended to avoid Freud's speculative account of repression, associated with a superseded model, and reached instead for the term *dissociation*. This is the concept which takes us from psychiatry after Freud to the pre-Freudian era: it derived from Pierre Janet's work in the 1880s and 1890s. In a formative paper a hundred years later, Frank Putnam declared that it was Janet that 'made the connection between dissociative psychopathology and traumatic experiences' and was one of the first to 'conceptualise dissociative reactions occurring in the context of acute trauma as an adaptive process that protects the individual and allows him to continue to function, though often in an automaton-like state'.[27]

Janet's model worked like this: a particularly shocking moment or event might produce a defensive response of a narrowing of the field of consciousness. This would become an *idée fixe*, held outside the recall memory of the conscious mind. It would accrue its own memory chain and associations, becoming a 'new system, a personality independent of the first'.[28] It was this act of splitting that created a double self, something that coalesced around the subconscious fixed idea. The subconscious (Janet's coinage) was not structural, then, as in Freud's notion of the unconscious, but was a specific product of traumatic hysteria: 'It is a special moral weakness consisting in the lack of power on the part of the feeble subject to gather, to condense, his psychological phenomena, and assimilate them to his personality.'[29] Something of this (without Janet's belief that the formation of the subconscious is a product of weak heredity) lies behind current theories of traumatic dissociation, although Janet dropped the term quite early in his career. One contemporary survey has confessed that the usage of dissociation now 'lacks a single, coherent referent or conceptualisation' and is often confused with repression.[30]

The late Victorian double self was consistently associated with supernatural powers. One of Janet's fellow researchers, Frederic Myers, firmly believed that the existence of the dissociations of double consciousness and 'multiplex' personality provided evidence of psychic powers, such as telepathy (a term Myers coined in 1882), and the ability to project a phantasmal double across time and space. Myers developed an elaborate synthesis of dynamic psychological research: his 'subliminal consciousness' was a major theory at the turn of the century which aimed to organise and naturalise the confusing mass of the supernatural and uncanny. In the 1930s, the leader of the Surrealists, André Breton, could still declare the movement more indebted to Myers's '*gothic psychology*' than to Freud.[31]

All of this is to say that we cannot understand contemporary trauma subjectivity or the uncanny in sole reference to Freudian psychoanalysis. The research that predates Freud informs the conceptualisation of PTSD in the 1980s. This is not an argument for jettisoning Freud; it is merely to state that there are other elements of the history of psychology that inform contemporary cultural representation. To illustrate this, I turn now to the work of Stephen King.

II Stephen King's trauma Gothic

Stephen King's prolific, bestselling horror writing is frequently the source of suspicion, celebrated by fans but ignored in the main by literary critics and disdained by experts in the Gothic. A problem for those who want to regard the Gothic genre as potentially subversive is King's conservatism; his novels invoke a coercive 'we' that David Punter considers 'at all points coterminous with US norms'.[32] Even worse, King seems to agree, seeing horror fiction as 'above all else an agent of the norm'.[33] Yet this is not so simple, for King's work registers exactly the pressure on those norms across a particularly turbulent span of American history. King's horrific tales are unusually sensitive to the depredations to contemporary subjectivity, and this historicity is nowhere more apparent than in King's relationship to the re-conceptualisation of trauma since the 1970s. If his conception of trauma keeps pace with psychiatric shifts from repressive to dissociative models of mind, then this also prompts the need to rethink the tendency of horror to rely on psychoanalytic concepts of the uncanny.

King's work might initially be regarded as routing the uncanny through trauma models in two ways. As we've seen, trauma psychology often resorts to the Gothic or supernatural to articulate post-traumatic effects. Genre fictions can become imbricated in the formation of new psychiatric subjects, since generic scripts can provide narratives for what Ian Hacking terms 'making up people', the dynamic interaction between subjects and psychiatric categories.[34] For instance, the apparatus of the horror and Gothic revival of the 1970s (of which King was an integral part) clearly surfaced in the descriptions of recovered memories of Satanic Ritual Abuse in the early 1990s.[35] That the Gothic might prove appropriate to provide scripts for trauma is perhaps because, as Robert Miles argues, the genre has from its foundation been 'embroiled within ... the history of the "subject"', presenting the self as 'dispossessed in its own house, in a condition of rupture, disjunction, fragmentation'.[36]

Second, King's trauma fiction could be read more literally as a body of work symptomatic of personal trauma. This project has been duly undertaken by Lenore Terr, one of the strongest proponents in the 1990s Memory Wars of the view that buried traumatic memory can be recovered in pure, unmediated form. Her suspicion that King's work has traumatic origins begins with the non-supernatural, rite of passage novella 'The Body' (filmed as *Stand By Me*), in which a handful of boys from variously abusive homes follow train tracks into the forest on the rumour that they will be able to see a dead body. 'The Body' is structured as a recollection of a writer on a defining incident in his adolescence, one which is suffused with death, and Terr takes the story as barely encrypted autobiography. Sure enough, King's autobiographical writings reveal an incident of which King claims to have no direct memory, only the indirect accounts of family lore: aged four, returning home from play silent and shocked, King was the possible witness to the death of his playmate on rail tracks, coping through amnesiac dissociation. How apt that King's traumatic origins as a writer are staged on this amnesiac site, the origin of trauma itself, the railway. King's account in *Danse Macabre*, however, is savage about decoding his career through this event. Such psychiatric speculation is 'jumped-up astrology': 'writers are made', he says, 'not born or created out of dreams or childhood trauma'.[37] Terr nevertheless traces this symptom with a dogged and literal determination. Mechanical monsters loom in King's work: possessed cars, demonic machines, zombifying mobile phones and always, always the train. King's characterisation and plotting knows 'how to present posttraumatic symptoms in his plots'.[38] King's well-known writing compulsion (and other addictions), his exploration of the same scenarios of menaced children, suggest rather that he is caught in cycles of traumatic repetition rather than mastery. Even the inordinate length of the novels that King produces has a traumatic origin for Terr: the over-accumulation of detail, the slowing of narrative time, all imply King is re-experiencing the timeless time of the traumatic event. Thus King's fiction is entirely the result of 'posttraumatic play': 'King is a trauma victim, struck terrified in his own childhood by a train.'[39]

Terr's account is a warning about the brutal reduction of text to autobiographical symptom, read with the alarming literalism driven by the belief that eidetic traumatic memory will never be seriously deformed or subject to revision, or even undergo any aesthetic transformation, but will simply repeat itself in the grain of texts as an open secret. Yet King is not an exemplification of trauma subjectivity; instead, his books are narrative vectors for its consolidation. I want to trace how King's attunement to the *Zeitgeist* very precisely shifts the locus and narrative form of subjective terror in the Gothic and the uncanny directly in response to the rise of the trauma paradigm, particularly in the early 1990s and most symptomatically in his novel *Gerald's Game*.

King writes self-consciously in the American Gothic tradition, in which domestic intimacy is menaced by its dialectical other, an unearthly, cosmic and always malignant force. In *The Shining* (1977), one of King's strongest books, the father is weak entry point in the family, taken over by the venomous spirits of the Overlook Hotel. For all the supernatural pyrotechnics of *The Shining*, its ambitions to render the hotel a repository of the monstrous underside of the American twentieth century, the book is also an impressive study of the father's psychic failings. His alcoholism, his guilty instant of physical abuse towards his son and his teaching job lost through an eruption of rage are traced back to an abusive father, whose exorbitant violence to his mother and siblings is recovered by Jack in a dissociative trance state in the symbolic basement of the Hotel, where all manner of forgotten histories accumulate. The precognitive flashes of future violence, picked up by his psychic son, are revealed to be repetitions of a traumatic scene from his father's childhood. They are instances of uncanny return. These traumatic motifs (the roar of '*come here and take your medicine*') cut across the narrative in distinct typographic intrusions that collapse linear temporality into the insistent presence of traumatic timeless time. This scene is coming, it is what propels the narrative, but it has also already taken place. This emplotment of psychic damage suggests an early recognition, on King's part, of psychological accounts of generational cycles of violence within the abusive family. It also indicates that King will always associate supernatural capacities with traumatic origins.

In the early 1980s, 'The Body' experimented with transferring Gothic affect out of genre trappings, locating its affect in early adolescent rites of passage. It was published in *Different Seasons* alongside 'Apt Pupil', a queasy investigation into the transmissibility of trauma. An adolescent boy, apparently a model student, discovers that an aged neighbour in his small American town has been living under a pseudonym, concealing his past as a concentration camp *unterkommandant* in Belsen, Aushwitz and Patin, where the Jews named him the Blood Fiend. Dussander is blackmailed by the boy to detail every element of crimes, a narrative that corrupts the listener and transfers the murderous impulse. The tale designedly walks a dubious line between the exploitation of historical horrors and a critique of our potentially unhealthy absorption in them. Punter observes that King offers his readers 'a series of opportunities to re-experience scenarios of childhood anxiety under conditions of relative safety',[40] but I see no reassurance in 'Apt Pupil', only a grim assessment of how unimaginable horrors can become vehicles of corrupting identification.

The 1990 long story, 'The Library Policeman', in *Four Past Midnight* signalled King's first explicit engagement with the recovered memory paradigm. The supernatural element of the story connects directly to a traumatic scene that the protagonist Sam must recover if he is to defeat the spectral figure who demands his life in payment of debt, a monstrous exaggeration of every child's fear of the punitive librarian. Sam is unaware that Junction City Library had employed a woman librarian in 1956 who had first traumatised children with a perverted storytelling hour before escalating her abuses to murder. A sort of vampiric creature occupying different human bodies, this figure has returned, the Library hovering between present day and 1956 incarnations, a haunted site that uncannily collapses back to the most traumatic moment in its history. This supernatural figure identifies Sam as a potential host because Sam's unacknowledged traumatic past leaves him with an exploitable psychic flaw.

Sam's recovery of his traumatic memories could almost be transcribed from a recovered memory therapy handbook. At forty years old, his functional life is thrown into doubt by his first encounter with the sinister woman librarian. Fragile defences are crushed and when he is forced to call on help, Sam recognises that his relationships fail, his social attachments are minimal, his business is only partially successful because his clients sense something in him is missing. The visit from the spectral library policeman sends him into a critical phase. Intrusive motifs begin to proliferate, signs of an occluded memory attempting to resurface. As in *The Shining*, these narrative anachronies are typographically marked off as urgent and insidious intrusions into linear narrative and are understood by the reader as anticipations of a recovered scene that will retrospectively rewrite Sam's life narrative. The recovery is too neatly done, emerging complete in 'a watching dream',[41] a symptom of dissociation, as Sam slumps unconscious. As a boy, returning in dread with a late book to the library, a figure claiming to be a policeman led Sam into the bushes and raped him, compounding the violence with shame and threats of death should he speak of the event. His dissociative strategy at the height of the attack is reinforced by an immediate forgetting. He becomes a post-traumatic automaton, marked by the encounter with psychic death, yet whose dissociative defences will be subject to all manner of uncanny menace. Remembering the traumatic scene, however, promises the complete reintegration that follows the emergency phases of recovering memory. Self restored, Sam slays the beast and gets the girl.

If the introduction of abuse recovery does not radically shift King's narrative mode, it might be worth wondering whether that is because popular narrative forms like King's actually inform abuse accounts and their 'clinical preoccupation with gothic scenes of sexual torture' rather than simply exploit them.[42] Even so, the supernatural elements in the story do not so much allegorise Sam's traumatic subjectivity as offer an oneiric, doubled account of it in ways that don't quite cohere. Reintegrated, Sam can cross into this other story and slay the vampire that bears the weight of other multiple traumatic histories, yet which perhaps only obscures his own story. The ambiguous function of the supernatural becomes starker in *Gerald's Game*, all the more because the text apparently shifts genre only for the horror mode to return, to problematic effect, in the final pages of the book.

Gerald's Game (1992) and the interlinked novel *Dolores Claiborne* (1993) moved King to the centre of the trauma paradigm, focusing on female terror but ultimate resilience in the face of paternal sexual abuse. Theresa Thompson has suggested that the two books were King's ripostes to charges of misogyny, but it is more I think that at the height of the impact of the feminist self-help recovery movement, King understood that these accounts had to be focalised through women. *Gerald's Game* is a narrative tour de force: in the opening pages, Jessie, handcuffed to a bed in a sex game in a remote cabin, kicks out at her husband and accidentally kills him, leaving the protagonist (and therefore the narrative focalisation) tied to a bed for the majority of the novel. The clue to escape starvation and death is buried, once more, in a traumatic memory she must confront, but since her adult life has been constructed around denial, passivity and dissociation, only extreme circumstances will force the issue.

Jessie is a thoroughly historicised subject, not just in the traumatic symptoms she displays in the narrative present. Her past typifies a certain trajectory of feminism. The abusive event occurs in 1963, the year Betty Friedan's *The Feminine Mystique* tried to express the nameless malaise American women experienced. This event is dissociated, only to obtrude dangerously now and then, forced to the surface during the era of feminist consciousness-raising in the early 1970s. Jessie suppresses and domesticates herself in marriage, giving up her teaching job on her husband's insistence, and by the 1980s, the era of conservatism and backlash, has become another post-traumatic automaton, with some attempts at therapy curtailed in panic at what they might disturb.

King's populism means that he constantly expresses aggressive anti-psychiatric opinions: Jessie dismisses talk of child abuse from 'whining Cult-of-Selfers, the Live-in-the-Pasts'.[43] Yet this only echoes the anti-establishment rhetoric of the recovery movement itself, and King's tracing of the traumatic subject seems to me very precisely worked out inside the new paradigm. The subject's minimally functioning defensive tactics are sent into crisis. This induces a disintegration: soon, the novel is driven by the competing voices in Jessie's head. These are given names and identities: the Goodwife and the countermanding Ruth, her long-lost feminist friend, Daddy's Little Girl, and a host of others sometimes termed 'UFO voices'. Early on, Jessie half-recognises that these uncannily repeat 'the voices you heard after the dark day', voices that splinter from the inaugurating trauma. [44] These selves are the 'multiples' or 'alters' that feature in the official diagnostic manuals – although multiple personality disorder was replaced in 1994 by dissociative identity disorder:

> Each personality state may be experienced as if it has a distinct personal history, self-image, and identity, including a separate name ... Particular identities may emerge in specific circumstances and may differ in reported age and gender, vocabulary, general knowledge or predominant affect. Alternate identities are experienced as taking control in sequence, one at the expense of the other, and may deny knowledge of one another, be critical of one another, or appear in open conflict ... Individuals with this disorder experience frequent gaps in memory for personal history, both remote and recent.[45]

Thirst and pain amplify these voices, but also send her into fevered states that begin to lift her mechanisms of defence: dreams, visions and hallucinations of visitors to her bedside merge with resurgent childhood memories. Here, King makes the path to recovery much more effectively crooked from resistance: screen memories from later in childhood protect the core event of 1963 from straightforward narrative reclamation. The event hovers at the margins of the text, not really a secret, and in this King also finds a narrative means to distinguish repression from dissociation, Janet's model of trauma that had become favoured by the late 1980s. King's narrator explains: 'The secret of that day had never completely sunk in her subconscious ...; it had been buried in a shallow grave, at best. There had been some selective amnesia, but of a completely voluntary sort.'[46] As this memory begins to move in from the margin, King uses his familiar tactic of increasing the anachronic intrusions of narratively dissociated phrases ('*to put out the sun*') that hint at the content of the traumatic memory. Exactly halfway through the book, the core traumatic memory emerges. It is a studiously un-Gothic scene: on the day of the 1963 eclipse, as father and daughter stare up through polarised glass at the sun, her father ejaculates against her back as he holds her on his lap. For the following two years, she later confesses, she existed 'in a kind of fugue state', 'sharing space in my head with a kind of whispering choir, dozens of voices'.[47]

Recovery does not prompt instant reintegration (as it had in 'The Library Policeman'), but a phase of further defensive reactions: denial and self-accusation, dramatic psychic splitting, all of which repeat childhood dissociative tactics. Yet after a passage of disintegration, where textual focalisation virtually disappears, Jessie begins to pull herself into coherence. She acknowledges her father's manipulations, the shift of blame to the daughter, the complicity of her mother and in classic trauma paradigm fashion sees the event as the determining pivot of her entire life: 'How many of the choices she had made since that day had been directly or indirectly influenced by what had happened during the final minute or so she had spent on her daddy's lap ... And was her current situation a result of what had happened during the eclipse?'[48]

Yet the unconscious prompts of the traumatic scene have also been grasped. The cuffs that bind her to patriarchal domination are made for male wrists, not female, and are thus looser than they should be. Her father's concern that Jessie not cut herself on the eclipse glass reminds her that blood can be a lubricant. She stabs at her wrists with broken glass in an act that, before recovery, would have been a symptom of self-mutilating masochism but is now recast as active and agential: 'I refuse to die this way.'[49] The escape from bondage to the marriage bed is painfully effected.

At this point, the reader might expect (as in *The Shining*) a brief coda depicting fragile recovery, the dispersion of uncanny psychic splitting and the tentative prospect of a post–post-traumatic life. Instead, *Gerald's Game* takes a very odd turn: one of Jessie's hallucinatory bedside visitors, a deformed nightmare creature, transpires to be an actual backwoods serial killer. The uncanny creature that looms over her in her delirium, a deformed double of her father, becomes weirdly literalised. In the closing movement of the book, Jessie must confront Joubert across a courtroom, a Gothic condensation of male violence created by gross family dysfunction: 'He was a victim of sex abuse himself, of course, his father, his stepfather, and his stepmother all apparently had a go at him.'[50] As if to countervail the predominantly domestic realism of the novel, Joubert's crimes are grossly excessive: grave robbery, corpse mutilation, serial murder and cannibalism. At his trial, Joubert constantly pulls Jessie back into her own traumatic moment: 'I was back in the lake house again – it happened with no lag whatsoever. Not remembering, do you understand?'[51] Jessie's final act of defiance, spitting in Joubert's face, completes her escape from repetition and marks the restitution of her Self.

Is this narrative move designed to make the text even more exemplary? The serial killer became, after all, another central icon of popular trauma culture. Mark Seltzer has argued that the serial killer is a subject constituted in modernity, acting out 'the form of public violence proper to a machine culture'.[52] The killer is a product, like the concept of trauma itself, of the statistical society that emerged in the late nineteenth century, a 'statistical person', who 'experiences identity, his own and others, as a matter of numbers, kinds, types'.[53] The blankness of empty serial actions prompts psychological profiles replete with traumatic indicators: abuse, violence, damaged attachments. King's use of an exaggerated Gothic mode for Joubert was hardly out of place in the 1990s when Thomas Harris's Hannibal Lecter series reached cultural saturation with *The Silence of the Lambs*, while films like *Seven* offered new levels of Gothic elaboration of serial killing and generated a ceaseless stream of imitative films, trading on the clichés of the psychological abuse profile.

Sympathetic feminist critics of *Gerald's Game* consider Joubert an 'apt symbol' or a monster 'of the realistic and plausible variety' that reinforces King's critique of patriarchy.[54] Yet the introduction of Joubert means the novel veers away from confronting the everyday story of domestic paternal abuse, replacing the father – *eclipsing* him, more aptly – with exorbitant Gothic horrors. In this regard, Joubert works as a narrative fetish: 'the serial killer serves the function of a *fetish* in public culture: he is the means of the disavowal of institutionalised violence, while the "seriality" of his acts of violence marks the place of recognition in this disavowal.'[55] This device means that intra-familial violence is half-acknowledged but at once covered over by exteriorising it in an abjected, monstrous figure defined as the very opposite of family. The clichés of the psychological profile killer as abused or damaged place him beyond ordinary social attachments, the marginal figure that defines and empties the norm of any transgressions, the exteriority that preys on the blameless model family. The homely is reconfirmed by this forceful expulsion of the unhomely, yet without any sense of that notorious instability with which Freud invests these terms. The serial killer therefore embodies King's sense of Gothic menace as always an external evil, what Bernard Gallagher sees in the work as 'the coercive influence of the external world on the individual psyche'.[56] And this also matches the model of trauma as something *done to* individuals, an event that breaches the integrity of the subject from an outside, turning them from agents to victims. Joubert's deformed body and collection of body parts distracts the force of King's critique of male violence in the family.

Dolores Claiborne corrects this mistake by revisiting the same moment of the 1963 eclipse: this time, the passage of visceral violence in this novel erupts exactly from within the abusive family dynamic, as Dolores gruesomely clubs her violent husband to death after she has discovered his predatory designs on his own daughter. In this scene, there is a brief occult or telepathic connection between Dolores and a girl she envisions sitting on her father's lap somewhere near by. King thus attempts to bind the novels together as uncanny doubles connected by the extremity of psychic trauma. *Dolores Claiborne* is a less interesting or at least less symptomatic text than its twin, however. The contradictions of *Gerald's Game* suggest how popular fiction can at once compellingly embody a narrative form of the insights of trauma psychology and at the same time work furiously to disavow them. The conventions of horror fiction can use the uncanny as fetish to deny rather than undermine the defensive fortress of dissociation.

The subjects of King's fiction are modelled as much through mechanisms of traumatic dissociation as Freudian repression. The splittings and doublings to which King insistently returns (this analysis could be extended to *Misery* and *The Dark Half,* fictions of the persecutory double King wrote at the same time) intertwine very different models of psychology. In unearthing a parallel tradition to the psychoanalysis that continues to be privileged by cultural studies, I am not hereby announcing that Freudian interpretation is inadmissible – far from it. But if Terry Castle is right to state that *'the uncanny itself has a history'*,[57] it is surely important that critics be aware of the full matrix of ideas that make up our modern, haunted, uncanny selves.

Notes

1. Sylvia Fraser, *My Father's House: A Memoir of Incest and Healing* (London: Virago, 1989), p. x.
2. Ellen Bass and Laura Davis, *The Courage to Heal: A Guide for Women Survivors of Child Sexual Abuse* (London: Vermilion, 2002), p. 22.
3. John E. Mack, *Abduction: Human Encounters with Aliens* (New York: Scribners, 1994).
4. Jane Smiley, *A Thousand Acres* (London: Flamingo, 1992), p. 228.
5. W. G. Sebald, *Austerlitz* (London: Hamish Hamilton, 2001), p. 76.
6. Ibid., p. 261.
7. Sandor Ferenczi, 'The Confusion of Tongues between Adults and the Child', in *Final Contributions to the Problems and Methods of Psycho-Analysis,* ed. Michael Balint (London: Hogarth 1955), pp. 164–5.
8. Ferenczi, 'Aphoristic Remarks on the Theme of Being Dead – Being a Woman', *Final Contributions,* p. 243.

9. Robert Jay Lifton, 'The Survivors of the Hiroshima Disaster and the Survivors of Nazi Persecutions', in Henry Krystal (ed.), *Massive Psychic Trauma* (New York: International Universities Press, 1968), pp. 171 and 183.
10. Robert Jay Lifton, *Death in Life: The Survivors of Hiroshima* (London: Weidenfeld and Nicolson, 1968), p. 517.
11. Judith Herman, *Trauma and Recovery: From Domestic Abuse to Political Terror* (London: HarperCollins, 1994), p. 96.
12. Janice Haaken, 'Traumatic Revisions: Remembering Abuse and the Politics of Forgiveness', in P. Reavey and S. Warner (eds), *New Feminist Stories of Child Sexual Abuse* (London: Routledge, 2003), p. 90.
13. Lenore Terr, 'Remembered Images and Trauma: A Psychology of the Supernatural', *Psychoanalytic Study of the Child*, 40 (1985), p. 528.
14. Sigmund Freud, 'The "Uncanny"', trans. Alix Strachey, *Penguin Freud Library*, volume 14 (Harmondsworth: Penguin, 1990), pp. 364–5.
15. Ernst Jentsch, 'On the Psychology of the Uncanny', trans. Roy Sellars, in *Uncanny Modernity*, ed. Jo Collins and John Jervis (Basingstoke: Palgrave Macmillan Ltd., 2008) p. 226.
16. Nicholas Royle, *The Uncanny* (Manchester: Manchester University Press, 2003), p. 24.
17. Mladen Dolar, '"I shall be with you on your wedding night": Lacan and the Uncanny', *October*, 58 (1991), p. 7.
18. Terry Castle, *The Female Thermometer: Eighteenth Century Culture and the Invention of the Uncanny* (Oxford: Oxford University Press, 1995), p. 18.
19. Mark Micale and Paul Lerner, 'Trauma, Psychiatry and History: A Conceptual and Historiographical Approach', in Micale and Lerner (eds), *Traumatic Pasts: History, Psychiatry and Trauma in the Modern Age 1870–1930* (Cambridge: Cambridge University Press, 2001), p. 10.
20. Wolfgang Schivelbusch, *The Railway Journey: The Industrialisation of Time and Space in the Nineteenth Century* (New York: Berg, 1986), p. 136.
21. Mark Seltzer, 'Wound Culture: Trauma in the Pathological Public Sphere', *October*, 80 (1997), p. 17.
22. Freud, 'The "Uncanny"', p. 370.
23. For one of the best, short accounts, see Wilbur J. Scott, 'PTSD in DSM-III: A Case in the Politics of Diagnosis and Disease', *Social Problems*, 37: 3 (1990), pp. 294–310.
24. Mitchell Wilson, 'DSM-III and the Transformation of American Psychiatry: A History', *American Journal of Psychiatry*, 150: 3 (1993), pp. 399–410.
25. The strong claims about the biology of trauma are explored in Allan Young, *The Harmony of Illusions: Inventing Post-Traumatic Stress Disorder* (Princeton: Princeton University Press, 1995).
26. Wilson, 'DSM-III', p. 408.
27. Frank Putnam, 'Pierre Janet and Modern Views of Dissociation' (1989), in M. Horowitz (ed.), *Essential Papers on Posttraumatic Stress Disorder* (New York: New York University Press, 1999), pp. 116 and 120.
28. Pierre Janet, *The Mental State of Hystericals: A Study of Mental Stigmata and Mental Accidents*, trans. C. Corson (New York: Putnam's, 1901), p. 492.
29. Ibid., p. 502.
30. Etzel Cardena, 'The Domain of Dissociation', in S. Lynne and J. W. Rhine (eds), *Dissociation: Clinical and Theoretical Perspectives* (London: Guildford Press, 1994), p. 15.

31. André Breton, 'The Automatic Message' (1933), in *What is Surrealism? Selected Writings*, ed. Franklin Rosemont (London: Pluto Press, 1978), p. 100. For lengthier discussion of Myers, see my *The Invention of Telepathy* (Oxford: Oxford University Press, 2002).
32. David Punter, 'Problems of Recollection and Construction: Stephen King', in V. Sage and A. Smith (eds), *Modern Gothic: A Reader* (Manchester: Manchester University Press, 1996), p. 122.
33. Stephen King, *Danse Macabre* (London: Hodder, 1991), p. 64.
34. Ian Hacking, 'Making Up People', in T. Heller et al. (eds), *Reconstructing Individualism: Autonomy, Individuality, and the Self in Western Thought* (Stanford: Stanford University Press, 1986).
35. See Lawrence Wright, *Remembering Satan: Recovered Memory and the Shattering of a Family* (London: Serpent's Tail, 1994).
36. Robert Miles, *The Gothic 1750–1820: A Geneaology* (London: Routledge, 1993), pp. 2–3.
37. King, *Danse Macabre*, pp. 103–4.
38. Lenore Terr, 'Terror Writing by the Formerly Terrified: A Look at Stephen King', *Psychoanalytic Study of the Child*, 44 (1989), p. 379.
39. Terr, 'Terror Writing', p. 389.
40. Punter, 'Problems of Recollection', p. 123.
41. Stephen King, *Four Past Midnight* (London: Hodder, 1990), p. 685.
42. Haaken, 'Traumatic Revisions', p. 90.
43. Stephen King, *Gerald's Game* (London: New English Library, 1992), p. 141.
44. Ibid., p. 40.
45. American Psychiatric Association, *Diagnostic and Statistical Manual*, 4th revised edn (Washington: APA, 2000), p. 526.
46. King, *Gerald's Game*, p. 100.
47. Ibid., p. 383.
48. Ibid., p. 215.
49. Ibid., p. 292.
50. Ibid., p. 378.
51. Ibid., p. 380.
52. Mark Seltzer, *Serial Killers* (London: Routledge, 1998), p. 17.
53. Ibid., p. 4.
54. Theresa Thompson, 'Rituals of Male Violence: Unlocking the (Fe)Male Self in *Gerald's Game* and *Dolores Claiborne*', and Carol A. Senf,'*Gerald's Game* and *Dolores Claiborne:* Stephen King and the Evolution of an Authentic Female Narrative Voice', both in Kathleen Margaret Lant and Theresa Thompson (eds), *Imagining the Worse: Stephen King and the Representation of Women* (Westport, CT: Greenwood, 1998), pp. 55 and 99.
55. Carla Freccero, 'Historical Violence, Censorship, and the Serial Killer: The Case of *American Psycho*', *Diacritics*, 27: 2 (1997), p. 48.
56. Bernard J. Gallagher, 'Breaking Up Isn't Hard to Do: Stephen King, Christopher Lasch, and Psychic Fragmentation', *Journal of American Culture*, 10: 4 (1987), p. 60.
57. Terry Castle, *The Female Thermometer*, p. 7.

7

'Neurotic Men' and a Spectral Woman: Freud, Jung and Sabina Spielrein

Jo Collins

> [The uncanny represents] the return of the repressed.[1]

> *Heimlich*: 'Concealed, kept from sight, so that others do not get to know about it, withheld from others. To do something *heimlich*, i.e. behind someone's back ... to behave *heimlich*, as though there was something to conceal; *heimlich* love-affair, love, sin ...'[2]

Freud's investigations into the etymology of the uncanny in his 1919 essay lead him to consider how *das Unheimliche* (the unhomely) is inextricable from its antonym *heimlich* (the homely). Freud surmises that 'what is *Heimlich* ... comes to be *unheimlich*',[3] as the two terms coincide around the sense that what is familiar, cordial, and comforting may transpire to be equivocal, estranged, and treacherous. Freud here identifies the ambiguity inherent in 'the uncanny'; his conceptualisation designating something at once recognisable and strange, simultaneously 'known' but alien.

If, for Freud, the uncanny signifies the transparency of what is apparently intimate and dependable becoming clouded, then such a proposition has resonance within Freud's own personal history. The genesis of Freud's paper, alongside Freud's ruminations on the meaning of the uncanny, is imbricated with Freud's relationship with Jung. On a metaphoric and metonymic level, displaced and condensed elements of their relationship fed into Freud's essay. Furthermore, according to John Kerr, Freud had embarked upon the paper after Jung's second visit to Vienna between 25 and 30 March 1909, but subsequently abandoned it until 1918.[4] The events of this visit depict in synecdoche the dissensions and suspicions which led to the final break between Freud and Jung in

1913. Jung brought disruption to Freud's house (*heim*) with his insistence on the credibility of parapsychological theories which Freud wished to reject. His visit is also notable as it occurs between the revelation of Jung's affair with his patient Sabina Spielrein to her parents, and Jung's confession of the affair to Freud. At the time of his visit Jung is concealing this partially unveiled secret, and it is his surreptitious behaviour which certainly caused Freud in hindsight to question Jung's faithfulness to his mentor and to the cause of psychoanalysis. The events of this visit and their ramifications encode complex relations between Freud and his then 'disciple' Jung, where burgeoning power struggles emerge not only between the men, but also in relation to psychoanalysis. Furthermore, while Freud was unaware of it, Sabina Spielrein was in the background of their relationship from its very inception, a presence which for Jung 'ought to have remained secret and hidden'.[5] Freud does not directly engage with these events in his essay. Nevertheless, the constellation of concealed secrets, theories of the occult, and the disruptive potential of the libido surrounding the Freud/Jung/Spielrein triad reappears in figurative form in Freud's essay. The outcomes of their interactions inveigle their way into the text as shadowy distorted forms, displaced allusions and repressed elements. The genesis of Freud's essay is tied to circumstances of duplicity (doubled motives) masked by congeniality, concealed secrets, and betrayal.

+ + +

From the beginning of their professional association in 1906, Jung kept certain things hidden from Freud. The inception of the professional relationship between Freud and Jung occurred in Jung's writing to Freud about Spielrein: a deliberate strategy on Jung's part of which Freud was unaware. Jung's second letter of 23 October 1906 uses Spielrein as a pretext to interest Freud: he requests Freud's opinion about an unnamed patient's neurosis.[6] Indeed, it transpires that, if circumstances had been different, Spielrein's case might have brought Jung into contact with Freud even earlier. On 25 September 1905, Jung wrote a letter for Spielrein's mother to enable her to engage Freud to treat her daughter.[7] However, Freud never received this letter and Jung instead instigated the correspondence in April 1906, sending Freud a copy of *Diagnostic Association Studies*, which he had edited, and which contained his paper 'Psychoanalysis and Association Experiments'.[8]

Sabina Spielrein, a Russian Jew, 'was the first woman psychoanalyst of significance, and she was until very recently almost forgotten'.[9] A nervous and withdrawn teenager, she originally moved to Zurich in the summer of 1904 in order to study medicine, but a breakdown led to her becoming a patient at the Burghölzli. Her coming under Jung's care would have far-reaching repercussions not only for his own philosophy, but also for the subsequent development of psychoanalysis. Following her decisive yet enigmatic intervention into psychoanalytic history, Spielrein would return to Russia in 1923 to practice psychoanalysis until it was banned in 1936. She was killed in 1941 during the Nazi occupation of Rostov on Don.[10] Spielrein is important to the foundation of Freud and Jung's professional association as she was a test case for Jung's practicing of the psychoanalytic method at the Burghölzli.[11] However, it is also significant that Jung chooses to present Spielrein by way of concealment. She is an offering to elicit Freud's approval, but within the letter there is also an implicit suppression of the actual circumstances of Jung's relationship with his patient. According to Appignanesi and Forrester: 'It is probable that the intensity of Jung's relationship to Spielrein was the immediate, if not the only, cause of his writing to Freud in 1906, thus initiating a triangular relationship which was to prove fateful both to the two men and the history of psychoanalysis.'[12] If Jung's letter indicates his ambitions regarding entry into the psychoanalytic field, it also encodes impropriety in his relationship to his patient, a circumstance from which Jung attempts to vindicate himself by paradoxically concealing the facts from Freud. Jung describes Spielrein as a 'twenty year old Russian girl', 'a hysteric' and 'a difficult case' whose 'recent experience' he feels he must 'abreact'.[13] Bruno Bettelheim suggests that the letter is unfaithful to the actual case history. While Jung implies that he has only just begun treating Spielrein, he had been engaged in her case since her arrival at the Burghölzli in August 1904.[14] Furthermore, according to Bettelheim, while Spielrein's is described as a 'difficult case', 'compared to those of most of the patients treated at the Burghölzli, her case was a relatively mild one'.[15] The 'difficulty' (i.e. inappropriateness) of his relationship with Spielrein (at this stage) is transferred into a difficulty of 'case'. That which requires 'abreaction' has been transferred from the relationship between Jung and Spielrein to the patient herself. Jung, a virtual stranger to Freud, duplicitously seeks a confidence, and Spielrein becomes that which is hidden in the correspondence. This letter is indicative of the tone of Jung's self-presentation in correspondence to Freud before the exposure and termination of the affair: congenial yet mendacious. If it is possible to read Jung's correspondence as in some way echoing Freud's suppositions about the uncanny quality inherent in concealed secrets, then according to Freud's conjectures Spielrein must surely have been uncanny to Jung, albeit in a different way. Spielrein represented that which was all too '*heimlich*'; she is too close to Jung, too familiar, too intimate. Furthermore, she is also 'obscure, inaccessible to knowledge' in Jung's correspondence,[16] but always threatening to return to disrupt the precious harmony of Jung's professional integrity.

Indeed, two and a half years after the Freud/Jung correspondence began, Spielrein did resurface to jeopardise Jung's reputation. During these years friendship was burgeoning between Freud and Jung, Jung visiting Freud on 3 March 1907 at his Vienna home, and Freud staying at Jung's Burghölzli flat between 18 and 21 September 1908. Freud began addressing Jung as 'friend' by 15 November 1907, cast off the appellation 'colleague' by 17 February 1908, and interpellated Jung as 'dear friend and heir' on 15 October 1908.[17] Jung declared an '"unconditional devotion" to Freud's theories and his "no less unconditional veneration" of Freud's person'.[18] However, just prior to his second trip to visit Freud in Vienna, Jung sent the following unexpected letter to Freud on 7 March 1909:

> a woman patient whom years ago I pulled out of a very sticky neurosis with unstinting effort has violated my confidence and my friendship in the most mortifying way imaginable. She has kicked up a vile scandal solely because I denied myself the pleasure of giving her a child. I have always acted the gentleman towards her, but before the bar of my rather too sensitive conscience I nevertheless don't feel clean, and that is what hurts the most because my intentions were always honourable. But you know how it is – the devil can use even the best of things for the fabrication of filth. Meanwhile I have learnt an unspeakable amount of marital wisdom for until now I had a totally inadequate idea of my polygamous components despite ... self analysis. ... The relationship with my wife has gained enormously in assurance and depth.[19]

Jung wrote to Freud under the guise of a wronged and indignant doctor whose ungrateful patient (Spielrein) has accused Jung of infidelity. However, what Jung omits from this account is the fact that he has already virtually admitted the impropriety of his relationship with Spielrein to her mother. While Spielrein had been discharged on 1 June 1905, she had remained in Zurich to pursue her medical studies. She had also continued to meet with Jung in secret.[20] In January 1909 Spielrein's mother received an anonymous letter, probably from Jung's wife, 'warning her to save her daughter from Jung'.[21] Jung subsequently wrote to Bleuler tending his resignation from the Burghölzli.[22] He also wrote the following to Spielrein's mother: '[y]ou understand, of course, that a man and a girl cannot possible continue indefinitely to have friendly dealings with one another without the likelihood that something may enter the relationship'. He even suggested to her: 'I could drop my role as doctor the more easily because I did not feel professionally obligated for I never charged a fee. This latter clearly establishes the limits imposed upon a doctor.'[23]

Jung's declaration of integrity to Freud, where he suggests he has acted as gentleman and doctor in treating the neurosis, effectively transfers guilt to Spielrein. Jung's duplicity compels him to declare to Freud that '[e]xcept for moments of infatuation my affection is lasting and reliable. ... [F]or the past fortnight the devil has been tormenting me in the shape of neurotic ingratitude. But I shall not be unfaithful to ΨA [psychoanalysis] on that account.'[24] Jung thus declares his fidelity to Freud and psychoanalysis. Nevertheless, he confesses: 'Now and then, I admit, the devil does strike a chill into my – on the whole – blameless heart.' What must Freud have made of this statement? Surely it is not possible to be 'partially blameless'; one must be either free from blame or guilty. It seems as if Jung is here partially conceding culpability. Indeed, Jung reveals to Freud that he feels himself to be beleaguered by an uncanny 'devil'. In hindsight this might possibly represent Jung's struggle with suppressed guilt, or perhaps the figure of Spielrein herself (Jung used the designation 'devil' in his previous letter about Spielrein and this was a word that Spielrein used to describe herself in therapy with Jung).[25] This reference to 'the devil' can also be read as the uncanny figure of the double, as Jung acknowledges in his letter that another woman has declared herself to be Jung's mistress and is publicising this rumour.[26] Jung confides to Freud: 'Such stories give me the horrors.'

The emergence of Jung's relationship with Spielrein caused him angst as it undermined the semblance of the professional integrity upon which he had founded his relationship with Freud. Jung inadvertently characterised the threatening situation as if it were uncanny: he saw himself as facing torment and horror from something which, once familiar, had become estranged and hostile. Nevertheless, such a comparison to the terms of Freud's 1919 essay must take account of the fact that, in Jung's case, it was the element of *familiarity* which was all too threatening and had to be kept concealed from Freud. If Freud was unaware of the nature of Jung's anxiety, 'the uncanny' nevertheless came to Freud's home with Jung's visit of 25–30 March. While discussing parapsychology and precognition in Freud's study, both men heard a peculiar noise which emanated from a bookcase. Jung correctly predicted that this sound would be repeated as he believed that he himself was producing the noises: the noises registered his rebellion against Freud's dismissal of 'catalytic exteriorization phenomenon'.[27] Jung's autobiography also suggests that 'this incident aroused his [Freud's] mistrust of me, and I had the feeling that I had done something against him'.[28] Jung's suspicion about Freud's mistrust hints at another factor in this incident: Jung's anxiety about Spielrein, the pressure involved in his suppression of the affair. As such, it seems possible to read Jung's repression of Spielrein's presence (his effective 'ghosting' of Spielrein) as contributing to the emergence of this uncanny incident of occult activity. John Kerr speculates that the crisis Jung had yet to describe to Freud brought the former to a world beyond his own experience, to an 'other world of premonition and strange coincidence'.[29]

The poltergeist phenomenon is also notable for another resonance with the uncanny: Jung's interest in the occult. By the admission of Freud (letter of 16 April 1909) and Jung[30] the men had been engaged in a discussion about occult phenomena before the 'loud reports' occurred. This topic was a subject of dispute between the two – Freud disapproved of Jung's desire to use psychoanalysis to investigate the occult. (While October 1909 would see Freud registering his disapproval of Ferenczi's experiments in telepathy with a medium, Freud himself did not entirely dismiss the occult. He attended séances in 1913,[31] and carried out experiments in thought transference in 1925,[32] and wrote four short papers on 'Occultism', much to Jones's chagrin.) Jung's interest in the occult also signified to Freud the former's reluctance to fully commit to the concept of a sexualised libido.[33] In his autobiography, Jung recalls a conversation with Freud from '1910' on the subject:

> Freud said to me, 'My Dear Jung, promise me never to abandon the sexual theory. That is the most essential thing of all. You see, we must make a dogma of it, an unshakable bulwark.' ... I asked him, 'A bulwark – against what?' To which he replied, 'Against the black tide of mud ... of occultism.'

Jung's autobiography depicts his response to this appeal as a recognition of the formation of a rift: '[this] struck at the heart of our friendship. I knew that I would never accept such an attitude.'[34] What is interesting about Jung's recollection is the erroneous date he gives the conversation: no encounter between Freud and Jung took place during 1910. Jung's biographer Gerhard Wehr speculates that Jung meant to refer to his second visit to Vienna from 25 to 30 March 1909.[35] Jung apparently forgets that the poltergeist incident and his decisive discussion with Freud occurred during the same time frame. It seems that the schism which the events foreboded is reproduced in Jung's narrative inscription of them. The early fissures in relations between Jung and Freud become literally separated in Jung's retrospective reworking. Indeed, what Freud saw as Jung's deviant 'Occultism' and his doubts over the sexual basis of the libido coincided with Jung's working through alternative theories using in part material from discussions with Spielrein. As Sayers indicates, 'Jung was inspired to develop his theory of the anima because he fell in love with one of his patients.'[36] This patient was Spielrein. The intellectual/soul connection which both experienced prompted Jung to consider a wider hypothetical basis for his theories than what he felt to be psychoanalysis's narrow sexual foundation.[37] While Jung only set about formulating his own definitive doctrine after the split in 1913, these ideas would have been simmering (in some form) in 1909.[38]

According to Jung, the poltergeist incident was never discussed again.[39] However, it seemed that Freud felt his authority to have been undermined, and he dispatched a gently admonishing letter to Jung (perhaps occasioned by Jung's reference to 'the oppressive sense of your paternal authority' to Freud on 2 April 1909). While acknowledging that Jung's 'experiment made a deep impression on me', Freud dismissed the phenomenon. Although the noises continued after Jung's departure, Freud did not believe that they were of supernatural origin. He wrote to Jung: 'my credulity ... vanished with the spell of your personal presence'. The episode prompted Freud to attempt to reaffirm his paternal authority. He appealed to Jung in a letter of 16 April 1909, 'dear son ... keep a cool head', adding in reproach:

> it is remarkable that on the same evening that I formally adopted you as an eldest son, anointing you as my successor ... that then and there you should have divested me of any paternal dignity, and that the divesting seems to have given you as much pleasure as investing your person gave me.[40]

Freud, sensing rebellion in his disciple, 'fall[s] back again to the role of father', and goes on to provide Jung with examples of his own experiences of the unknown (such as the 'uncanny' coincidences surrounding the numbers 61 and 62 in his life), ostensibly to assuage potential discord developing around the topic.[41] For Freud, Jung was an asset, a non-Jewish academic prepared to align himself with psychoanalysis in an anti-Semitic climate. Freud hoped that Jung would become his successor, his 'crown prince'.[42] Besides, Jung, Freud anticipated, would 'apply to psychoses what Freud had done for neuroses'.[43] This scenario was, however, not to be. The events of Jung's visit, as well as impelling Freud to begin his paper on the uncanny,[44] foreboded the gradual unravelling of the relationship.

After two months of cordial if intermittent exchanges, Spielrein entered into the correspondence. On 30 May 1909, Spielrein assertively wrote to Freud requesting an audience.[45] Freud, guessing that this was the lady Jung had written about, sent her a stalling letter (4 June 1909) while in the meantime requesting more information from Jung (letter of 3 June 1909). Jung's reply of 4 June 1909 truthfully describes Spielrein as his 'test case'. He also suggests that after 'devoting a large measure of friendship to her', '*gratissime*' and over a number of years, his discontinuance of their 'friendship' led her to 'seek revenge'. He tells Freud, 'She was, of course, systematically planning my seduction.'[46] If 'seduction' did represent an apparently natural outcome of their ambiguous relationship (which oscillated between medical care and 'friendship') then Jung is not 'on the whole' 'blameless'. Indeed, Jung confides that a 'compulsive infatuation' which intermittently afflicted him had permeated into his relationship with Spielrein. Jung tells Freud that this compulsive infatuation is an ongoing unconscious response to his first visit to Vienna. Jung's allusion to the 'very long unconscious aftermath' of his Vienna visit is an implicit reference to complexes he claims he develops as a result of attempting to assimilate the concept of a sexualised libido into his thinking.[47] Jung wrote in his letter of 31 March 1907 (his first to Freud after the visit):

> Up till now I had strong resistances to writing because until recently the complexes aroused in Vienna were still in an uproar ... The most difficult item, your broadened conception of sexuality, has now been assimilated up to a point ... [However, this still evokes] emotional inhibitions which make any kind of teaching quite impossible.[48]

Thus, Jung's denial, with its partial confession to infatuation with Spielrein, is also implicitly a veiled critique of Freud's theorising of the libido. It is as if Jung is accusing Freud of being somehow responsible for his own misjudgements because Freud forced him into (partially) accepting a theory of a sexualised libido that entailed confronting his own 'emotional inhibitions', 'resistances' and 'complexes', and even led to Jung's acting out his libidinal impulses (through his infatuation).

Jung seems to be implicitly suggesting that Freudian theories have affronted him with these impulses and thus he is compelled to act upon them. This then implies that Jung's apparent affection for psychoanalysis is effectively supplanted by his 'compulsive infatuation' with Spielrein ('Except for moments of infatuation my affection is lasting and reliable').[49]

If Jung's letter of 4 June 1909 was a partial confession replete with oblique recriminations, then his letter of 21 June 1909 entailed a series of retractions, as Spielrein had confronted Jung and obliged him to write a truthful account of events to Freud.[50] Jung wrote:

> I took too black a view of things ... It transpired [that] the rumour buzzing round me does not emanate from her ... Although not succumbing to helpless remorse, I nevertheless deplore the sins I have committed for I am largely to blame for the high-flying hopes of my former pupil ... Caught in my delusion that I was the victim of the sexual wiles of my patient, I wrote to her mother that I was not the gratifier of her daughter's sexual desires, but merely her doctor ... My action was a piece of knavery which I have reluctantly confessed to you, my father ... You and she know of my 'perfect honesty'.[51]

While this letter represents a revision of Jung's previous story, it is full of elisions and concealments. Jung's letter to Spielrein's mother did not state that Jung was 'merely Spielrein's doctor', but rather that he *was not* her doctor – since he was unpaid – which logically suggests he *was* potentially the 'gratifier of her daughter's sexual desires'. The sins he deplores are not those of his infidelity, but rather of being 'too good a doctor', reconstructing his patient's ego too well, being too upright in his defence of his integrity by writing to her mother. His declaration of 'perfect honesty' was inscribed in English in a letter otherwise entirely written in German, a declaration of truthfulness, which rather represents 'a foreign element in the letter'.[52] Indeed Jung concedes in the process of trying to vindicate himself that, while he 'imagin[ed] that I was talking theoretically ... naturally Eros was lurking in the background'.[53] Here, Jung's use of the term '*natürlich*' implies the inevitable and even intuitive fruition of an 'improper' relationship with Spielrein. Despite Jung's evasions, Freud now knew that Jung was not 'on the whole' 'blameless' or '*unbescholtenen*' ('spotless') and furthermore that he had been disingenuous in his presentation of the facts. Freud wrote to Spielrein on 24 June 1909 to apologise, conceding: 'I had construed [matters] wrongly and to your disadvantage ... I was wrong and ... the lapse has to be blamed on the man and not the woman.'[54]

The pledges of trustworthiness, dependability and fidelity upon which Jung had founded his relationship to Freud and psychoanalysis had been undermined by the revelations about the affair. Here Jung's infatuation, as he had warned, had meant that his affection for psychoanalysis and Freud had not been 'reliable'. While Freud wrote in a conciliatory tone to Jung, suggesting 'the matter has ended in a manner satisfactory to all' (30 June 1909), subsequent events suggested otherwise.[55] The two men met again on 20 August at Bremen, as they were due to sail to America to lecture at Clark University Massachusetts.[56] Their lunch on this day (with Ferenczi) was interrupted by an 'ominous episode'.[57] During the meal, Jung animatedly discussed Northern German peat bog corpses. Freud unexpectedly fainted. According to Jung, '[Freud] said to me that he was convinced that all this chatter about corpses meant that I had death-wishes towards him.'[58] Freud's diary meanwhile treated the incident as trivial, stating briefly: 'I broke into a bad sweat with a feeling of faintness.'[59] Notwithstanding the difference between these accounts, Bettelheim suggests that Freud's collapse represented a response to the psychic struggle he faced in attempting to assimilate Jung's actions regarding the affair. For Bettelheim, 'the affair had shaken Freud's trust in Jung and evoked conscious or subconscious fears that Jung might betray his pseudo-father as he had betrayed his lover'.[60] The incident then could be read as Freud's apprehension of his successor as uncanny; Jung, a familiar, threatened to become a stranger, a usurper. Not only had Jung undermined Freud's authority by his duplicity, but an Oedipal struggle also appeared to be breaking out between father and son over psychoanalysis.

A later incident on the boat to America serves to confirm this sense of rivalry, an incident which for Jung spelt the beginning of the break between the two men.[61] According to Gay:

> Jung ... had interpreted one of Freud's dreams as best he could without further details about Freud's private life. Freud had demurred at supplying them, looked at Jung suspiciously, and objected that he could not have himself analyzed; it would put his authority at risk. Jung recalled that this refusal had sounded the death knell of Freud's power over him. Freud, the self-proclaimed apostle of scientific candor, was placing personal authority above truth.[62]

If Freud *had* 'plac[ed] personal authority above the truth',[63] then Jung had also similarly sacrificed the truth in attempting to preserve personal integrity through his representation of Spielrein to Freud.[64] The mutual distrust displayed in this incident is not only allied with the aftermath of the Spielrein affair, it also indicates struggles for authority and power, effectively Oedipal competition for superiority within psychoanalysis. Jung was beginning to rebel against Freud's father figure.

The relationship between the two men returned to an even keel after the Clark trip (where Jung presented lectures which supported Freudian psycho-sexual theories). However, Jung continued to grapple with his resistances to Freudian libido theory.[65] Furthermore, 1910 saw Spielrein back in contact with Jung. Spielrein, who had registered for a medical degree after being discharged from the Burghölzli in 1905,[66] sought advice from Jung on her dissertation. Jung, while providing her with guidance during her study, was also analysing her, and discussing with her ideas about the 'death instinct' and ancestors.[67] It was these discussions with Spielrein which inspired Jung to formulate new strains of thinking beyond the Freudian framework. Spielrein's diary records how intense their meetings became,[68] Jung at one point apparently giving her his diary to read. She suggests that they developed almost telepathic parallels in thought and a mutual 'deep spiritual affinity',[69] characterisations which appear to correspond with Jung's own later theorisation of the anima. Jung saw the anima as an unconscious image which inhabited every man, an image which could be externally projected onto 'the Beloved' motivating attraction.[70] If the confluence of their thoughts contributed to Jung's development of the concept of the anima, then Spielrein was also for Jung what Carotenuto describes as 'the typical image of the anima', as she appeared to understand him with (what she describes as) 'an independently developed system of thought that is completely analogous to his own'.[71] As such, Spielrein appeared to confront Jung with elements of his own unconscious – she represented an externalisation of the more disruptive and unruly aspects of his psyche (again it is possible to read her as 'the uncanny' here, as a literalisation of the 'return of the repressed').

Spielrein's influence on Jung had a decisive impact on the development of psychoanalysis. Jung used Spielrein's dissertation extensively in composing his paper 'Transformations and Symbols of the Libido', a paper which moved away from Freud's viewpoint. However, while Jung was retreating from Freudian theories, Spielrein was advancing towards them. She joined the Vienna Psychoanalytic Society on 11 October 1911, approximately a month before Jung wrote to Freud to inform him that he intended to revise the libido theory. On 29 November 1911, Spielrein presented her first paper, 'Destruction As the Cause of Coming into Being' (published in *Jahrbuch* in 1912), essentially a precursor to the death drive which Freud would develop in 'Beyond the Pleasure Principle' (1920). While Freud's initial reaction to her paper was to overlook its value and use it to critique Jung's theories,[72] Freud's 'Beyond the Pleasure Principle' drew on Spielrein's ideas. The use of Spielrein's ideas in Freud's later paper is denied by the Vienna Psychoanalytic Society. The society's minutes record:

> At first glance it might seem that, under Jung's influence, Dr Spielrein had formulated, many years before Freud, the hypothesis ... of two opposing drives – the life instinct and the death instinct. Closer scrutiny, however, discloses that she does not express this theory at all, but rather believes that ... the creative instinct itself contains a destructive component.[73]

Here the society erases Spielrein's importance – she has not influenced Freud's work, and her work is only validated by her direct contact with Jung. Both Jung and Freud denied the legitimacy of her paper, Jung arguing that her conception of the death instinct was 'overweighted with her own complexes', Freud contending that 'her destructive drive is not much to my liking, because I believe it is personally conditioned. She seems abnormally ambivalent.'[74] Neither Freud nor Jung acknowledged the importance of Spielrein's hypothesis on the death instincts: Jung underplayed her influence in order to protect his private life, while Freud elided the effects of her insights as he saw her as affiliated with Jung.[75] Spielrein's shadowy and disavowed role in the genesis of the death instinct also links her to Freud's paper on the uncanny. Freud worked on 'Beyond the Pleasure Principle' and 'The Uncanny' simultaneously, and the end of the latter paper ends by enigmatically referring the reader to 'another place' – to Freud's 1920 essay. According to Nicholas Royle, the death drive and the uncanny double each other, as '[e]verything that "The Uncanny" has to say about the double, the demonic and the literary comes back in *Beyond the Pleasure Principle*'.[76] If Freud's notion of the uncanny is haunted by the concept of the death drive and vice versa, then Freud's essays are also haunted by the figure of Spielrein.

However, it was not the figure of Spielrein, but the spectre of Jung's resentment of Freud's position as 'old master'[77] and contentions over conceptualising the nature of 'the libido' that returned to disturb the Freud/Jung relationship in 1912. This culminated in 'the Kreuzlingen gesture', a mutual misunderstanding which led to a serious falling out in June 1912. By August 1912, Freud had authorised Jones and Ferenczi to form a secret committee of loyal members, independently of Jung.[78] Freud even consolidated the society by presenting a ring to each member (Jones, Sachs, Abraham, Ferenczi, Rank). In September, Jung was a successor turned betrayer, having given a series of lectures at Fordham University, New York, detailing his divergence from Freud's theories. Subsequent to this, while reconciliation was effected at the Munich conference of November 1912, Freud took to addressing Jung as 'Dr Jung' instead of 'Dear Friend'. The Munich conference also saw a disagreement between Jung and Freud over reading the ancient Egyptian ruler Amenhotep's relationship to his father.[79] As in Bremen, Jung's alacrity silenced Freud and Freud collapsed. In an uncanny repetition of the events of 1909, Freud's response to a crisis with Jung was to fall into unconsciousness. Freud's authority was no longer in place; Jung was 'the oedipal son who had struggled free'.[80] Shortly afterwards, in January 1913, the men discontinued their correspondence. Finally:

> [o]n 20 April 1914, Jung took the decisive step and sent off letters to the heads of each of the local psychoanalytic societies formally announcing his resignation as president of the International Association. On the copy sent to Freud, Jung marked '+ + +' at the bottom – the old symbol, used several times in their correspondence, to ward off the devil. The 'unedifying struggle' was finally over.[81]

+ + +

In the winter of 1918 Freud returned to his paper on the uncanny, an essay which had been fermenting since 1909. Accordingly, elements of the Freud/Jung relationship infiltrate the essay. These include references to discussions, as well as displacements and condensations of incidents which occurred during the professional association. Thus, in his essay, Freud refers to Hoffmann's 'The Devil's Elixir' as a narrative which produces uncanny effects.[82] This reference also (metonymically) alludes to the affair between Jung and Spielrein. In his letter of 11 March 1909, after denying culpability for the rumour of his disloyalty and pledging his fidelity to psychoanalysis, Jung proceeded to mention to Freud his having read this narrative. Kerr argues that the main strand of the story involves the protagonist 'waiting to be unmasked for his secret sins', which thus had a resonance with Jung's own situation which was 'truly uncanny'.[83] Here the reference in Jung's letter could be read as a partial (if unconscious) self-incrimination, indicative of Jung's unfaithfulness to both psychoanalysis and Freud. It is possible to read further evidence of Jung's betrayal surfacing in the essay with Freud's description of the uncanny coincidences surrounding the numbers 61 and 62. Freud had written to Jung about this in his letter of 16 April 1909, and in his essay he characterises the strange recurrence of numbers as 'involuntary repetition', and discusses his own unnerving experiences in the third person.[84] This aspect of the essay also encodes a displacement of the 'bookcase incident', which occurred during Jung's Vienna visit of 1909. Freud had originally written the letter to disabuse Jung of the notion that any supernatural activity had occurred, and to warn Jung against becoming too committed to pursuing occult investigations. However, Freud's description of the uncanny coincidences was also included in order to assure Jung that Freud would be willing to indulge some investigation of the occult (if only as a subsidiary activity and 'charming delusion').[85] Thus the reference signifies Freud re-establishing himself as a tolerant and supportive father figure (to balance the earlier admonishment).

It is also possible to read a further allusion to the bookcase incident in the essay, an allusion which represents a condensation of Jung's apparent externalisation of poltergeist activity and Freud's fainting at Bremen. Freud suggests in the essay:

> [w]e can also speak of a living person as uncanny, and we do so when we ascribe evil intentions to him. But that is not all; in addition to this we must feel that his intentions to harm us are going to be carried out with the help of special powers ... It was the pious Gretchen's intuition that Mephistopheles possessed secret powers of this kind that made him so uncanny to her.[86]

Here Freud is suggesting that a person may seem uncanny if he or she appears to be able to employ supernatural powers malevolently. For Freud, it is not the evil motives themselves which are terrifying, but rather the 'special powers' which can be used to achieve malign ends. Furthermore, not only is it the capacity for manifesting such powers that is frightening, the recognition of potential for supernatural activity in another is also an uncanny experience. Thus, it is prospective parapsychological activity which constitutes the uncanny here. It is this potential for parapsychological activity ('catalytic exteriorisation phenomenon') that Jung sets out to demonstrate with the unexplained bookcase noises. Jung told Freud that he was able to manifest telekinetic energy at will, and thus effectively made himself uncanny (in the terms set out above). Here, not only were the peculiar and unexplained bookcase noises uncanny (inexplicable, out of place), so was Jung's apparent determination to defy his mentor, his resolve to manifest supernatural activity at will. Freud admits to Jung that in spite of his incredulity, 'your stories and your experiment made a deep impression on me'.[87] Freud's dismissal of the phenomenon is not absolute; he acknowledges the power of Jung's presence and concedes that apparently mystical effects have occurred in his own life. He even (if condescendingly) sanctions Jung's future investigations into the occult. In this reading, it is possible to see Jung's actions as suggestive of the uncanny: inexplicable things had occurred in his presence, and even if Freud was not totally convinced that Jung had special powers Jung was certainly straining Freud's authority in troubling ways.

It is possible to speculate that Jung's erratic behaviour, his insistence that he could externalise his wishes, made such a pervasive impression on Freud that the 'venerable master' was unnerved by Jung when he met him again in Bremen. When Jung asserted his dominance over the subject under discussion, Freud fainted. Freud's passing into unconsciousness could be seen as a reaction against and/or a manifestation of Jung's conviction that he was able to actualise his desires externally. Even if Freud did not entirely believe that Jung could produce paranormal activity, he still knew that Jung was convinced of his own power to project his desires. Freud also knew that Jung probably resented his scepticism of parapsychology, and he most likely felt that Jung nonetheless wanted to verify the existence of his paranormal propensities to Freud. Freud's fainting was, then, a reaction against (or a literal 'blocking-out' of) Jung's implicit challenge to Freud's power from the domain of the supernatural, a domain Freud wished to exclude from psychoanalysis. Freud's fainting could also be seen as a defensive and fearful reaction to counter the sheer force of Jung's will (paranormal or not). Thus, it would seem that on some level, Freud's speculation (above) and comment '[l]et us take the uncanny associated with the omnipotence of thoughts, with the prompt fulfilment of wishes, [and] with secret injurious power',[88] refer to Jung. Moreover, the later connection of omnipotence of thought to wish fulfilment also supports the above reading of the Bremen fainting, where Freud accused Jung of harbouring death wishes against him.

Freud suggests in his essay that the uncanny impression produced by the omnipotence of thoughts may be attributed to a 'primitive' attitude which has not entirely been relinquished, an attitude which we still return to when we 'do not feel quite sure of our new beliefs'. Here Freud is linking uncanny feelings to 'old discarded beliefs', primitive systems of thought which have been substantially 'surmounted' but may unexpectedly return, the familiar which has returned from repression.[89] What is interesting about this speculation is that Freud's thinking here resembles Jung's theorisations on the 'collective unconscious', a storehouse of accumulated memories, symbols and ideas. Jung, in his 1919 lecture 'The Psychological Foundation of Belief in Spirits', suggested that previously surmounted ideas which resurfaced from the collective unconscious into consciousness cause uncanny impressions.[90] Freud states in his essay that the old beliefs 'still exist within us',[91] by implication echoing Jung's notion of a collective unconscious of shared ideas and complexes which are inherited from our 'primitive' forefathers. Furthermore, Freud's contention also resonates with the strain of thinking that Jung had started to develop from around 1909 (and in discussion with Spielrein), on phylogenetic memory.[92] Freud was initially resistant to this notion of genetically inherited memories, because it destabilised the consolidation of his own conception of the libido. It seems that Jung was instrumental in broaching this subject with Freud. Freud had been considering the idea of phylogenetic memory while reading Fraser's *Golden Bough*, as research for *Totem and Taboo*. Freud acknowledged to Jung that in his latest project he had 'unearthed strange and uncanny things' (letter of 20 August 1911).[93] He wrote to Jung on 13 October 1911 that Fraser's *Golden Bough* described the imaginative investment of afterbirth in ancient societies with human qualities (it was treated as 'twin'). This was significant he felt, as '[i]f there is such a thing as a phylogenetic memory in the individual, which unfortunately will soon be undeniable, this is also a source of the uncanny aspect of the *doppelgänger*'.[94] Freud's notion here was significant for the later development of his thoughts on the uncanny nature of the double in his 1919 essay. Freud argued that the double was threatening because, where previously in 'primitive societies' the double had functioned to ensure the immortality of the ego, in modern-day society this notion had been repressed. Thus the double could only return as an annihilator, that which would destroy the security of the ego by returning it to itself, showing the ego that it was not autonomous or sovereign.[95]

This idea of a store of inherited memories is thus important to some of Freud's main contentions in his essay. However, it also generates a schism in the paper, as Freud is unable to reconcile the idea of phylogenetic memory with his other source of uncanny experiences – repressed infantile complexes. While Jung developed his theories by relinquishing the sexualised libido and replacing it with a genetic libido, Freud seemingly conflates the two in his essay. For Ellen Peel, '[Freud] fails to construct a clear relationship between animistic beliefs and infantile complexes.'[96] If infantile and animistic psyches may be implicitly aligned as examples of the 'long known' which have been repressed, then what are we to make of these two aspects of the uncanny? How do they fit together? There appears to be a rift in the essay between infantile and genetic explanations which reproduces the rupture between Freudian and Jungian thinking. Furthermore, Freud's two theories of the uncanny – phylogenetic memory and infantile complexes – can also be read within his rift with Jung. We have seen that Freud's partial and troubled adoption of the notion of inheritance of 'racial' memories seems to have been instigated by his professional and personal relationship with Jung. In addition, Freud's insistence on conducting a father/son relationship with Jung also established the very possibility of Freud's identifying the Oedipal rivalry which he had already outlined as fundamental within his version of psychoanalysis.[97] By giving Jung a filial appellation Freud was also effectively designating him as a potential rival for psychoanalysis itself. Thus even Freud's profession of friendship (*heimlich*) paradoxically entailed that Jung was always already destined to become a sinister adversary (*unheimlich*), where ultimately Jung's theories could only ever inevitably become threatening.[98]

Alongside this undertone to Freud's essay, that the theoretical outlooks of the two colleagues were unmanageably different, there is another repressed aspect which deserves to be addressed – that which concerns Spielrein. Spielrein not only represents a disruptive factor within the Freud/Jung relationship, she also signals the subversive potential of a particular kind of femininity: the educated and assertive 'New Woman'. This kind of woman was increasingly visible in journals, newspapers and visual representations, and a few (such as Spielrein) found their way into psychoanalysis, as patients and/or practitioners.[99] These changing gender roles provide one context through which we can understand Freud and Jung's uneasiness about Spielrein. She is also a figure onto which the tensions between Freud and Jung were mapped. It is possible to suggest that Spielrein's role in the men's relationship can be read through Freud's elaboration of the uncanny, as precisely the point where *heimlich* and *unheimlich* coincide, the '[c]oncealed, kept from sight, so that others do not get to know of or about it', the hidden, 'behind someone's back', the 'love-affair, love, sin'.[100] It is this contention of Freud's essay, that the uncanny represents simultaneous the 'homely' and the 'strange', where meaning becomes strained. Here, Freud's claim that the uncanny signifies the coincidence of 'homely' and 'unhomely' is troubled by that which is too congenial, too familiar. It is possible to suggest that Spielrein was uncanny to

Freud precisely because she was too familiar, too intimate. However, such a contention also problematises the consolidation of the concept of the uncanny. How are we to understand the overlap between the two? Can we still possess a clear sense of 'the homely' when we recognise something alien within it that jeopardises its status? Thus the meeting point of the *heimlich* and *unheimlich* may also be seen as the vanishing point of logic within Freud's essay. Furthermore, if Spielrein becomes a vanishing point in this reading, then this is reminiscent of the representation of women in the essay as a whole. Freud's essay consistently overlooks women, where besides the automaton Olympia (and a fleeting reference to Clara) Freud's only reference to women in the essay is to the 'painted women' or prostitutes, who fuel Freud's own experience of the uncanny as a foreigner lost in Italy.[101] If women are denied the experience of the uncanny, that is because, for Freud, they *are* uncanny. They represent the vanishing point of logic, sense, and meaning, they are symbolised by the genitals which encapsulate their ascribed 'lack'.[102] This suggests another problem in Freud's essay, in that women *are* uncanny (because they are castrated, and because they are the 'former *Heim* [home] of all human beings'[103]), how do women *experience* the uncanny?

It seems that Freud's essay is riven by evasions and unresolved tensions. As an ambitious attempt to map the theoretical terrain in the unfamiliar 'province' of aesthetics through psychoanalysis, the essay was also a journey into Freud's own complexes, associations (conscious or unconscious) and repressions. The essay is a synecdoche of the paradox, inherent in psychoanalysis itself, that, as Samuel Weber suggests, unconscious processes cannot be theorised without 'leav[ing] their imprint on the process of theoretical objectification itself'.[104] Thus the uncanny can never be finalised or complete, as some aspect of it must be 'withheld', always somehow in 'another place'. Furthermore, what is 'withheld', or 'elsewhere', in Freud's essay is 'woman'. However, 'woman', like Spielrein, may be kept from sight, but is never entirely repressed. She does not simply vanish; instead, she returns at the margins, signalling the 'elsewhere' and the further possibilities at the edges of Freud's conception of the uncanny.

Notes

1. Nicholas Royle, *The Uncanny* (Manchester: Manchester University Press, 2003), p. 2.
2. Sigmund Freud, 'The "Uncanny"', in *Art and Literature*, The Pelican Freud Library, vol. 14 (Harmondsworth: Penguin Books, 1985 [1919]), p. 344.
3. Ibid., p. 345.

4. John Kerr, *A Most Dangerous Method: The Story of Jung, Freud and Sabina Spielrein* (London: Sinclair Stevenson Publishers, 1994), p. 490.
5. Freud, p. 345.
6. William McGuire (ed.), *The Freud/Jung Letters: Abridged* (London: Penguin Group, 1979), p. 46.
7. Bernard Minder, 'A Document. Jung to Freud 1905: A Report on Sabina Spielrein', in Coline Covington and Barbara Wharton (eds), *Sabina Spielrein, Forgotten Pioneer of Psychoanalysis* (Sussex and New York: Brunner-Routledge, 2003), pp. 137–42.
8. Peter Gay, *Freud: A Life for Our Time* (New York and London: W. W. Norton and Company, 1988), p. 196.
9. Lisa Appignanesi and John Forrester, *Freud's Women* (London: Phoenix, 2005), p. 204.
10. Avery F. Gordon, *Ghostly Matters, Haunting and the Sociological Imagination* (Minneapolis: University of Minnesota Press, 1997), pp. 59, 60.
11. Kerr, p. 104.
12. Appignanesi and Forrester, p. 204. See Bruno Bettelheim 'Introduction', in Aldo Carotenuto, *A Secret Symmetry: Sabina Spielrein between Jung and Freud,* trans. by Arno Pomerans, John Shepley, Krisha Winston (London and Melbourne: Routledge and Kegan Paul, 1984), Aldo Carotenuto (*A Secret Symmetry*, p. 166) and John Kerr (pp. 112–13) for speculations on the genesis of this relationship.
13. See Janet Sayers on Spielrein's case history (Janet Sayers, *Divine Therapy: Mysticism and Psychoanalysis* (Oxford: Oxford University Press, 2003), pp. 68–9).
14. Bettelheim, p. xxii.
15. Ibid., p. xxii.
16. Freud, p. 346.
17. McGuire, pp. 87, 97, 124. See also Gay, Chapter 5, section 1.
18. Gay, p. 204.
19. McGuire, p. 139. See Bettelheim on further connotations of the letter (p. xxvii).
20. Sayers, p. 72. Whether Spielrein and Jung engaged in a sexual relationship is still an open question.
21. Ibid., p. 72.
22. Jung was plotting his escape from the Burghölzli since spring 1907 (Kerr, p. 165). However, according to Zvi Lothane and Kerr, p. 212, Jung tended his resignation and wrote to Spielrein's mother simultaneously in Jan 1909 (Zvi Lothane, 'Tender Love and Transference: Unpublished Letters of C. G. Jung and Sabina Spielrein', in Covington and Wharton (eds), *Sabina Spielrein*, pp. 189–223; 206.
23. Carotenuto, p. xxix.
24. McGuire, p. 142, letter of 11 March 1909.
25. Minder in Covington and Wharton, p. 88.
26. Jung does not think that this is Spielrein (McGuire, pp. 141–2), and there is no evidence that Spielrein approached the neurologist Muthmann with a story about Jung, as Freud reported the incident in his letter of 9 March 1909.
27. Carl Gustav Jung, *Memories, Dreams, Reflections*, trans. by Aniela Jaffé (London: Harper Collins, 1995 [1962]), pp. 178–9.

28. Jung, p. 179.
29. Kerr, p. 213.
30. Jung, p. 178.
31. See letter of 23 November 1913 (no. 436), Eva Brabant, Ernst Falzedor and Participial Grampien-Deutsch, (eds), *The correspondence of Sigmund Freud and Sandor Ferenczi, Vol 1, 1908–14*, trans. by Peter T. Hoffer (Cambridge, Massachusetts and London: The Belknap Press of Harvard University, 1993), p. 523.
32. See letter of 15 March 1925, in R. Andrew Paskauskas, ed., *The Complete Correspondence of Sigmund Freud and Ernest Jones 1908–1939* (Cambridge, Massachusetts and London: The Belknap Press of Harvard University, 1993), pp. 420–1.
33. See Jung's autobiography (pp. 172–3); Kerr, p. 270.
34. Jung, p. 173.
35. Gerhard Wehr, *Jung: A Biography* (Boston, MA: Shambhala Publications Inc., 1985), p. 514.
36. Sayers, p. 61.
37. See Sayers, p. 75.
38. See Kerr, Chapter 7. For Freud's feeling that Jung's work on the libido was an infidelity to psychoanalysis see Freud's letter 95 to Jones, 22 September 1912 (Paskauskas, p. 162).
39. Jung, p. 179.
40. McGuire, p. 143.
41. Jung waits for a month before replying to this letter, and then admits ruefully that he has committed a 'sin of omission' (McGuire, p. 146).
42. Wehr, pp. 104, 103.
43. Sayers, p. 66.
44. Kerr, p. 490.
45. Carotenuto, p. 91.
46. McGuire, p. 150.
47. Ibid., pp. 151, 56.
48. Jung wrote to Freud after his first visit to Vienna after a gap of a month (letter of 31 March 1907, in McGuire, p. 56).
49. Jung wrote: 'Meine Zuneigung ist, solange sie keine Verliebtheit ist, von Dauerhaftikeit und Verläßlichkeit' (William McGuire und Wolfgang Sauerländer, *Sigmund Freud, C. G. Jung: Breifwechsel [letters]* (Frankfurt: Fischer, 2001), p. 102). McGuire's English edition translates Verliebtheit (in love) as infatuation. In the letter of 4 June 1909, Jung describes his relationship with his patient as 'Zwangsverliebung' (McGuire und Sauerländer, p. 111), 'a compulsion to fall in love'. As such, the 'affection' that Jung harbours for psychoanalysis is overwhelmed by more compulsive feelings towards Spielrein.
50. Kerr, p. 221.
51. McGuire, pp. 154–5.
52. Bettelheim, p. xxxi.
53. McGuire, pp. 154–5.
54. Carotenuto, p. 115.
55. McGuire, p. 156.
56. See also Saul Rosenzweig's *The Historic Expedition to America (1909), Freud, Jung and Hall the King-maker* (St Louis: Rana House, 1994 [1992]).

57. Gay, p. 208.
58. Jung, p. 180.
59. Rosenzweig, p. 53.
60. Bettelheim, p. xxxii.
61. Jung, p. 182.
62. Gay, p. 225.
63. Jung, p. 182.
64. Gay elaborates on this theme of mistrust, suggesting that Jung believed the undisclosed aspect of the dream included evidence of Freud's affair with his sister-in-law (footnote, p. 225). Thus, Jung's reading of the dream links to his own recent infidelity, his having deceived Freud about the nature of the relationship, and his being obliged to confess. The situation Jung interpreted in the dream was then the inverse of his own. Freud, he assumed, had deceived him, but would not be forced to confess. In withholding confession Freud also wielded power, while Jung had effectively renounced his own power by admitting his misrepresentation of Spielrein to Freud.
65. Kerr, p. 270.
66. Coline Covington, 'Introduction', in Covington and Wharton (eds), *Sabina Spielrein*, pp. 1–14; 1.
67. Carotenuto, pp. 15, 14, 20.
68. There is a dearth of evidence to contradict this account as Jung's letters to Spielrein have not been published.
69. Carotenuto, pp. 12, 20, 12.
70. See Jung, p. 411.
71. Carotenuto, pp. 190, 20.
72. Kerr, pp. 350, 364, 371.
73. Minutes III, 330, Number 4, cited in Carotenuto, p. 142.
74. Carotenuto, p. 146.
75. Appignanesi and Forrester, p. 220.
76. Royle, p. 89.
77. Letter of 9 January 1912, McGuire, p. 255.
78. See Paskauskas, p. 147.
79. Kerr, pp. 428–9.
80. Gay, p. 238.
81. Kerr, pp. 469–70.
82. Freud, p. 355.
83. Kerr, p. 211.
84. Freud, pp. 359–60.
85. McGuire, p. 146.
86. Freud, pp. 365–6.
87. McGuire, p. 144.
88. Freud, p. 370.
89. Ibid., pp. 371, 370.
90. Carl Gustav Jung, 'The Psychological Foundation of Belief in Spirits', in *Psychology and the Occult*, trans. by R. F. C. Hull (London: Routledge and Kegan Paul, 1977 [1919]), pp. 108–25; 118.
91. Freud, p. 371.
92. According to Kerr, since 1909 'Jung had been trying to anchor his reflections on libidinal development on a phylogenetic, evolutionary basis, as

opposed to the personal-historical past' (pp. 340–1). Kerr suggests that by 1910 Jung is discussing these ideas with Spielrein (p. 310). On 8 November 1911, Spielrein talked about phylogenetic memories at a meeting of the Vienna Psychoanalytic Society. Freud responded to her ideas reprovingly and with caution (pp. 359–60).

93. McGuire, p. 234.
94. Ibid., p. 240. Jung's response to this letter outlined his own definite (and increasingly independent) views on the matter. He asserted: '[the] "early memories of childhood" are not individual memories at all but phylogenetic ones' (McGuire, p. 240, 17 October 1911).
95. Freud, pp. 356, 358–9.
96. Ellen Peel, 'Psychoanalysis and the Uncanny', *Literary Studies* 17.4 (1980), pp. 410–17 (p. 411).
97. See Sigmund Freud, *The Interpretation of Dreams* (Oxford: Oxford University Press, 1999), pp. 201–4. See also Sigmund Freud, 'A Special Type of Object Choice made by Men', in *On Sexuality: Three Essays on the Theory of Sexuality and Other Works*, trans. James Stratchey, The Pelican Freud Library, vol. 7 (Harmondsworth: Penguin Books, 1977 [1910]), pp. 227–42.
98. Furthermore, if Jung was always already 'uncanny' to Freud, designated as 'son' precisely when Freud claims he has been 'divested of paternal dignity', then this uncanniness again is tied to Spielrein. As already outlined above, these events of April 1909 were intertwined not only with Freud's commencing his paper on the uncanny, and the beginning of the dissolution of the Freud and Jung relationship, but also with Jung's unfaithfulness to psychoanalysis, due to his affair with Spielrein. Thus it seems that Jung might be guilty of another considerable crime: as Freud's rival for psychoanalysis, he was also ostensibly inconstant in his affections.
99. Appignanesi and Forrester note that 'a significant number of Freud's women 'patients' made that cross-over [to practitioner]: ... at a time when women's access to the profession was surrounded by difficulty' (p. 5).
100. Freud, p. 344.
101. Freud, p. 359.
102. See Jane Marie Todd, 'The Veiled Woman in Freud's "Das Unheimliche"', *SIGNS* 11.3 (1986), pp. 519–28 (p. 527).
103. Freud, p. 368.
104. Samuel Weber, *The Legend of Freud* (California, Stanford University Press, 2000), p. xiv.

8
The Urban Uncanny: The City, the Subject, and Ghostly Modernity

Julian Wolfreys

> [T]he city of Venice ... was drowned in trees. Dark, ghostly trees crowded the alleys and squares, and filled the canals, Walls were no obstacle to them. Their branches pierced stone and glass. Their roots plunged deep beneath paving stones. Statues and pillars were sheathed in ivy. It was suddenly – to Strange's senses at any rate – a great deal quieter and darker ... Yet none of Venice's inhabitants appeared to notice the least change.[1]

I

We find ourselves confronted by a somewhat surreal image, that of an oceanic city, famous in the imagination as well as the experience for its waterways, 'drowned', as my epigraph puts it, in trees. In a city already 'compromised' as it were by being neither wholly solid nor liquid, but a precarious amalgam of architectural presence and reiteration on the one hand, and watery provisionality on the other, the identity of place is transmogrified by a spectral forest that is no respecter of boundaries. Already a liminal place or, rather say a place where place is constantly dissolved through the endless juxtaposition of differing liminalities, the implicitly uncanny nature of Venice, an aspect on which writers from Otway to Wilkie Collins, from Collins to Du Maurier, from Du Maurier to Winterson and beyond have traded, is made all the more manifest, material, by this paradoxically ghostly transformation. All the more startling, however, in this historical narrative set in the first two decades of the nineteenth century, is that the city of Venice is made all the more odd to one person and one person only. If representation is staged as uncanny therefore, it is staged as uncanny for a single subject, in whom and to whose 'senses' the already eldritch city is revealed from within itself as all astounding, arresting, bizarre, otherworldly. The picturesque is heightened until defamiliarized, and with that, the familiar becomes morbidly unfamiliar as there emerges to one isolated individual a 'landscape of difference'.[2]

II

My title assumes a great deal. First, that we understand what we mean when we speak of the 'uncanny'; second, that there is such a 'thing', a phenomenon at least repeatable and available to experience by different people at different times, and which in turn can be subdivided, identified according to the principle of genus and species, and part of which can be named therefore 'urban uncanny'. This is still to assume much. For, if nothing else is recognized, the supposition is that the 'urban' and 'uncanny' are related *a priori*. One of the connections I am making, doubtless too easily, is that a relation does exist and that the thread binding the two terms, however tenuously, has itself a tenuous relation between the idea of the urban and the idea of the home or, to put this another way, between the topography and culture of cities and the architecture of familiarity and the family that goes by the names 'dwelling', 'building', 'house', and so on. In such implicit and given concatenations, the pull of underground currents pertaining to translation holds sway, dictating along the passageways of memory eddies of translation.

As Sigmund Freud was all too obsessively aware, whatever one might wish to call or signify by the terms the 'uncanny', *das 'Unheimlich'*, the 'unhomely' quite literally in German, one must proceed cautiously, never assuming absolute knowledge of that which slips away from you as soon as you attempt to define it, whether etymologically, psychoanalytically, or by narrative example. Rather like seeing someone you believe you know, or who recollection convinces is familiar to you, you pursue the glimpsed stranger through streets and turnings that become less and less familiar, as in the pursuit your surroundings begin to let you down, losing you in a labyrinth of contiguous but chance relations. Obsession is perhaps the key there. One need only see a stranger twice to find that figure familiar, or to invest that fleeting being who is other than oneself with the specious familiarity that memory can, on occasions, invest. Consider Donald Sutherland's architect, John Baxter, in Nicholas Roeg's 1973 *Don't Look Now*, set in the labyrinthine topography of Venice, a city that typifies the quandary of simultaneous familiarity and defamiliarization, in that every alley leading on to another just like it, opens the city not as knowable place but as abyss in which the iterability of the self-same only serves as a reminder that nothing is the same, and that each and every street is wholly other, in which one comes to find oneself adrift, without bearings, lost. Cinematic grammar and syntax conforms in its baroque frustrations to the disturbing, unrelenting enigmatic condition of the city. Nothing is to be found, nothing known, and anxiety twinned with obsession is exponentially generated in the face of the uncanny persistence of resistance to any epistemological mode that will comfort or make familiar. Architecture as practice and metaphor for rational ordering – and therefore explanation – is only confounded, made to seem inadequate as explanation, clarification, or ordering principle. Yet, one persists in searching, as does Roeg's architect. And this is all the more obsessive when that search, and the desire and obsession that drive it, are tied to traumatic memory and the passing encounter with a small red-cloaked and hooded human form, human enough, and yet strangely inhuman too. So the architect is swallowed by the city, he loses his bearings, his identity, and, ultimately, his life.

The very condition of the uncanny experience, then, is that there is always the inexorable slide, inescapable as well as ineluctable, from the familiar to the unfamiliar, the homely to the unhomely, the 'canny' or 'known' to the 'uncanny'. And this equally has to do with one's 'self', one's identity or being and one's location, where location or context determines who one thinks one is, and how the subject is orientated or disorientated not only in the present but in relation to the past, to personal, and to cultural memory. In this, and in all motions associated with spatial orientation and disorientation, structural, topographical, and, inevitably (on occasion), architectural figures and tropes serve to illustrate what takes place. Topography becomes or is already haunted by tropography. Space, place, and displacement vie uneasily in the same location, situation, site, or locus. As soon as there is a form with repeatable if irregular shapes, the experience or occasion of the uncanny has its chance. Turning this around, the uncanny is *there*, as soon as undifferentiated space gives way to even the most haphazard construction of place. For the uncanny experience may take place as soon as there is *a* place for the occasional, jarring encounter. And this encounter is a reminder, a *mémoire de lieu* if not a *lieu de mémoire* (to borrow and invert French cultural historian Pierre Nora's now well-known phrase), all the more disturbing because it is a memory, a surfacing *souvenir* (something which returns, which comes [*venir*] from the other, the unconscious or just simply underneath [*sou*]; all the while there, under the surface and invisible, the trace of the other can surface at any time to capsize one's being) borne up by the undercurrent of the structure of place from some urban unconscious to remind us that we cannot bear in mind that which is at the heart of any familiar locale – its strange otherness, its persistently disorientating alterity.

Yet, as we know and as Freud demonstrates insistently, as soon as there is an example, the 'uncanny', so-called, has fled. When definition takes place, it does so belatedly. Departed, on the run like the red-hooded dwarf of *Don't Look Now*, ahead of its definition or by determination of its identity or meaning, the 'uncanny' is only to be acknowledged belatedly by the recounting, the witnessing, of an effect as after-effect; that is to say, as the somewhat ghostly generator of untimely narrative that takes place in the very place where 'uncanny' (whatever 'it' is, even though it is nothing as such) is not. Freud's essay is too well known to require yet one more demonstration of the effects it both describes, narrates, accounts for, and performs, entering as it does in that odd semi-fictional condition of belated testamentary inadequacy and supplement to the singularity of an experience that can never be shared directly. What is uncanny for you may not be for me, and vice versa. Something haunting has to be perceived, again indirectly, as that which touches one or moves one, and which one can only recount in the hopes that the auditor for one's narrative can say, somewhat feebly, I see what you mean, I've had similar experiences.

Then it must be admitted that 'uncanny' is not singular itself even though each and every experience that we name or describe as uncanny is, and indeed must be perforce. For 'uncanny' names on the one hand, an effect, an experience as should be clear already. On the other hand, in giving definition to this phenomenon, 'uncanny' comes to take on the appearance of that most familiar 'possession', what I call a name, that which supposedly belongs to me, and which is mine and no other's. It is then also a name, a proper name if you will for all that is most improper, all that surfaces where something should have remained hidden, and all that appears to return in a defamiliarizing fashion in the places with which one is, supposedly, most familiar, most at home. Lastly, 'uncanny' signifies or identifies, however provisionally, in however precarious or fluid a manner, a concept, at once all too obvious and yet simultaneously frustratingly enigmatic, paradoxical. Its hazy conceptuality, its very play with the idea of the conceptual as epistemological mode marks out – even as it erases – a boundary, a border or limit between the known and the unknown, the familiar and the unfamiliar, that which can be given a name and that which is unnameable. The uncanny is, we might say, that which at the limit, names all that cannot be named and so comes to haunt the proper, the familiar, and the concept of conceptuality itself.

Which brings us to, or rather say *back* to, the urban (which has been here all along), and, with that, one non-synonymous cognate to which this essay addresses itself: the city. If the city, any city, can be said to be uncanny, and if, reciprocally, the uncanny is often represented or experienced as a condition of that conglomeration of architecture, transport, communication, and topography over decades, generations, and centuries that we call *city* or *urban* (perhaps *urbanism*), this is because the city, if it is anything, is 'indeed an open non-totalizable set of idioms, singularities, styles: a place to welcome the other within oneself, a place open to what is coming, the very coming of what is to come, open to imminence'. But this very condition of being open to the other is an uncontrollable opening that admits to the unexpected, the arrival of the unfamiliar, the unhomely, all, in short, which cannot be programmed or anticipated, uncanniness itself. For the city, it must be understood, takes place according to and on the condition of an '*axiom of incompleteness* ... [it is] a set which must remain indefinitely and structurally non-saturable'.[3] In this, the subject to be open to the city must also remain indefinite, provisional in his or her identity, and thus subject to the uncanny arrival of some other. As with that in the idea of the city that remains inimical and irreducible to any architectural planning, organization or erection, so there is that in the idea of the modern subject, which remains, in each of its articulations, provisional, given to slippage and translation, and, itself, incomplete, not at home with itself, with the idea of a self which would be determined as architectonically or ontologically finite or stable.

The provisionality of which I am speaking is given specific voice apropos Macao. Speaking of Macao, but in a generalizing mode of reflection that admits of thinking the universal singularity of place, Philippe Pons, Tokyo Correspondent for *Le Monde*, writes that 'cities are fragile constructions, fluid realities: like a precipitate' he continues, 'they're the result of a constellation of elements converging at a given moment in time'.[4] Unequivocally a momentary arrangement dictated temporally through the occasion of convergence, city-precipitates lose that otherwise indefinable quality by which their spirit, their most haunting aspects, are generated. Once this happens, Pons asserts, the city vanishes. The material structures remain, to be sure, the concrete, the wood, the architecture, the streets, the topography: all remain in place, to be razed to the ground and subsequently rebuilt in haphazard, serial, or planned fashion, time after time. But what is properly the 'city' (properly the city yet improperly difficult to define except as an experience or event belatedly recalled and subsequently narrated), this – whatever it is – has disappeared, 'existing', as Pons puts it so eloquently 'in the archipelago between memory and imagination'.[5]

Moreover, so temporally marked a phenomenon is the event (the taking place, the rhythms, oscillations, and temporalities) of city as that which, having taken place and now having always already vanished, that it is felt 'oppressed by the weight of time', which in turn causes 'one's mind to flit continually between present and past', producing 'muffled echoes resonating in the present ... from an imagined past or else one that you read about in books'. In the remains of the city, in what we name 'urban' as an adjective for the imprecision of a feeling, you feel 'the beating hearts of so many vanished lives ... so many ghosts whispering their stories that past and present could only blur'.[6] Past, present, and it has to be remarked, the future also: for, if in the urban space what touches and haunts me is what has vanished, then it follows that I must, necessarily also experience that uncanny encounter with myself, my other or double, arriving to me from some future-present as being the trace of the always already vanished, the disappeared, the phantom figure of the city's pulse.

Far from being a narrowly modern experience therefore, one belonging let us say to the last one hundred years exclusively, the uncanny experience of the encounter with all that haunts the city is to be found in texts that address the city as the locus of the individual and isolated subject, the urban figure who comes to reflect that he or she is, as Matthew Arnold has it, 'in the sea of life enisl'd' ('To Marguerite, Continued'). Arnold's perhaps overused phrase has that virtue perhaps in that in overturning John Donne's equally overworked 'no man is an island' (Meditation XVII), it gives a topographic location and thus a certain historically grounded modernity to subjectivity and consciousness, even if that modernity has an arc of over 300 years at least.

Writers as distinct as Descartes, Heidegger, and Derrida appreciate this. They give formal acknowledgement to the seemingly intuitive obsession *and* anxiety that is articulated through the architect of Nicholas Roeg's *Don't Look Now*. In giving voice to their urban experience, to their unsettling encounter with the city's spectral solitude *and* uncanny iterability, they announce and affirm the subject's haunting urban adventure as a coming to awareness of modernity, a modernity that spans, if not participating in the articulation of, the history and historicity of the subject's individual subjectivity and modernity. To be modern is to be alone wherever one is, and wherever one dwells; but this 'aloneness' is unlike any other isolation, for it is, as I shall conclude, that isolation-in-coming that my being-in-the-world shares with every other being. In having this revealed to me, I recognize the perpetual condition of isolation and so the uncanniness of being's singularity, a singularity iterable from and for everyone to every other one.

As soon as there is the city then, *there*, we might say – and in so doing indicating proximal place, which, however near remains at an interval – *there* is the subject. 'I' am placed; 'I' has a stage for its reflection and so takes place. The subject, thus understood, is the event of the urban yet paradoxically not its centre, merely one of a potentially infinite number of centres. It is this centre-decentred of self-conscious urban being that brings about a concomitant awareness of the sense of one's uncanniness. This perhaps initial perception arises because of the equally paradoxical sensation of isolation, if not invisibility. More than this, and herein lies the perception, or the growing awareness at least, of one's subjectivity having uncanniness imposed upon it. The impression might grow therefore that being-in-the-city, being a subject of the modernity that is urban topography and the architectural complex, leads to the possibility that one may gain the imaginary insight into what it might feel like to be other. Of Amsterdam, in a remark that echoes the sentiment meditated on in the *Discourse* shortly to be cited, Descartes writes that 'in this great city ... everyone is so attentive to his own profit that I could live here my entire life without ever being seen by anyone'. Continuing he remarks that 'I take walks every day amidst the confusion of a great multitude, with as much liberty and repose' as there is to be found in the countryside.[7]

The city effectively spectralizes the philosopher therefore. Making him invisible, it erases, in his reflection on the condition of urban living, his material and corporeal presence, to leave behind only a disembodied cogito. *I am* a thinking entity. Thinking determines me to myself, and it determines me in my reflection on my isolation from everyone else 'so attentive' to their material pursuits, from whose lives I am excluded and to whom I do not exist, either spatially or temporally ('my entire life'). For the Descartes of the *Meditations*, existence in the city opens to me, in a moment of reflexive cogitation the fictional encounter with myself 'as if I had lived quite alone and retired as in the most remote deserts', with the strange paradox nonetheless that I am not deprived of 'any of the conveniences to be had in the most frequented cities',[8] a material plenitude therefore that only enforces a metaphysical solitude. *I think*, one might venture, *therefore I am*, but more significantly, the city gives me the possibility of thinking, reflexively, on the otherwise invisible being-to-oneself by which thought can circulate around itself, thereby 'enisl'ing' the subject in its urban modernity. More than 200 years before Arnold's spiritual cry, Descartes appreciates the condition of the modern subject's location *qua* dislocation. This is the uncanny revelation of the city, and vouchsafed by the city in its strenuous, ceaseless energies: that the self is afforded a place for becoming as a private and unseen consciousness to itself. Descartes is given a vision of the subject therefore, unavailable elsewhere, and projected by the event of urban epistemological generation. Doubtless, it would be going too far to argue that without the encounter with the urban the Cartesian cogito, and so a decisive turn, if not a break, in the history of western thought could not have taken place. Indeed, there are no grounds for such a hypothesis. Yet, there is undeniably a fascinating and somewhat unnerving, if not actually uncanny epiphany, which, whether Descartes knows it or not, is the gift of the city, a being given by the other, to which he cannot but help be open, in not knowing that this is the uncanny experience of the other-to-come.

Perhaps what is most troubling in the relationship of the city to the birth of the modern subject is the paradox that the crowdedness of modern life to Descartes is also a mode of inescapable solitude. The city comes to be a constellation of experiences in which the subject is a precipitate (to recall Pons's definition of the city), but one without a centre or ground. The self cannot provide the centre even as its encounter with the urban is its central and recurring experience. Everywhere one is, one is centred on oneself. And yet, in the urban space, wherever one is, one is always different, different from oneself, and from others who surround one. There is no stable location, no resting or dwelling place, no home. Thus, while Descartes may espouse the alleged superiority of the 'centrally planned city' over the organic, heterogeneous, and piecemeal urban locus in the *Discourse on Method*, the latter topography and architecture is at once both an accurate macrocosmic mediation of subjectivity, while simultaneously being the distorted reflection of the truth of being. And while countless masses, confused as to identity and number, go about the city on business and for their profit,[9] free from work or labour, the meditating subject moves through the networks of the city as an incorporeal thought taking place separate from yet conditioned by the materiality of the city's body. Put this another way: inadvertently or not, Descartes affirms how the modern subject is the uncanny and invisible by-product, the phantasmic possibility and the absent difference of the 'detailed presence of the domestic, economic, and [other material] networks', which constitute the 'loci of distribution'.[10] The self is a product as much as it is a projection. Just as the city is that precipitate given articulation as the result of a constellation of elements converging at a given moment in time, so too is the reflexive coming to consciousness of one's self, as the historical by-product of determinate material factors and conditions, generated by the general economy of the urban.

III

Where does this lead us, in conclusion? Where do we find, or how can we orientate, ourselves?

Of Los Angeles, Jacques Derrida writes, 'L.A. n'est pas *anywhere*, mais c'est une singulière organisation de l'expérience du "*anywhere*"'/'L.A. is not anywhere, but it is a singular organization of the experience of "anywhere"'.[11] That single English word *anywhere*: why, one wonders, why this eruption in the surface of an otherwise calm grammar and in the midst of a meditation on a city perceived in its 'singular organization', indeed just as this singularity? *Anywhere*: apparently resistant to a domesticated rendering in French, and articulated in relation, at least implicitly, to the idea of topography or geography, if not more generally to space and place themselves, and then, to the subject's *experience* of that 'anywhere' – the sentence is the map, a map on which cognizance and *connaissance*, knowledge as an auto-cognizance and reconnaissance are staged *at the limits of subjective perception*.

And note, if you will, that re-emphasis, and with it, intensification: first time italicized, marking out the foreignness, the strangeness or otherness, then, as if we had somehow overlooked such an effect of alterity, materially marked in the sentence. It is as if *Anywhere* were a monument, a landmark in the otherwise undifferentiated topography. The diacritical materiality of the word's placement is then supplemented. Itself doubled, its own other appearing, from place to place it is displaced from its initial appearance, as if it were the uncanny ghost of itself in its foreignness, in a strangeness that is strange (to) itself. Its oddity is amplified through the placeholders of quotation marks, inverted commas surrounding the italicized foreign language as if to provide the reassuring signs of mappable coordinates for a place. It is as if the uncanny double, the stranger, could be given an identity, which in its singular organization and experience, cannot otherwise be mapped, save for that heterogeneous tongue placed rudely in another's mouth, a forced, shocking confrontation, unexpected and immediate, then remembered and re-marked.

Derrida's sentence effectively, economically marks and maps, records and performs the singular organization *and* experience of the uncanny-urban or urban-uncanny. The economy is all the more *affective* too, for it bespeaks both empirical experience and phenomenological registration. Moving between two epistemological registers as much as there is that oscillation between languages, the sentence opens – perhaps disturbingly, if not uncannily – the 'truth' (for want of a better word) of the uncanny: that it cannot be assigned simply either to experience or interpretation, world or subject. Belonging neither to one nor the other, irreducible to and yet partaking of both, uncanny is nothing as such, indescribable, without some event, some moment of *taking place* and with that, a taking place for someone. The city, a constellation of architectures and a gathering of lines, intersections, and motions, guarantees familiarity and repetition as the possibility of unfamiliarity, estrangement, and eruption. Something – as that invisible force – passes between place and experience of place. In this *event*, this taking place marked by place and momentarily held 'in place' by the graphic elements of language in Derrida's sentence that arrive belatedly as the weak memory of the uncanny shock, the subject, otherwise invisible except as observer, is marked. He or she comes into being through relationship, only to be thrown from any familiarity with his or her surroundings, *as the very condition of subjectivity's modernity*. Remarking experience, the subject remarks on him- or herself as marked by the other, in this case the city, its singular organization. What is uncanny precisely in this might be expressed as follows: in the moment that I recognize or apprehend the singularity of an encounter with the city, the uncanny arises as a condition of the urban because I apprehend the world not as objective but as a nearness, a proximity to me in a present moment where my unthinking passage through that world is suspended. The constellation and experience take me out of the time of the everyday, and in that instant, the proximity of the urban forces itself upon me in such a fashion that I am separated, as Martin Heidegger argues of *Dasein*, 'by the slightest interval',[12] which in that interval unveils my being's materiality, my being-in-the-world. Place takes place in me as an encounter with alterity, epiphanic in its touching on the material intimacy of my being with an environment that exists without the illusory comfort of organic life.

In the countryside, I can always comfort myself with the illusion that I am part of 'nature', I belong to a greater, possibly ineffable but nonetheless experiential life (so I tell myself). I can see the mountains, sunsets, or ocean horizon seen by Wordsworth, Kant, Coleridge, and others. Undifferentiated continuity as life is vouchsafed, rather than the truth that only in the 'fellowship of death' is there such undifferentiation and such unbeing. With the city, it is another matter. Every step I take reminds me that 'in walking on the street we touch and come in contact with the ground with every step, but we do not really live in what is touched and brought near in such touching'.[13] And what I touch is not the street, as Heidegger avers, but the intimate acquaintance with the other with whom I share 'in-being'. My very 'being-in-the-world' in all its differentiated, intervallic singularity can be revealed to me at any instant in the city, through the 'environing world in which I constantly am. For it is the spatiality [and not the undifferentiation of a chauvinist Nature] which belongs to my very being-in-the-world, which I constantly take with me, and, as it were, cut out from "objective world-space" everywhere that I am, at every place.'[14] Hence the always uncanny possibility inherent in the 'singular organization of the experience of "anywhere"', even as Heidegger, consciously or no, responds in the thrownness of that grounded *I am* to the Cartesian cogito. The uncanny experience moves the modern subject from reflecting that 'I think therefore *I am*' to the sensuous apprehension that everywhere, 'at every place' that I experience the 'environing world' as such, *there* is the place 'in which *I constantly am*' and '*I am, at every place*'. And this *I am* can only have its chance if, in disembodied form it can translate the experience of the city, and the encounter with the urban that causes one to pause and reflect on the unbearable strangeness of being-given through belated perception in the form of 'written linguistic embodiment and its historical transmission'[15] as the only basis for affirming one's subjectivity.

Is the experience described by Derrida not true, in principle, for every subject, for everyone's experience of any city, at any given moment therefore? Does what Derrida have to say about his impression of Los Angeles not go for any other person's encounter with any other city? Can it not be said that there are innumerable uncanny moments in that potentially endless series of singular encounters of every subject's experience of the urban, from say Descartes to Derrida? Of course, this is as inescapable as it is unprovable. There is always the possibility, to recall Pons, 'of a constellation of elements converging at a given moment in time', and converging, as Pons, Derrida, Descartes, and the architect Baxter affirm and attest, each in their own singular observations and responses. And this is why one can always experience the uncanny. Experiencing the city, any city always implies an encounter with a singular organization irreducible to any logic or explanation. What we encounter however, what we experience also, is a strange disruption. As that sentence of Derrida's with which I began this concluding section of the essay illustrated, what is uncanny is neither the absolutely unfamiliar nor the absolutely familiar either. Neither one thing nor the other, and yet a little of both: the un/familiar, with our experience and language, our aesthetic and phenomenological registration simultaneously inserting the '/' even as our registration crosses the boundary, offering to erase it at least in part. Derrida's reflection on and mediation of Los Angeles demarcates as precisely as is possible the way the modern subject, the urban subject, founders *in the instant of recognition*, as there arises, and as language carries in it 'a barely concealed tropical anxiety'.[16] Such anxiety is betrayed (given away and traced) in Derrida's italics, in his reiteration and in the intensification of the other through the placeholders of inverted commas.

As Swati Chattopadhyay suggests, such 'anxiety appears at the moment of slippage between desire [or memory] and experience, between representational mastery and inadequacy of the representative strategy, and takes the form of the uncanny'. While Derrida, and before him Descartes, speak to the question of aesthetic response, what each writer's representation fails or refuses to acknowledge is the extent to which experience is irreducible to representation. For this reason our encounter with the urban manifests itself not primarily as an 'aesthetic strategy, but as an unexpected outcome of the *process of representation*', to cite Chattopadhyay once more.[17] It is in the act of seeking to speak or write adequately that anxiety emerges, and the subject is confronted with an abyss at the heart of the encounter, an abyss within the self to which the city gives access. Even though Freud did not speak of the urban or cities in his famous essay, this is what he perceived in unpacking the mechanisms of *unheimlich* experience. And in this, he intimated why the uncanny can always take place, again, and again.

Notes

1. Susanna Clarke, *Jonathan Strange & Mr Norrell* (London: Bloomsbury, 2004), p. 792.
2. Swati Chattopadhyay, *Representing Calcutta: Modernity, Nationalism, and the Colonial Uncanny* (London: Taylor and Francis, 2005), p. 32.
3. Catherine Malabou et Jacques Derrida, *Jacques Derrida: La Contre-Allée* (Paris: La Quinzaine Littéraire Louis Vitton, 1999), p. 110. Trans. David Wills as *Counterpath: Traveling with Jacques Derrida* (Stanford: Stanford University Press, 2004), p. 109.
4. Philippe Pons, *Macao*, trans. Sarah Adams (London: Reaktion Books, 2002 [1999]), p. 9.
5. Ibid., p. 9.

6. Ibid., p. 9.
7. René Descartes, *Oeuvres de Descartes*, ed. Charles Adam and Paul Tannery (Paris: J. Vinn, 1965), vol. I, pp. 203–4.
8. René Descartes, *Discours de la méthode* (Paris: Garnier Flammarion, 1966 [1637]). Trans. John Veitch, Int. A. D. Lindsay, as *A Discourse on Method* (London: Everyman, 1969), p. 25; translation modified. (See also Kevin Dunn, '"A Great City is a Great Solitude": Descartes's Urban Pastoral', *Yale French Studies*, 80 (1981): pp. 93–107.)
9. Descartes, trans. Veitch, p. 25; Descartes, *Oeuvres de Descartes*, vol I., p. 203.
10. Françoise Choay, *The Rule and the Model: On the Theory of Architecture and Urbanism.*, ed. Denise Bratton (Cambridge, MA: MIT Press, 1997), p. 143.
11. Malabou et Derrida, p. 115; Wills, p. 114.
12. Martin Heidegger, *History of the Concept of Time: Prolegomena*, trans. Theodore Kisiel (Bloomington and Indianapolis: Indiana University Press, 1985 [1979]), p. 231.
13. Ibid., p. 231.
14. Ibid., p. 232.
15. Claudia Brodsky Lacour, *Lines of Thought: Discourse, Architectonics, and the Origin of Modern Philosophy* (Durham: Duke University Press, 1996), p. 70.
16. Chattopadhyay, p. 33.
17. Ibid., p. 33, emphasis in original.

9

Profane Illuminations, Delicate and Mysterious Flames: Mass Culture and Uncanny Gnosis

Michael Saler

I The uncanny and modern gnosis

Those early twentieth-century thinkers who believed that modernity was 'disenchanted' were unlikely to perceive the uncanny as a source of genuine knowledge, but rather as an immature affect that needed to be explained away. It is possible to discern this sentiment in Max Weber, for example. Weber did not discuss the uncanny specifically, but he alluded to something comparable in a revealing aside in *The Protestant Ethic and the Spirit of Capitalism* (1905). Deriding the 'fashionable' idea that specialists ought to be 'degraded to a position subordinate to that of a seer', he sneers in response, 'He who yearns for seeing should go to the cinema.'[1] For Weber, rationalized science yields not only scientific specialists, but also the disenchantment of the world; both 'seers' and the cinema belong to the marginal and irrational sphere of mass culture. Thus the 'uncanny', associated with the mysterious powers of the seer, is implicitly dismissed as a relic of the premodern, enchanted world.

Many of Weber's contemporaries also thought that positivism and materialism had disenchanted the world.[2] They would have agreed with his assertion that 'principally there are no mysterious incalculable forces that come into play, but rather that one can, in principle, master all things by calculation'.[3] Sigmund Freud was one such figure. His famous discussion of 'The Uncanny' (1919) attempted to exorcise the frightening, indeterminate nature of this experience by reducing it to the 'production of that infantile morbid anxiety from which the majority of human beings have never become quite free'.[4] But would they ever become free of the uncanny? One suspects that Freud believed this was possible, at least – *pace* Weber – 'in principle'. After all, the disenchanting practice of psychoanalysis had demonstrated that the lived experience of the uncanny was neither extraordinary nor marvelous: 'for this uncanny is in reality nothing new or foreign, but something familiar and old-established in the mind that has been estranged only by the process of repression'.[5] Freud acknowledged that his psychoanalytic definition might not encompass all manifestations of the uncanny, but the exceptions tended to be those 'taken from the realm of fiction' rather than those experienced directly.[6] In terms of everyday life, the uncanny could be 'surmounted' if it was due to residual animistic beliefs; if it were due to more intractable infantile complexes, one could at least be reassured that this manifestation was 'not of very frequent occurrence in real life'.[7]

Indeed, for many early twentieth-century intellectuals, the uncanny only thrived in the delimited space of fiction, that sphere of the aesthetic 'irrational' that Weber had distinguished from the disenchanted realm of rational procedures and bureaucratic administration. Freud and Weber acknowledged that the irrational remained a potent force to contend with, but 'in principle' the uncanny could be explained away by reason. The uncanny was no more a source of positive knowledge than was mass culture; neither seers nor the cinema would produce insights about the nature of reality.

But the sorts of experiences that Freud classified as 'uncanny' were precisely those that were cultivated by a number of thinkers in the twentieth century as a source of knowledge, different from but compatible to reason. Even those who may not have read Freud's essay were attracted by the same incidents he described: the confusion between the animate and the inanimate, the appearance of mysterious doubles, and the marvelous yet frightening collocation of circumstances that seemed to transcend coincidence. These thinkers believed that such occurrences yielded important knowledge about reality beyond the purview of positivism, which Freud himself adhered to. For them the quotidian was uncanny, if perceived correctly; they did not believe that the domain of the uncanny was primarily that of fiction. They wanted to identify and perpetuate the uncanny in the everyday, to savor and reflect upon the indeterminacies it elicited, rather than explain it away.

Thus, while Freud's account of the uncanny has been enormously influential, it does not do justice to the diverse ways the concept has been used in the past century. The surrealists, for example, used experiences similar to those Freud discussed to undermine the positivistic pretensions of psychoanalytic theory itself. (André Breton acknowledged his debt to Freud's pioneering explorations of the unconscious, but nevertheless dismissed his reductive explanations: 'we reject the greater part of Freud's philosophy as *metaphysics*.')[8] For them, the uncanny was consonant with the findings of the 'new physics' that challenged the mechanistic foundations of nineteenth-century science. As Breton wrote in 1937,

> I have endeavored to show how the *open rationalism* which defines the present position of scholars (as a sequel to the conception of non-Euclidean and subsequently a generalized geometry. Non-Newtonian mechanics, non-Maxwellian physics, etc.) cannot fail to correspond with *open realism* or *surrealism* which involves the ruin of the Cartesian-Kantian edifice.[9]

Quantum theory was positively uncanny to Breton: it revealed that the fundamental constituents of matter could be indeterminate and that bizarre coincidences might in fact be meaningful 'actions at a distance'. As he wrote in 1935, 'I regard the consideration of current scientific developments to be more worthwhile than that of the psychological movement, which always lags behind the former. Of all sciences, modern physics seems particularly to require our attention.'[10]

While the uncanny is often linked reflexively with Freud, the surrealists and others in effect decoupled this link. They presented the uncanny as a legitimate source of knowledge compatible with, yet distinct from, Western rationality, rather than as an expression of repressed desires and atavistic attitudes. The knowledge engendered by the uncanny was often more intuitive than logical, more felt than deduced, more indeterminate than defined. Salvador Dalí, for example, attempted to codify his technique of evoking uncanny perceptions – the 'paranoiac-critical method' – as 'a spontaneous method of *irrational knowledge* based on the critical and systematic objectification of delirious associations and interpretations'.[11] Uncanny experiences can be empirically observable, but also logically ineffable; the uncanny can be understood as a modern gnosis that expands one's apprehension of reality, and undermines rigid schemas, Weber's 'iron cage' of rationality.

This essay will explore the uncanny as modern gnosis by examining selected writings of the French surrealist André Breton, the American science fiction writer Philip K. Dick, and the Italian semiotician and novelist Umberto Eco. While the knowledge revealed by the uncanny is by its very nature uncertain, for these authors it does clarify certain issues. For Breton and many of the surrealists, the uncanny reveals that the modern world is not disenchanted and deterministic, but rather replete with marvels that incite wonder. For Dick and Eco, as well as

Breton, uncanny experiences also challenge consensual reality and suggest that other possibilities are accessible to reasoned reflection. For all three, the uncanny is complementary to rationality, rather than a negation of it.

There is another important way that the uncanny accords with modernity, and thus deserves to be seen as modern gnosis: in its direct association with mass culture. All three authors frequently locate the uncanny within mass culture, echoing Weber's conflation of 'seers' with the 'cinema'. But just as they converted Freud's irrational uncanny into a source of legitimate knowledge, they inverted Weber's dismissive attitude toward mass culture: as a central locus of uncanny experiences, mass culture was neither trivial nor banal, but important and even profound.

These thinkers turned to mass culture as a principle source of the uncanny for three reasons. The first was simply practical and pragmatic. Mass culture (broadly defined to include mass-produced commodities) was a constituent part of modernity for many in the West by the early twentieth century; reality was mediated through its numerous manifestations. If the uncanny was to be revelatory about modernity, it would have to take into account this pervasive aspect of everyday life, one ignored or belittled by most contemporary intellectuals. The second reason followed from this: for many, the pleasures of childhood were intimately tied to the pleasures of mass culture, and it was the formative experiences of childhood – intense, strange, frightening, marvelous – that uncanny sensations often evoked, and that partisans of the uncanny wished to restore to a 'disenchanted' modernity. Mass culture could inform adulthood no less than childhood, rendering the world ever strange and new. Finally, thinkers located the uncanny in mass culture because to do so was itself a performative act that rendered mass culture uncanny. By deliberately seeking revelations ('profane illuminations', in Walter Benjamin's words, 'Mysterious Flames' in Umberto Eco's) within a sphere of culture widely derided as banal, they situated it between incompatible registers – inert yet vital, trite yet profound, homogeneous yet complex, profane yet spiritual. These were the disturbingly indeterminate conditions that Freud attributed to the uncanny. Commodities, therefore, need not be alienating, as Karl Marx had maintained; once defined as uncanny, objects lost their reified status and became fluid. For Breton, Dick, and Eco, commodities seen as uncanny had the potential to alienate us from our alienation and suggest new worlds to inhabit: the peculiar gnosis derived from the *unheimlich* would disclose the *heimlich*.

In their cultural pessimism, Weber and Freud represent a well-known trajectory of modern thought that attempted to marginalize both the uncanny and mass culture. The three thinkers to whom we now turn are representative of an alternate tradition that found in some people's 'trash' the treasure of modern gnosis.

II Uncanny gnosis and modern re-enchantment: André Breton

As Hal Foster has noted, the French surrealists of the interwar period delighted in many of the experiences that Freud defined as uncanny, although they may not have been familiar with his eponymous essay until at least the early 1930s.[12] Whereas Freud tried to explain away the uncanny through reasoned analysis, Breton sought to perpetuate its estranging effects as a form of knowledge. As he wrote in the first 'Manifesto of Surrealism' (1924), 'Fear, the attraction of the unusual, chance, the taste for things extravagant are all devices which we call upon without fear of deception.'[13] Breton argued that these impulses sprang from the imagination, or the unconscious – he used the terms interchangeably – and that they expressed the 'marvelous', which can be thought of as his equivalent of the 'uncanny'.

He and his fellow surrealists developed techniques in the interwar period to bypass reason and access the marvels of the unconscious directly. Automatic writing, trance states, and unforeseen encounters with people, situations, and 'found objects' that catalyzed unconscious desires ('objective chance') – all were used toward expanding the mind's awareness of reality. Breton maintained that Western knowledge of its fundaments had been artificially circumscribed by the 'Greco-Roman' tradition of logic and nineteenth-century positivism. Surrealism would restore access to the foundational realities of desire, love, and beauty, forces that included and transcended the individual ego and its limited rational perceptions. 'The imagination is perhaps on the point ... of reasserting itself', he wrote in 1924, and reaffirmed in 1935 that 'it is positivist rationalism that we continue to oppose'.[14]

For Breton, the knowledge that surrealism found through its evocation of uncanny experiences was ineffable in terms of traditional logic, yet nonetheless comprehensible as a totality. On the one hand, the ontology exposed by surrealism seemed radically 'other' and apparently without limits: according to the first Manifesto, 'The mind becomes aware of the limitless expanses wherein its desires are made manifest', and 'Existence is elsewhere.'[15] On the other hand, Breton also claimed that surrealism exposed an underlying unity to existence that effaced all false antinomies. In 'The Second Manifesto of Surrealism' (1930), he stated that surrealism sought the point at which apparent oppositions met and were resolved into a totality.[16] Once the artificial boundaries between the 'subjective' and the 'objective' were dissolved, Breton claimed, humanity would be made whole again; the '*one original faculty*, of which ... one still finds a trace among primitives and children' would be restored.[17]

Breton's idealist and romantic presuppositions are apparent in these considerations. He could conceive of the uncanny as yielding a form of knowledge because he believed that there was a metaphysical order waiting to be recovered, one that accorded with unconscious desires. He acknowledged that unleashing the primordial energies of the unconscious from rational control could be frightening; it might even lead to madness if not tempered by 'minimal common sense'.[18] But throughout his lifetime Breton had an unwavering faith that the underlying motive force of the unconscious was love, its material expressions that of 'convulsive beauty'.

Breton's rejection of conventional logic and positivism, and his turn to uncanny experiences as gnosis, did not constitute an anti-modern stance. Uncanny knowledge could be reconciled with the rational, secular, and even commercial tenets of modernity. The surrealist explorations into the unsettling experiences of dreams, psychic automatism, and objective chance were complementary to reason, he claimed, refuting charges from both the public and the French Communist Party that surrealism was irrational if not mystical.[19] Both before and after his attempted *rapprochement* with the communists, Breton made substantial room for reason even as he criticized the reductive spirit of positivism. As early as the 1924 Manifesto he wrote, 'If the depths of our mind contain within it strange forces capable of augmenting those on the surface ... there is every reason to seize them – first to seize them, then, if need be, to submit them to the control of our reason.'[20] And in 1936, he continued to embrace a degree of instrumental rationality, provided that it was used as a tool rather than adopted as an epistemology: 'Predetermination of the end to be attained, if this end is the order of knowledge, and the rational adaptation of means towards this end, are enough to defend surrealism against all charges of mysticism.'[21] While it is easy to assume that Breton repudiated modern science and reason, this is belied by many of his writings and activities: from the creation of the 'Bureau of Surrealist Research' in 1924, to the fact that his magazine *La Révolution surréaliste* was modeled on the popular science journal *La Nature*, to his expressed desire to 'give *Nadja* an atmosphere as dispassionate and clinically objective as one of Freud's case studies', to his characterization of the surrealists as 'chemists and as technicians' rather than as 'literary men and artists'.[22] As his biographer noted, 'For Breton, any revolution to be waged must first pass through the intellect; despite his opposition to Western logic, his passion was still the passion of reason.'[23]

Everyday life, especially as found within mass culture and the hidden byways of urban life, was another facet of modernity embraced by Breton, who identified the quotidian as a principle site of the uncanny. Whereas Freud had argued that fiction was the privileged locus of the uncanny in the modern world, the surrealists sought it in common experience and common objects: modernity itself was uncanny, if perceived in a receptive way. Those uncanny sentiments of fear, ambiguity, and wonder evoked by everyday objects or chance encounters were for Breton literal sources of illumination: 'a very delicate flame highlights or perfects life's meaning as nothing else can'.[24] Because the surrealists were committed to recovering experiences that intellectuals ignored or disdained, mass culture was a particularly fruitful site for such 'profane illuminations', as Walter Benjamin characterized them.[25] They turned to films as a form of waking dream; Breton recounted how he and his friends would go from cinema to cinema at random, not even knowing which film they were viewing, seeking illumination from the chance juxtaposition of cinematic images that flitted before them in dreamlike succession.[26] When he did single out films for their subject matter, they tended to be uncanny in orientation: horror films like *Nosferatu*, or serials about criminal heroes with seemingly supernatural powers, like *Les Vampires* and *Fantômas*.[27] A tawdry grand-guignol play involving lesbianism and child murder, poorly acted in a run-down theatre and widely condemned by critics, particularly excited Breton by its uncanny ambiguities. He found it haunted his dreams and revised his waking perceptions of life: through such forms of mass culture, 'certain powerful impressions are made to play, in no way contaminable by morality, actually experienced 'beyond good and evil' in the dream, and, subsequently, in what we quite arbitrarily oppose to the dream in the name of reality'.[28]

Breton also haunted flea markets in the hope of coming across 'found objects', everyday items that helped him objectify his unconscious desires or catalyze his inchoate ideas. These were indeterminate things, inert yet alive, the detritus of the objective world corresponding uncannily to the subjective life of individuals. In *Mad Love* (1937),

Breton recalled two alluring objects he and Alberto Giacometti chanced upon at a flea market:

> The two objects ... of whose existence we were ignorant some minutes before, and which imposed with themselves this abnormally prolonged sensorial contact, induced us to think ceaselessly about their concrete existence, offering to us certain very unexpected prolongations from their life.[29]

These found objects answered the needs of both men: Giacometti's indecision about how to proceed with a work of art was resolved by the item he found; Breton's object, a wooden spoon whose handle ended with a shoe, corresponded to an earlier desire he had of obtaining a sculpture of Cinderella's slipper. He doesn't realize this until he places the spoon in his home, when it springs to life: 'I suddenly saw it charged with all the associative and interpretive qualities which had remained inactive while I was holding it. It was clearly changing right under my eyes.'[30] The spoon becomes uncanny, changing shape in his mind's eye, and suggesting the existence of another order of reality that had both generated Breton's original desire and fulfilled it through this chance encounter:

> The wood, which had seemed intractable, took on the transparency of glass. From then on the slipper, with the shoe heel multiplying, started to look vaguely as if it were moving about alone ... Then it became clear that the object I had so much wanted to contemplate before, had been constructed outside of me, very different, *very far beyond* what I could have imagined ...[31]

Thus for Breton commodities, and mass culture as a whole, had the potential to be uncanny and therefore revelatory of another order of being. Indeed, this was precisely the lesson Walter Benjamin took from the surrealists when he embarked on his history of modernity, 'The Arcades Project', with its focus on the vital utopian longings that lay dormant, waiting to be awakened, in nineteenth-century commodities.[32] Benjamin, like Breton, was often critical of consumerism, but both strove to find meaning and enchantment within modernity.[33] But Breton, perhaps more than Benjamin, was specifically concerned with those experiences Freud labeled 'uncanny', finding in their mass cultural carriers a gnosis that in many respects was compatible with the rational and commercial tenets of modernity.

III 'A Flurry of Breath in the Weeds in the Back Alley': Philip K. Dick

The American science fiction writer Philip K. Dick (1928–82) wrote about uncanny experiences in many of his works, focusing obsessively on the themes of 'what is reality?' and 'what is human?'[34] His novels center on the ambiguous boundaries between machines and humans (*Do Androids Dream of Electric Sheep?*), doppelgangers (*A Scanner Darkly*), life and death (*Ubik*), and in nearly every case, a consensual reality that becomes undone, the *heimlich* become *unheimlich*. Dick described his central theme in a 1970 letter:

> I set up my character; I set up his world; then I begin to have him lose his world as he knows it, finding himself at last in an alien world, which has replaced the former one (not 'real' one but decidedly former). Each novel of this sort that I do describes a trip by someone going from familiar territory into what in German is called *fremd* – uncanny, strange.[35]

The destabilizing effects of the uncanny are put to use in his novels as a form of knowledge: reality is not how his characters initially perceive it to be, but is radically other, ever strange. Although his work was published as fiction, Dick did not think of the uncanny experiences he limned as imaginary, but rather as integral to the modern condition, calling us to account at every moment. To be at home in the world is to be complacently ignorant about one's true condition; to be not-at-home is to be on the royal road to legitimate knowledge. Looking back on his work, Dick – like Breton – thought of it as revealing an ontology that only uncanny experiences could elicit: 'I am a fictionalizing philosopher, not a novelist ... The core of my writing is not art but *truth*.' The readers he appeals to 'cannot or will not blunt *their* own intimations about the irrational, mysterious nature of reality, & for them, my corpus of writing is one long ratiocination regarding this inexplicable reality'.[36]

As if to certify that he was not writing fiction, Dick underwent a series of mysterious revelations in the months of February and March, 1974, that undermined everything he took to be real. He spent the rest of his life puzzling out these disturbing events – visual and auditory hallucinations, seeming coincidences that were fraught with meaning – filling over 8000 pages of a journal he called *Exegesis*. The uncanny instability between reality and fiction he had portrayed in his works became his lived experience; as an entry from 1978 relates, 'My God – my life – which is to say my 2-74/3-74 experience – is exactly like the plot of any one of ten of my novels or stories. Even down to the fake memories & identity. I'm a protagonist from one of PKD's books.'[37] At times he felt he had The Answer, one that involved (among other things) his being the reincarnation of a Christian from the first century AD, the subject of a Manichean cosmic struggle between an evil demiurge and a loving deity who attempts to reveal the true nature of reality through Dick and his works. At other times, he felt he might simply be deluded, and a healthy skepticism occasionally appears among his entries. At one point he claims that he shares with the readers of his fiction a 'mutual realization that no answer of this mysterious reality is forthcoming'.[38]

Two points remain constant in Dick's work before and after his '2-3-74' epiphanies, linking him to Breton's understanding of both the function and location of the uncanny in the modern world. The first is Dick's belief that the uncanny is a legitimate form of gnosis, one often ineffable in terms of conventional logic but nevertheless compatible with rationality. Dick, after all, was a science fiction writer, and his works, like those of Breton, express ambivalence about science rather than a repudiation of it. He had no sympathy with the occult or other forms of pseudo-science; his fondness for imaginative theories was tempered by strict analysis.[39] The second has to do with the sources of uncanny gnosis: Dick, like Breton, found it in the quotidian world, that of mass culture and everyday life – the 'trash' ignored or despised by the elite. 'I do seem attracted to trash, as if the clue – the clue lies there', Dick wrote in *Exegesis*; 'you wind up encountering ultimate deity cooking & riding pop tunes on the radio & popular novels, & a breath of wind in the weeds in the alley'.[40]

Dick's preoccupation with uncanny incidents began at an early age. His sister Jane, a fraternal twin, died within weeks of being born, and her absence – his lost 'Other' – haunted him throughout his life. His biographer traces the roots of Dick's preoccupations with dualities and alternative realities to this early trauma.[41] His own mental instability – frequent periods of depression and paranoia, deep-set insecurities and repeated recourse to drugs – contributed to his awareness of the instability of human perceptions. His wide-ranging curiosity about metaphysics, philosophy, religion, science, and literature, together with a powerful imagination, predisposed him to entertain unconventional theories; he tended to equate orthodoxies with authoritarianism. And then there were the visions. Even before his epiphanies of 1974 he was troubled by uncanny experiences, notably in 1963, when he witnessed briefly a malevolent visage floating in the sky (the inspiration for *The Three Stigmata of Palmer Eldritch*, 1965). Perhaps, he thought, he had seen the evil demiurge, described by Gnostic writers, who had created an illusory world obscuring the genuine creation of a loving God. And perhaps not: Dick could swing from credulous enthusiasm to skepticism and self-mockery; *Palmer Eldritch*, like so many of his novels, is a black comedy.

In Dick's fictional worlds, the uncanny is frequently associated with everyday items, especially those from the mass culture of his youth. In *Now Wait For Last Year* (1966), the 130-year-old Virgil Ackerman has recreated on Mars the Washington neighborhood of his youth, right down to local movie theaters, Big Little Books, and a robot simulacrum of Steve, the janitor he had known in 1935. Another character finds this recreation of Steve uncanny: 'God, to think that the actual man's been dead a century ... I don't like it. I like things to appear what they really are.' Another character disagrees, noting that people don't object to recorded music, which itself is an illusion of something actual: 'We live with illusion daily, he reflected.'[42] The uncanny is a constituent aspect of modernity, in which reality and illusion are frequently indistinguishable.

Dick also shows that while obvious illusions – like Steve the robot – can generate uncanny sensations, that which we assume to be real can also become uncanny, revealing its illusory aspects. In many of his novels, mass cultural artifacts, seemingly unremarkable, become uncanny for his protagonists, suggesting that reality is radically different from the way it appears. In *Time Out of Joint* (1959), the apparently stable world of 1950s suburbia literally falls apart around Ragle Gumm: everyday objects disappear, to be replaced by tiny pieces of paper describing what they were: Soft Drink Stand, Gas Station, Bowl of Flowers. Magazines have pictures of actresses that never existed in his world, like someone named Marilyn Monroe. These are among the clues that lead Ragle to discover that the world he has taken for real is counterfeit; it is a simulacrum from his childhood designed by the government to make him think he is living securely in the 1950s, whereas he is living decades later in the midst of a nuclear war. In *Ubik* (1969), messages about the deceptive nature of reality come to the protagonist through advertisements on television sets and matchbook covers.

Mass culture had positive connotations for Dick: he never relinquished his love of the radio premiums, pulp magazines, and fantastic novels of his youth. He thanked the author of a book on nostalgia for bringing back memories of his own Little Orphan Annie Decoder Ring: 'How well you brought back to me those days, their spirit, how deeply some of it touched me – pierced me through the heart, in fact.'[43] He invested in a nine-hundred pound safe to protect the pulp magazine collection he had started in adolescence, for 'after my wife and daughter these mean more than anything else I own – or hope to own'.[44]

But there was more to his use of contemporary mass culture in futuristic novels than nostalgia. Dick, like Breton and Benjamin, turned to mass culture for knowledge about modernity because it was a prime constituent of modernity. Writing to the Polish author Stanislaw Lem, who had noted the persistence of mass cultural references in his work, Dick observed:

> ... there is no culture here in California, only trash. And we who grew up here and live here and write here have nothing else to include as elements in our work. How can one create novels based on this reality which do not contain trash, because the alternative is to go into dreadful fantasies of what it ought to be like ... This is a world of hamburger stands and Disneyland and freeways and gas stations ... it's like living in an endless TV commercial ... Hence the elements of such books of mine as UBIK. If God manifested Himself to use [sic] here He would do so in the form of a spraycan advertised on TV.[45]

Like Breton, Dick also turned to mass culture for knowledge because by doing so he transformed it from the 'trivial' to the uncanny, from something banal to something ambiguous and thus potentially revelatory. In some ways he identified with mass culture: he was sensitive to the divide between 'high' and 'low' cultures fostered by many intellectuals during his lifetime, because he felt that he fell on the wrong side of the divide. Dick lacked a college degree, and his own attempts to write 'serious', modernistic fiction failed. And while he was quite successful at placing his science fiction with genre publishers, he had difficulty getting these works reviewed by mainstream critics. To add injury to insult, the paltry sums most science fiction publishers paid meant that he was frequently in debt as well as ignored. He tried to make the best of it – 'I am uncomfortable around power and money, and am happy in what we call the street' – but he knew that in the literary world, science fiction itself was usually thought of as 'trash', devoid of serious insights.[46] Dick, like Breton, performed a transvaluation of values by insisting that mass culture was not superficial or escapist, but rather a locus of mysterious clues concerning fundamental aspects of reality. Simply making that claim destabilized the conventional view about mass culture, in effect rendering this sphere uncanny. However, Dick and Breton went farther than making mass culture more ambiguous that most assumed it was: they argued that the uncanny affects it could generate expressed the uncanny nature of modernity itself, which did not correspond to positivist and materialist descriptions.

Breton indicated that the uncanny nature of mass culture was not merely an artifact of his writings, but could be experienced in everyday life by anyone who followed surrealist techniques. One might argue that this was not true for Dick, because his novels established a clear demarcation between the uncanny experiences of their protagonists, which were set in the future, and the contemporary lives of his readers. Freud had observed that fairy tales were not uncanny because they leave the readers' world behind, and this might be said of science fiction as well, for all its claims to extrapolate from the laws of known science.[47] However, many of Dick's works were expressly about the present rather than the future, for all their futuristic trappings. He was more of a surrealist than a 'hard' science fiction writer who creates carefully crafted worlds based on scientific plausibility. In a journal entry, he acknowledged that, 'I certainly see the *randomness* in my work, & I also see how this fast shuffle of *possibility* after possibility might eventually, given enough time, juxtapose and disclose something important, automatically overlooked in more orderly thinking. Pataphysique. No wonder my stuff is popular in France – the surreal, the absurd.'[48] He intended his works to induce his readers to think about their realities in a different way, to apply the insights his characters derive from uncanny experiences to their own lives. In *The Man in the High Castle* (1962), for example, the reader is plunged into an alternate history in which the Axis powers won the Second World War. The protagonists seek out the author of a proscribed book, *The Grasshopper Lies Heavy*, which argues that the Allies actually won, and that the present reality is false. The funhouse mirror effect of this is to make the reader's reality uncanny: if in the alternate world *The Grasshopper Lies Heavy* is true, might not *The Man in the High Castle* be 'true' in this world, at least metaphorically? Popular protesters during the 1960s, of whom Dick was one, often accused America of being 'fascist' or 'totalitarian', and *The Man in the High Castle* is very much a book of its times. Many of his readers recognized this, voting it the best science fiction novel of the year.

The direct connections between Dick's fiction and contemporary reality only became more pronounced after his epiphanies in February and March, 1974, when he thought it possible that a benign deity was contacting him to reveal the Manichean nature of reality. Contemporary reality is false, his visions and dreams seemed to say, the creation of a malevolent demiurge; a benevolent divinity has prepared a genuine and bountiful reality that humans must assist in realizing. As he continued to reflect on his uncanny experiences of those months, several of which came through mass culture ('God talked to me through a Beatles tune'), he suspected that his own 'trashy' novels were the means by which this Power expressed the truth: 'my writing is *not* fiction but a form ... of revelation expressed not *by* me but through me'.[49] His novel *Ubik* had presented salvific messages encoded in mass culture; thinking about this novel in the light of his recent strange experiences, Dick determined that his *oeuvre* accomplished in reality what the novel had presented as fiction: 'I restore Gnostic Gnosis to the world in trashy form, like in UBIK.'[50]

Like some of the characters in his novels, Dick admitted to himself that his visions might have been a form of psychosis.[51] They remained uncanny for him: incapable of being explained completely, challenging the Western divisions between appearance and reality, reason and the imagination, fiction and truth, high and low culture. Indeed, his suspicions that he might be living one of his own novels gives his own life story an uncanny quality: factual biography becomes metafiction. Even if Dick had never taken this particular turn in his thought, his novels of the 1950s and 1960s would stand as exemplars of the uncanny nature of modernity. In them, categories become contested but not resolved, and the detritus of everyday life heralds exalted possibilities of being. In his case, 'trash' did become gnosis, the uncanny a route to knowledge.

IV Mysterious flames and practical knowledge: Umberto Eco

'Who Am I?'[52] The opening line of Breton's *Nadja* evokes the unheimlich nature of modernity, the sense that the self is not rooted or at home with itself but contains, as Walt Whitman claimed, 'multitudes': or, as Arthur Rimbaud famously celebrated, 'I is another.' Philip K. Dick's works also addresses similar questions concerning the mysteries of selfhood and the ambiguous nature of reality. For both men the marginalized sphere of mass culture revealed potential answers: it generated uncanny sensations, which in turn suggested other realities beyond that postulated and reinforced by 'official' culture. We have seen that Walter Benjamin referred to such moments as 'profane illuminations', and this conceit is explicitly adopted by Umberto Eco in *The Mysterious Flame of Queen Loana*. The protagonist of the novel engages in a similar quest for truth about himself and his world: 'I cannot let myself go, I want to know who I am.'[53] But whereas Breton and Dick's alternate realities tend to be esoteric and at times ineffable, Eco's novel presents the alternatives to 'consensus' reality in a more straightforward manner. The uncanny knowledge that mass culture provides is consonant with modern reason. But it is never definite or finished: otherwise it could not be uncanny.

The novel concerns Yambo, a middle-aged dealer in rare books, who suffers a stroke and loses his 'episodic memory'. He is in a perpetual fog, for although he can remember 'general' knowledge shared by others, his 'personal' knowledge, which is tied to his emotions, has been lost. But Yambo can at least sense the presence of the personal knowledge that had once belonged to him, through the strange sensation it provokes. His neurologist explains, 'certain images spark something in you', and Yambo himself comes to describe this feeling as 'a mysterious flame'.[54] These experiences, combining what is strange with what is familiar, Yambo likens to the *unheimlich*: 'It is awkward, revisiting a world you have never seen before: like coming home, after a long journey, to someone else's house.'[55]

Revealingly, the items that most often trigger these 'mysterious flames' are from mass culture. Yambo returns to his childhood home in search of his lost time, and finds old comic books, adventure novels, pulp magazines, stamp albums, and other artifacts from his bookish youth (what he calls his 'paper memory'). One of his first revelations concerns the very phrase 'mysterious flame': it comes from the title of a prized comic book from his youth, 'The Mysterious Flame of Queen Loana'.[56]

As he pores over this material, he realizes that it is neither trivial nor escapist. It provides him not only with clues about his self-divided nature, but also reveals itself to be a source of counter-knowledge to the prevailing orthodoxies of Italy under Mussolini. As a child during the Second World War, Yambo had read 'Mickey Mouse Runs His Own Newspaper' at a time when the government opposed a free press.[57] He also listened to popular songs on the radio extolling the beauties of Hawaii, while contemporary newspapers celebrated the Japanese bombing of Pearl Harbor.[58] His stamp collection, with its alluring depictions of foreign lands, contradicted the provincial images the State promulgated concerning Nationalist Italy. Yambo suspects that other Italian citizens must have been experiencing everyday life as uncanny during the war, just as he had:

> I had been trying to imagine the divided self of a boy exposed to messages of national glory while at the same time daydreaming about the fogs of London, where he would encounter Fantômas battling Sandokan amid a hail of nailshot that ripped holes in the

> chests and tore off the legs of Sherlock Holmes's politely perplexed compatriots – and now here I was learning that in those same years the radio had been proposing as an ideal the life of a humble accountant who longed for nothing more than suburban tranquility.[59]

Uncanny, strange, ambiguous: but not without determinate meanings, genuine knowledge, either. Yambo believes that the mass culture he was exposed to provided an alternative morality to the 'consensus reality' of fascist Italy: 'Clearly I was encountering heroes in those ungrammatical [comic books] who differed from the ones put forward by the official culture, and perhaps in those garish (yet so mesmerizing!) cartoons I had been initiated into a different vision of Good and Evil.'[60] He concludes that it was these comic books, with their multicultural settings and individualistic heroes – Mickey with his free press – that inoculated him from fascist rhetoric and enabled him to construct 'a social conscience'.[61]

Through Yambo's profane illuminations, Eco illustrates the ways in which mass culture recasts consensual reality as strange, and indicates other possibilities of being. Yambo's 'mysterious flames', unlike those related by Breton and Dick, have a prosaic, common-sense character to them: readers who have not encountered spoons transforming into slippers, or Beatles' lyrics morphing into providential commandments, can conceivably relate to the utopian aspirations and antinomian attitudes Yambo locates in the mass culture of his childhood. (Ernst Bloch found similar expressions in those forms of popular and mass culture he labeled as 'colportage'.)[62] But the uncanny, like wonder, disappears once it is clearly defined. Breton and Dick found that mass culture opened the world to possibilities hitherto unforeseen, but they also found these to be largely indeterminate: the gnosis generated by mass culture remained Other. It would appear that once Yambo recovered his memories through his re-exposure to the detritus of his youth, the mysterious flames would expire, and his world would cease to be uncanny.

Eco anticipated this, for at the moment when Yambo has pieced together many of the forgotten shards of his past and seems to be moving out of his stroke-induced fog, he has another stroke. This event restores all his memories but one: the face of the girl he learned he had loved as an adolescent, and who had haunted his life ever since. The second stroke is more severe than the first, it would appear, for Yambo now finds himself existing within a perpetual present, in which all his memories swirl around him in no chronological sequence; he is cut off entirely from the real world. He who had sought 'my truest, most hidden memories' is now condemned to exist with them in solipsistic isolation.[63] Characters real and fictional – including the figures from his comics and novels, as well as advertising icons and movie stars – swirl around him in a chaos of unlimited possibility.[64] He takes advantage of this semiotic anarchy by appealing to 'Queen Loana' for a vision of his lost love, which will at least provide his existence with significance and closure: 'I will see what I have looked for all my life ... and I will be reunited. I will be at peace.'[65] We have seen that Breton and Dick had similar desires for a transcendent unity, and made similar invocations to mass culture to provide them with such gnosis.

Eco pulls out all the stops at this point, parodying Dante's vision of Beatrice at the conclusion of the *Paradiso*. Yambo is nearly overwhelmed by the heavenly choir of figures from mass culture who parade before him. Flash Gordon, The Dragon Lady, Mandrake the Magician, and many others prepare a staircase to Paradise (accompanied by Tin Pan Alley tunes: 'I'll build a stair to Paradise ...'), and Yambo anticipates seeing his lost love, 'lovely as a rose', at its pinnacle.[66] But at the last moment, the fog returns; all becomes dark; no final, beatific vision is forthcoming, and the novel ends abruptly with the uncanny gestures of mass culture toward the inexpressible.

* * *

Within modernity, the uncanny can be conceived as a disturbing sensation that has the potential to expose overlooked or unimagined possibilities about the nature of existence. It does not simply reflect atavistic impulses, as Freud maintained. The knowledge the uncanny provides is complementary to that of modern rationality, suggesting potentials that positivism could not postulate. Mass culture is an apt vessel for such uncanny gnosis, an ambiguous arena at once trivial and profound, inert and alive, material and spiritual. Even Freud perceived the uncanny nature of everyday objects, although his insights concerned the 'mass culture' of the classical period. He was an ardent collector of the detritus of the ancient world: by 1939 he had amassed over 3000 statuettes, scarabs, and rings, which he kept in constant view in his office. In 1939, terminally ill and fearful of the Nazis, he left Austria for London, taking his beloved objects with him. But he knew his collecting days were over, and that both he and his objects were expiring. As he wrote to a friend, 'There is just one thing: a collection to which there are no new additions is really dead.'[67]

Thus, until 1939, his collection has been 'alive' – but in what senses? Freud would undoubtedly have responded in psychoanalytic terms. But with the examples of Breton, Dick, and Eco in mind, he can no longer have the last word.

Notes

1. Max Weber, *The Protestant Ethic and the Spirit of Capitalism*, Talcott Parsons, trans. (New York; Scribner, 1958), p. 29.
2. Weber's own position on positivism was ambiguous. In his distinction between fact and value, he rejected positivism as ontology, but in his own works he employed a positivist methodology and often emphasized the importance of scientific causation. See George E. McCarthy, *Objectivity and the Silence of Reason: Weber, Habermas, and the Methodological Disputes in German Sociology* (New Brunswick, New Jersey; London: Transaction Publishers, 2001).
3. Max Weber, 'Science as a Vocation', in H. H. Gerth and C. Wright Mills, ed., *From Max Weber: Essays in Sociology* (New York, Oxford: Oxford University Press, 1946), p. 139.
4. Sigmund Freud, 'The Uncanny', in *Studies in Parapsychology* (New York: Collier Books, 1963), p. 66.
5. Ibid., p. 47.
6. Ibid., p. 53.
7. Ibid., p. 55.
8. André Breton, *What is Surrealism? Selected Writings*, Franklin Rosemont, ed., (New York: Pluto Press, 1978), p. 147.
9. Ibid., p. 153.
10. Ibid., p. 147.
11. Mark Polizzotti, *Revolution of the Mind: The Life of André Breton* (New York: Farrar, Straus & Giroux, 1995), p. 353.
12. According to Hal Foster, there are no references to Freud's writings on the uncanny in surrealism before 1929, and 'The Uncanny' itself was not translated into French until 1933. Hal Foster, *Compulsive Beauty* (Cambridge, MA; London: MIT Press, 1993), pp. xviii, 13.
13. André Breton, *Manifestoes of Surrealism*, Richard Seaver and Helen R. Lane, trans. (Ann Arbor: The University of Michigan Press, 1972), p. 16.
14. Ibid., pp. 10, 237.
15. Ibid., pp. 37, 47.
16. As he famously stated in the 'Second Manifesto of Surrealism': 'Everything tends to make us believe that there exists a certain point of the mind at which life and death, the real and the imagined, past and future, the communicable and the incommunicable, high and low, cease to be perceived as contradictions. Now, search as one may one will never find any other motivating force in the activities of the Surrealists than the hope of fixing this point' (Breton, *Manifestoes of Surrealism*, pp. 123–4). In 1934, he commended Louis Aragon's characterization of 1924: 'there are other relations besides reality, which the mind is capable of grasping and which also are primary, like chance, illusion, the fantastic, the dream. These various groups

are united and brought into harmony in one single order, surreality' (Breton, *What is Surrealism?*, p. 126).

17. Breton, *What is Surrealism?*, p. 109.
18. André Breton, *Nadja*, Richard Howard, trans. (New York: Grove Press; Evergreen Books: London, 1960), p. 143.
19. In 1934, he went so far as to distinguish the early, 'intuitive epoch' of surrealism from its succeeding 'reasoning epoch'. Breton, *What is Surrealism?*, p. 116.
20. Breton, *Manifestoes of Surrealism*, p. 10.
21. Breton, *What is Surrealism?*, p. 149.
22. Polizzotti, pp. 226, 281; Breton, *What is Surrealism?*, p. 139. Unlike many of his fellow surrealists, Breton had had a scientific rather than classical training.
23. Polizzotti, p. 235.
24. André Breton, *Mad Love*, trans. Mary Ann Caws (Lincoln: University of Nebraska Press, 1987), p. 25.
25. Walter Benjamin, 'Surrealism: The Last Snapshot of the European Intelligentsia', in *Walter Benjamin: Selected Writings, Volume 2 1927–1934*, Michael W. Jennings, ed. (Cambridge, MA; London: Belknap Press, 1999), p. 209.
26. Breton, *Nadja*, p. 37.
27. Polizzotti, p. 68; Robin Walz, *Pulp Surrealism: Insolent Popular Culture in Twentieth Century Paris* (Berkeley; London: University of California Press, 2000).
28. Breton, *Nadja*, p. 51.
29. Breton, *Mad Love*, p. 30.
30. Ibid., p. 33.
31. Ibid., p. 34.
32. Susan Buck-Morss, *The Dialectics of Seeing: Walter Benjamin and the Arcades Project* (Cambridge, MA; London: MIT Press, 1991).
33. For Breton's participation in a 1965 exhibition attacking consumerism, see Polizzotti, p. 616.
34. Lawrence Sutin, *Divine Invasions: A Life of Philip K. Dick* (New York, 1991), p. 3.
35. Philip K. Dick, *The Selected Letters of Philip K. Dick 1938–1971* (California: Underwood Books Inc, 1996), p. 269.
36. Philip K. Dick, *In Pursuit of Valis: Selections from the Exegesis*, Lawrence Sutin, ed. (California: Underwood Books Inc, 1991), p. 161.
37. Ibid., pp. 175–6.
38. Ibid., p. 161.
39. Sutin, p. 150.
40. Ibid., pp. 146, 160.
41. Ibid., p. 12.
42. Philip K. Dick, *Now Wait for Last Year* (New York: DAW, 1981), p. 29.
43. Philip K. Dick, *The Selected Letters of Philip K. Dick, 1972–1973* (California: Underwood Books Inc, 1993), p. 353.
44. Sutin, p. 35.
45. Dick, *Selected Letters, 1972–1973*, p. 298.
46. Sutin, p. 78.
47. Freud, pp. 56–7.
48. Dick, *Exegesis*, p. 147.
49. Ibid., p. 135.

50. Ibid., p. 79.
51. Ibid., p. 38.
52. Breton, *Nadja*, p. 11.
53. Umberto Eco, *The Mysterious Flame of Queen Loana* (Orlando, FL: Harcourt Brace & Company, 2006), p. 419.
54. Ibid., pp. 24, 67.
55. Ibid., p. 245.
56. Ibid., p. 253.
57. Ibid., p. 241.
58. Ibid., p. 203.
59. Ibid., p. 170.
60. Ibid., p. 240.
61. Ibid., p. 242.
62. Ernst Bloch, *The Principle of Hope, Volume One*, trans. Neville Plaice, Stephen Plaice, and Paul Knight (Cambridge, MA: MIT Press, 1995), pp. 352–69.
63. Eco, p. 154.
64. Another novel that effectively uses advertising icons for uncanny effects is Haruki Murakami, *Kafka on the Shore* (New York: Alfred A. Knopf, 2005).
65. Eco, p. 448.
66. Ibid., pp. 435, 444.
67. John Forrester, '"Mille e tre": Freud and Collecting', in *The Cultures of Collecting*, John Elsner and Roger Cardinal, ed. (Cambridge, MA: Harvard University Press, 1994), p. 227.

10
Terrorism and the Uncanny, or, The Caves of Tora Bora

David Punter

To address the notions of terrorism and the uncanny requires a thinking in terms of the unfamiliar, or more specifically of that which brings the unfamiliar into the heartland (or, as we might now refer to it in the era of 'homeland security', the homeland) of the family. We might be familiar with the headline 'Terrorists are also family men'; perhaps less so with the equally thinkable proposal, 'Family men are also terrorists' – or, indeed, and more contentiously, 'Men are also family terrorists'. Yet what might be uncanny in terrorism already appears here in one form: that a 'terrorist' is not always or only simply a 'terrorist', he or she is other things as well, not assimilable to a simple, single, quasi-eternal category. Yet in order to cope with terror, we need to reduce the phenomena to a single line: we cannot have 'terrorism and', or 'terrorism because', we have the need to isolate the moment of the terrorist, the 'day of the jackal'.

We might consider the issue of terrorists in literary history; one who springs most rapidly and vividly to mind is the character in Conrad's *The Secret Agent* (1907) known only as the Professor. Within a group, or cell, of terrorists, the Professor stands out as the most single-minded, the most extreme, a lone nihilist amid the comparative harmlessness of the idealist anarchism of his companions. The question raised, troubled, but not settled by Conrad is: is this a pathology, in any intelligible sense of that word, or does it bring us to the brink of a different realm, a dark, cold realm (even if it can also be rendered as in some ways laughable) where pathology's writ does not run? The Professor is an early avatar of the suicide bomber: he goes everywhere in the darkened spaces of the city with explosives strapped to his body. But what is even more distinctive about the Professor, if such a thing can be, is that he has no 'cause', in either of the more obvious senses of the word: no clear motive and no obvious origin. He is, so Conrad claims, a natural 'force',[1] a necessary efflorescence of the inhumanity of the city, a figuration constructed from alienation; but as such he is also, presumably, an aspect of a wider malaise, a part object with which the reader can curiously empathise even while attempting to put him at the farthest reach from the lightened world of reason and order.

In encountering the Professor, therefore, we as readers make a simultaneous gesture of the *heimlich* and the *unheimlich*: we exile him while welcoming him, which is indeed, among other things, the fate of the immigrant, which is clearly something Conrad obscurely – through his use of his names (Verloc is perhaps the oddest and most emblematic), through his strange but multiple geographical scenarios – attempts to embody in *The Secret Agent*. In encountering the terrorist, we are taken to the limit of understanding, to the end of inscription: nothing but death is written on this body, and death is not interpretable, it is the liminal case which simultaneously forbids all thought of the threshold. In the fate of the immigrant, we see the limitations of understanding, or of being understood; the inescapability of stereotyping and prejudice; the impossibility of ever being fully 'at home'. And thus the fates of the terrorist and of the immigrant are already, in an uncanny way, indissolubly entwined.

But in general the description of the terrorist is also, in a sense, the description of something which all of us imagine we shall come to know, the body at the end of its tether, the body about to be fearfully liberated into a different, unimaginable realm, the possibility of an inconceivable freedom around which the ghosts of martyrdom and posterity hover in as yet undecidable shapes. 'Terror', we may need to be reminded, is an ancient term, with an ancient history: its very recital serves to reincarnate unassimilable states of being, being-at-the-brink, being towards non-being, being-understood as an always ungraspable gesture towards the limits of the human.

Is the terrorist human, one question might go? Psychoanalysis – or some of its variants – say that we might consider the essence of the human to be perversion, in the sense that perversion continuingly tests the limits, and thus forms and patrols the shape of what being human might mean;[2] it frames and gives shape and urgency to the soggy liberal morass of conventional opinion. It is worth wondering whether the same might be true of terror: without terror, as Aristotle implies, how would we begin the process of soul-forming, how would we know what is 'appropriate' to the human, how would we know what is forbidden? Or, perhaps better: how would we find a tremulous language in which to express these limits, a primitive torch to shine out into the darkness where otherwise there would just be the eyes of the wolves, seeking their endless reflection in our own?

Terror, let us then say, is in part 'reflection': it is reflection, in the sense of mirroring, in its purest form because it is also reflection, in the sense of thought, taken to its utmost extreme – where all thought appears to have failed and only 'direct action', whatever that might mean (and it can have many different meanings), appears to suffice. And so an accounting for, a way of coming to accounts with, the human will also mean a raising or settling of accounts with terror, in an uncanny doubling – it would be convenient to claim, or pretend, that each terrorist is *sui generis*; instead, we might suggest, they enact a tedious repetitiveness, an endlessly recurring mark of the limitations of human violence, of human folly. A gun is, in one sense, always the same gun, a bomb always the same bomb; its work is always the same, the images of destruction always reduce human differentiation to an identical chaos of mangled corpses, torched shops, scraps of flesh and clothing and, at the end of it, a crying child.

This is so whether, of course, the terrorism is performed by the individual or by the State; and clearly there can be no consideration of one kind of terrorism without the other. It is not a question of the figures, of the numeration of the dead in Rwanda, in Darfur, in Palestine: it is a question of what is permitted, what is taken on as allowable within the supposed confines of law and order. Let us consider a poem by Kamal Mirawdeli called 'Tora Bora 2002' (2001):

> The name is so familiar
> Sounding so close, so ancient, so complex
> As the cave complexes witnessing the conflict
> Between the latest highest most lethal modern technology
> And the most primitive, backward, pointless theology
>
> Yet there is a grey area between the two
> Images and echoes from Tora Bora
> Which have such allure, such endurance, and such enigma
>
> They almost lead me to a trance
> And I see tears on the cheeks of history
> And I see stars withering in the wrath of a semi-nuclear storm
> And I see an Afghan child
> Hungry, helpless, homeless
> Reminding me of my martyred little brother
> And of the orphans of Anfal

Here comes the New Year
And Tora Bora is an enigma
Resisting to be opened by daisy bombs

And Tora Bora is an echo
Reaching beyond the boundaries of history.

And Tora Bora is the most advanced form of death
Which makes the caves laugh at the madness of mortal man.[3]

In this marvellous poem the caves of Tora Bora figure as an impossible meeting place, reminiscent perhaps of the war-torn meetings in T.S. Eliot and Wilfred Owen,[4] a location where worlds collide. It is, of course, impossible to separate this, in the first place, from the enormously resonant question of caves in general, and it is perhaps worth mentioning just a few of the parameters. The exploration of caves, for example, stands as a testing of the limits of human endurance, of what pressure – of rock, of isolation – can be withstood. Then again, the symbolism of caves is in part as entrances to, or exits from, the underworld, places from which strange exhalations breathe, and to enter which might involve encounters with monsters. Also, caves have historically and mythically given the sense of being fissures in the world's apparently seamless surface, locations which challenge our desire for firmness and security. Yet caves are also places of refuge, places where our ancestors, so we assume, found sanctuary from the terrors of the outside world; places where, if recent reports from the rock of Gibraltar, for example, are accurate, Neanderthal man managed to continue to 'live on' beyond what was previously thought to be his allotted span. And also, of course, things are preserved in caves: fossils, relics, ancient paintings – all of them testimony to the deep roots of humanity, to the skills of our ancestors, as well as to the processes of anxiety and propitiation.

From the insides of caves, voices speak: perhaps they are human voices, perhaps they are the voices of the gods, perhaps they emerge from that curious semi-human, semi-divine hinterland which we refer to under the heading of the 'oracular'. Yet again, perhaps all these possibilities are, as Mirawdeli suggests, aspects of the echo: within the cave, voices are strangely lost and just as strangely reproduced. And so voices, and names, become uncanny, they become 'familiar' and 'unfamiliar';[5] they enter into the windings of an unimaginable 'complexity', where there may be no origin and no ending but just the always tempting, always unfulfilled, prospect of that crucial unimaginable journey, a journey to the centre of the earth.

This, then, would be part of the poem's assignation of 'enigma'; in a kind of inverted – or inside out – version of the sublime, caves threaten us with a limit to how far the world may be explored or mapped. But they also, of course, more immediately menace us with the terrors and psychological complexities (or is it better in this speleological context to say 'complexes'?) of claustrophobia; they relate directly to the fear of being 'buried alive', of disappearing and leaving no trace by which we may be remembered, of being for ever unheard as we bang on the lid of our coffin. Thus, in an uncanny way, caves are both a source of memory and a promise of forgetting. In the key representation of this in Christian mythology, the cave becomes also the tomb, and then also the possible site for an improbable resurrection, a letting forth of the secret, which is the secret of a life beyond life, of a new beginning – but also, naturally, of a return to the womb and a hoped-for rebirth, the foundational myth that incarceration in a cave might provide absolution from all our sins. Now, however, we have the prison service and chimerical notions of rehabilitation to address this mythological need.

The analytical psychologist James Hillman distinguishes helpfully between the 'underground' and the 'underworld'.[6] The underground, while frightening, is nevertheless populated – with spirits, with gods, with souls. It is alive and it teems – perhaps not with 'life as we know it', but nonetheless with life of a sort, life on the 'other side' of the Styx, the Lethe. The underworld, on the other hand, is empty, cold, desolate: there is nothing there – or rather, 'nothing' is what is there, limbo, the void, a dead, frozen realm where the sun can never shine. And so, as well as being in some sense 'natural', caves are also an anthropological prompt towards the artificial, towards the need for light to see by, the need for fire to warm us. For Mirawdeli, these particular caves can never be fully opened, never fully laid out in the light: they are symbolically crucial in the history of Afghanistan, yet at the same time they are an 'enigma', a puzzle, 'resistant' to interpretation, whether by violent or any other means.

What, then, do we actually appear to know of these caves of Tora Bora? Not, we might conclude, a great deal. We know that their name means 'black dust'. We know that there were 'natural' caves in this region of the White Mountains in eastern Afghanistan, but we do not know whether these caves were referred to as 'Tora Bora' before they were transformed in the early 1980s. They were transformed then, with the assistance of the CIA, for use by the mujahideen during the Soviet occupation of Afghanistan: thus the cold caves become an agent of the Cold War, and another step in the 'great game' of Afghan regional politics – or rather, of what the strategic location of Afghanistan has signified for conflicts which have raged around it for several centuries.

We know that it is supposed that, in its most recent incarnation, the cave complex was suspected to be the headquarters of Osama bin Laden, but we know surprisingly little of what this complex actually consists of, or indeed what might be, or have been, in it. Rumours abound of stocks of weaponry and ammunition left behind in the 1980s; but perhaps what we are seeing here is an all too 'familiar' story of the 'buried treasure' which caves might harbour. We know that when the caves were 'captured' – if, indeed, caves can be captured – by US and other forces in 2001, they were said to be far less extensive and intimidating than had been previously supposed; it is to this day not clear whether it would be apt to describe them as a 'headquarters', or better to see them as a well-known temporary refuge from battle.

And another thing we know is about their future:

> Tora Bora Tourist Resort
>
> Osama bin Laden's secret caves hideout is being converted – into a £5.3 million tourist resort. Hotels and restaurants are being constructed on mountains overlooking the al-Qaeda chief's Tora Bora refuge in Afghanistan, reports *The Sun*. Former warlord Gul Agha Sherazi, now a local governor, said: 'Tora Bora is world famous – but we want it to be known for tourism, not terrorism. It was known as a picnic spot long before anyone had heard of Osama bin Laden'. Bin Laden, who hid there in 2001 after the Taliban government was ousted, is believed to have fled after a US bombing blitz. Two journalists were killed there this month but Mr Sherazi insisted: 'Tora Bora is 100 percent safe'.[7]

If nothing else – and the dead journalists might, under other circumstances, have had something to say about the 'safety' of Tora Bora – this report might lead us to speculate on the uncanny relationship between the 'secret' and the 'known'. The scenario might lead us back, for example, to the famous image of Edgar Allan Poe's purloined letter, topic of exchanges between Lacan and Derrida, which is, of course, eventually found in the most obvious place of all – in a letter rack.[8] Just so, one might think that if one is in need of preserving a 'secret', why not go to a place which is 'known'– but known 'otherwise', known differently, and therefore too obvious a hiding place. It might also offer to us some thoughts on the nature of modernity.[9]

At least since the Enlightenment, and in some cases before, modernity has signified a process of 'bringing to light'. The dark spaces of superstition and prejudice must be made to quail before the light, just as the wolves must be made to stand back from fear of the fire. No secrets are to be left untold; transparency is all. If you take to hiding in a cave, your motives are no longer to be seen as an understandable defence against incursion; rather, you are choosing, unacceptably, to renounce the onslaught of the modern and to remind us of a past which modernity wishes above all things to forget. The cave is redolent of an unenlightened primitivism, but in this case, as we see, all this can be transformed via the helping hand of commerce-driven tourism towards a different kind of regeneration.

The lineage goes back, of course, in many directions, but one direction is towards Berchtesgaden and Hitler's tunnel complexes. One of the cultural/military lessons now taught in the informational tourism which now attends those 'caves' is that the larger and more destructive the bombs become, the deeper and more elaborately we have to dig. Another is that this tactic is rarely successful. It is very unusually in military history that fortifications, however complex, can withstand siege: relative immobility, as Paul Virilio so often rehearses,[10] is not – and probably never has been – a credible tactic in the face of the always increasing speed and depth of weaponry and military operations. The trouble is not that 'you can run but you can't hide', but rather the reverse: you can hide, but unless you are supernaturally privileged you cannot also run – you have, more or less literally, dug yourself into a hole.

Hence the Western exasperation when, in the face of this well-tried formula, Osama bin Laden did indeed appear to find a way out of the caves of Tora Bora, and the ill-disguised feelings that in order to do so he must have had 'unnatural' – or we might say uncanny – help; or, of course, we might have to conclude that this help was purely local, but that would threaten to unseat Western protestations of 'liberation'. Another source of Western frustration is, of course, that if indeed it is true that it was CIA money that engineered and adapted the cave complex, then where are the charts and maps which should have recorded the caves' entrances and exits? Or, we may feel, has another hand been at work here? Just as the CIA 'inscribed' itself on the previous arrangements of the 'natural', have successive waves of insurgents, George W. Bush's 'bad guys', performed a further reinscription, altered the map, thereby deceiving those who thought they knew as much as was possible about the admittedly shaky ground on which they stood?

We shall probably never know. Mr Sherazi, after all, is a 'former warlord' who is now a 'local governor'. It is, of course, possible for people to change; what is more certain, however, is that circumstances change, and thus that yesterday's hunter may well be today's gamekeeper. And so, for example, old terrorists come in out of the cold and become responsible for policing their former allies; old allies (in this case, perhaps the mujahideen) become apparently vicious enemies (even though their agenda might be quite different from our own), in a series of uncanny mirrorings and reversals. And a location of fear is exposed to the light, rebuilt – the darkness of the caves succumbs to the lightness of the mall or atrium in an apparently inexorable process of modernisation, even though this modernisation is precisely a key, biased player in the conflicts it is supposed neutrally to resolve.

One of the major features of the uncanny, we may need to remember, is repetition:[11] as we think we are about to escape into freedom, we find ourselves challenged by the thought – or feeling, as emblematically in the phenomena of *déjà vu* – that we have been here before, that our sense of newness, of progress, is not what it seems. And this calls to mind the whole panoply of ways in which we try to 'understand' the past, especially in the literal sense of getting behind or below it, so that we can minimise its threatening aspects. Would it be possible to understand the plight of an orphaned Afghan child by probing the caves to their depths? Is it possible to 'explain away' the disturbing presence of repetition by a simple clearing of the ground, by saying that this question of repetition is just a matter of delusion – we may feel that we have been here before but we have not really, it is just our (collective) memory playing its usual tricks?

But I fear I begin to repeat myself (whatever that might mean). To start again: the 'repetition' of Tora Bora is about the old finding itself again within the new; but it is also about the new becoming subsumed into the old, about, we might say, 'old habits dying hard'. In this hallucinatory concatenation of the ancient and the modern, nothing is clear. Everything solid has just gone, left the moment before we were due to discover the secret; we are left, to use that grand Victorian phrase which still has so many references, with smoke and mirrors. Perhaps, therefore, in search of some less illusory truth, it is time to turn to a different, but all too obvious, cave: Plato's. Here, of course, we are on old and apparently familiar territory; the scenario is about the limitations of our perception of the real as we become absorbed with all of the world we can ever know, the flickering firelit shadows which combine representation and delusion.

Indeed, it would not be going too far to say that Baudrillard's notion of the simulacrum is simply an updating of Plato for our times. The Gulf War, Baudrillard for example tells us, never really happened.[12] Within the cave, we might surmise, time works differently; we are deluded by phantoms and lose our purchase, if we ever had any, on the real. Or, to put it in an opposing way, everything in the simulacrum is of the surface: there is no cave, no cavity beneath or within which might be filled with substance.

These are some verses from a long poem called 'A Dead Terrorist', published in 1996:

> He had a long
> Police record; and around his rooms were found
> Shotguns, ammunition; he was precisely
> In the centre, one shoe pointing
> North-east, the pistol eighteen inches away
> From his hand. Blood more pallid than
> Is usual. No two of his passports recorded
> The same name. No two of his
> Camouflaged tape recorders displayed a
> Consistent voice
>
> ...
>
> In Port Said, a naval attaché with pointed
> Shoes signed the first cheque; or a registrar
> With drooping moustaches and a dented crystal
> Ball, throwing out a line to the future.
> Where did he imagine he would go, where could have been
> Large enough, nameless, for the long aftermath
> Of intrigue? Or was there always a terminus,
> In Holland Park or Detroit, twitching net
> Curtains, and an oversized bank balance to
> Drag through the dripping streets? What savour,
> What signet ring?
>
> ...
>
> Belief is endless, and transferable; bullets
> Are blown back in the angelic winds. We took comfort
> In the storm, and rattled the jet sticks
> Of chance. In his kitchen was nothing, like an
> Exploded universe. Planets swung before him like a bell,

> And the air tore. We jumped through the gap, but
> Were caught, broken in to the kaleidoscope, encased
> In a various gaze. No, for the bells, nightly,
> We sang, but it did not stop him, nor he us,
> Swinging from the ridiculous firmament, pushed by
> The mafia of stars. And now there can be no renewal
> From his life; the snake-cup leaks, and the fracture
> Will not mend.[13]

Here, then, might be the aftermath of terrorism, or more exactly the aftermath of the terrorist – seen in the poem as a whole as a parallel to other kinds of crisis, other kinds of 'little death' at a more personal level. Whose 'precision' is being described in the first stanza – the precision of the terrorist, staple of a thousand tabloids; the precision of the police investigation which we are to presume has followed the terrorist's death; the more basic *desire* for precision, born of the hope that thus we might be able to 'explain' the chaos, the irreconcilable destruction, make it again 'familiar' by bringing the uncanny back under the sign of law and order?

Nothing, though, is truly certain about the life offered to us (and withheld from us) in this poem: in the second quoted stanza, various options are offered, but none are judged as accurate or feasible accounts. Graham Greene and John LeCarré have long made us familiar with how difficult it is to know one crucial detail in the life of the terrorist, the spy, the 'secret' agent: the identity of the paymaster. We might speculate on how even the terrorist him- or herself, the secret agent, may die unsure of where the 'bank balance' comes from. In an era where the concept of the 'signature' still retains an outmoded totemic status, despite forgery and 'chip-and-pin', the idea of the 'signet ring' is perhaps a gesture towards authentication, towards verisimilitude; but perhaps it too enters into the hall of mirrors signified in the multiple passports, the uncertainty of voices.

And the last stanza, clearly, is an act of mourning. We might think of Freud's attempts to connect mourning with the uncanny, but they are unclear, broken, 'fractured'. If the uncanny frequently takes the form (through ghosts, phantasms, revenants and so forth) of a 'reminder' of what has apparently passed, then it should be inseparable from mourning's complexity, from mourning's 'cave complex'. It is not, of course, that we mourn the terrorist; but we can nonetheless be in mourning, especially in the era of the suicide bomber, for explanation, and this will also have a more personal resonance. If the dead terrorist 're-minds' us of the inexplicability of human action, then we are simultaneously reminded that our own actions may well go unexplained; that, despite the best efforts of biographers, there is no single, true account of a life, that there will always be secrets which haunt it – and of which we are, always, variously proud and ashamed. Do we wish our 'true story' to be told, or not? How much of a hand, as 'ghost writer', would we want to have in the narrative in order to be satisfied, or to be content in the grave?

What this poem might also remind us of is, again, modernity, and we might ask this question: does modernity wish to answer questions, or to foreclose them? Is there, in the end, any difference? 'What signet ring', indeed: but also, what would it mean if we were to be privileged to unravel the uncanny secrets of this man's life – would it tell us anything we do not already know, or that we need to hear? We need also, and perhaps quite urgently, to address what has happened to the concept of mourning in an age characterised by the term 'closure'. We are surrounded in contemporary discourse by this curiously thin notion of closure, or rather, perhaps, by the hope and fear of closure. What the term 'closure' appears mainly to mean at the moment (although this has not always been its meaning) is detection and retribution: as though the archaic notion of 'an eye for an eye' can be resurrected in modern terms. We need to be clear on this point, as was Freud: mourning cannot be closed down or banished, it does not go away.[14] It becomes instead an integral part of the weft of life, it is sewn in to the quotidian, it becomes assimilated to the 'dark background'. The thought of closure is not possible unless one realises its inseparability from denial. From here it would be possible to entertain a good many thoughts about the ambiguities of trauma; but like rebirth, that will have to await another day.

On this point of closure, of course, Melanie Klein would differ from her melancholy forebear, and would claim that there is a way to 'make it right', to effect reparation: and that is through art, through the achievement of a surrogate unity which can replace the 'damage done', whether in the real world or in our childhood fantasies of our wished-for treatment of our parents.[15] Leo Bersani has taken Klein to task, in *The Culture of Redemption* (1990), for what he takes to be this dangerous optimism.[16] We might cite examples like Goya, Kafka and Beckett as instances of an art which is thoroughly non-redemptive, stark, able to own to and articulate its own stricken-ness. But perhaps neither of these arguments goes quite deeply enough into the 'underworld', into the bare, dark, cold place where articulacy has no purchase and where the echo has no origin and no hold. The function of the uncanny here would not be to remind us of what has gone before in terms of human time or action, but rather of that which encompasses such anthropocentrism, that which lies always beyond and further back. In *déjà vu*, then, it would not be that we 're-live' the moment, but more that we receive a shivering intimation of what Russell Hoban refers to as 'the moment under the moment', the moment which is already dead.[17]

And what of the terrorist, '*hypocrite lecteur, mon semblable, mon frère*'?[18] Let us consider, in this context, the passion of self-righteousness, or perhaps of 'righteous anger'. If we were to look at anger as a psychological concept, we would need to tangle with concepts that, on the one hand, abut onto freedom, and on the other onto addiction. The 'release' of anger, its sense of liberation and self-justification, the cold turkey we do when we realise the damage caused, all of these are redolent of the realm of the addicted, and therefore of the possibility of the suspension of moral law. But is the terrorist angry? In what sense might he or she be angry, and how would we know? Conrad's Professor was probably not angry in any sense in which we can readily recognise it: rather he is a practitioner of cold method. He knows that while he is carrying, or wearing, his armoury, he is untouchable. Perhaps, at the end of the day, what the suicide bomber most wishes for is to avoid a hangover.

I feel I am ricocheting about here between terrorism and the uncanny. This seems more than appropriate. The first *OED* entry under 'ricochet' is from a book on British gunnery: 'The smaller the angle, under which a shot is made to ricochet, the longer it will preserve its force and have effect.' There are various ways to think this. First, it is undeniably the case, even if this is an unpalatable truth, that terrorism is, in a sense, low in the scale of immediate lethal impact. The numbers of deaths in the Twin Towers or in the Bali bombings do not stack up statistically against, to take a deliberately non-neutral example, the deaths of one million Filipinos in the US/Philippine War of 1900. But this, of course, is not the end, or perhaps even the beginning, of the truth: because terrorism depends on the effects of ricochet. Thus a single image, on television news, of a Western national bound, gagged and blindfolded, waiting under the sword, cannot be equated with the faceless thousands killed by other means. This is not to say, obviously, that the smaller the act the larger its consequences: but it is to say that the question of leverage is all-important, and that one of the crucial oppositions in the question of terrorism is between the facelessness of the terrorist and the faciality (especially when partially erased) of the victim.

And this would in turn raise some further interesting and important questions about the uncanny; because one of the several things which are not often said about the uncanny is that it is so frequently *trivial*. Of course we may believe in omens and portents, despite Freud's painstaking excision of such thoughts from his interpretation of dreams;[19] but in the main we do not regard *déjà vu* as important in the sense that it is likely to tell us special, extra-natural truths about our life; but rather because it is so weird, it appears to arrive in the form of a message without content, as though one were to open, with excitement, a clearly addressed envelope, perhaps in a handwriting one thinks one recognises, to find nothing whatever inside it.

So perhaps the unlooked-for moment in the interpretation of the uncanny is its absence of meaning. Obviously, this is a controversial and contentious thing to say, especially in view of Freud's attempts to connect it with childhood anxieties. But the fact remains that the uncanny is an irruption, an intrusion: although it demands interpretation, it also, rather comically, flaunts its ability to resists our efforts at interpretation. Perhaps we might find a useful analogy in Coleridge's extremely strange poem, 'Limbo' (1817), which he concludes thus:

> No such sweet sights doth Limbo den immure,
> Wall'd round, and made a spirit-jail secure,
> By the mere horror of blank Naught-at all,
> Whose circumambience doth these ghosts enthral.
> A lurid thought is growthless, dull Privation,
> Yet that is but a Purgatory curse;
> Hell knows a fear far worse,
> A fear – a future state; – 'tis positive Negation![20]

What Coleridge is trying to capture here is, as so often in his poetic and philosophical writing, a sense of absence, of negation, of nothingness. Probably we now equate this structure with the depression, dejection, melancholy which were clearly Coleridge's lot in life, but which more importantly have become seen as a significant marker of the 'romantic moment'. What seems more important, however, is that we are here at the limit of interpretation and of articulacy: mere 'privation' (which we may interpret as 'suffering', 'absence of resource' or indeed, rather bizarrely, 'secrecy') is, paradoxically, 'as nothing' beside the condition Coleridge is here describing (while, crucially and knowingly, failing to describe it).

What, in the uncanny, is trivial, what is important? Is the individual terrorist trivial, or important? Do our psychic lives, and especially our dream lives, respond to the trivial, or to the important? Is it not customary to wake up full of frustration that our dreams have been so composed of apparently minor matters from the 'day's residues' and that we cannot see how more significant matters have been attended to? This, then, might be a measure of the obliquity of the figure of the 'terrorist' to our conscious lives, but at the same time an intimation of how close such a figure might be in the different realm of the underworld, and how, therefore, it stretches and strains, in an uncanny way, our *heimlich* assumptions and reminds of the paradoxes which emerge when we try to sort through the questions attendant on what has been 'known' and what is to remain, always, 'unknown'.[21]

Notes

1. Joseph Conrad, *The Secret Agent*, introduction M. Seymour-Smith (Harmondsworth, Middlesex: Penguin, 1984), p. 269.
2. See, Vanessa Campos Santoro *et al.*, 'Perversion and Infancy and Adolescence', *International Forum of Psychoanalysis*, XIV: 3–4 (2005); Danuza Machado, 'Phobia and Perversion', *CFAR Journal*, II (1993); Judith Feher-Gurewich, 'A Lacanian Approach to the Logic of Perversion', in *The Cambridge Companion to Lacan*, ed. J. -M. Rabaté (Cambridge: Cambridge University Press, 2007).
3. Kamal Mirawdeli, 'Tora Bora 2002', *Kurdish Media: United Kurdish Voice* (internet publication, 2001). The apparent oddity of the dates is perhaps explained by the fact that this poem was proleptically published on Christmas Day 2001.
4. See T. S. Eliot, 'Little Gidding', II, in *Collected Poems 1909–1962* (London: Faber and Faber, 1963), pp. 216–19, and Wilfred Owen, 'Strange Meeting', in, e.g., *The Penguin Book of Contemporary Verse*, ed. K. Allott (Harmondsworth, Middlesex: Penguin, 1950), pp. 106–7.
5. Here, as elsewhere, I am referring to Freud, 'The "Uncanny"', in *The Standard Edition of the Complete Psychological Works of Sigmund Freud*, eds J. Strachey *et al.* (24 vols, London, 1953–74), XVII, pp. 217–52.
6. See James Hillman, *The Dream and the Underworld* (New York; London: Harper & Row, 1979), pp. 35–45.
7. *Ananova* (2007).
8. See Edgar Allan Poe, 'The Purloined Letter', in, e.g., *Selected Tales*, ed. D. van Leer (Oxford: Oxford University Press, 1998), pp. 249–65; *The Purloined Poe: Lacan, Derrida and Psychoanalytic Reading*, eds J. P. Muller and W. J. Richardson (Baltimore, MD: Johns Hopkins University Press, 1987).
9. See my *Modernity* (London: Palgrave Macmillan, 2007).
10. See, e.g., Paul Virilio, *Speed and Politics*, trans. M. Polizzotti (New York: Semiotext(e), 1986); *The Art of the Motor*, trans. J. Rose (Minneapolis; London: University of Minnesota Press, 1995).
11. See Freud, 'The "Uncanny"', p. 237; Andrew Bennett and Nicholas Royle, *Introduction to Literature, Criticism and Theory* (2nd edn, London: Prentice Hall Europe, 1999), p. 42.

12. See Jean Baudrillard, *The Gulf War Did Not Take Place*, trans. P. Patton (Bloomington, IN: Indiana University Press, 1995).
13. Jiao Shou Pan De, 'A Dead Terrorist', in *Asleep at the Wheel*, David Punter (London: Amani, 1996), pp. 13–15.
14. Freud, 'Mourning and Melancholia', in *Standard Edition*, XIV, pp. 243–58.
15. See Melanie Klein, 'Love, Guilt and Reparation', in *Love, Guilt and Reparation and Other Writings 1921–1945*, ed. H. Segal (London: Vintage, 1988).
16. See Leo Bersani, *The Culture of Redemption* (Cambridge, MA; London: Harvard University Press, 1990).
17. See Russell Hoban, *The Moment under the Moment* (London: Jonathan Cape, 1992).
18. Eliot, 'The Waste Land', in *Collected Poems*, p. 65.
19. See Freud, *The Interpretation of Dreams*, in *Standard Edition*, IV, pp. 2–5.
20. Coleridge, 'Limbo', in *Poetical Works*, ed. E. H. Coleridge (London: Oxford University Press, 1967), pp. 430–1.
21. See Freud, 'The "Uncanny"', p. 220.

11
Document: 'On the Psychology of the Uncanny' (1906)[1]: Ernst Jentsch

Translated by Roy Sellars

Translator's preface

[In his famous essay on the uncanny, first published in 1919,[2] Sigmund Freud begins by complaining that aesthetics has hitherto not paid much attention to the aberrant and the repulsive. This complaint is also an expression of anticipatory pleasure on the part of Freud the writer, in so far as the uncanny in particular has no 'literature' with which to contend – but he has to admit that there is one exception, namely the essay translated below.[3] Jentsch emphasises that the uncanny arises from a certain experience of the uncertain or undecidable, and this seems intolerable to Freud. Freud decides, in other words, that the undecidable cannot be tolerated as a theoretical explanation, but it nonetheless recurs in his own essay, undecidably.[4] He also pays close attention to Jentsch's argument about the uncanniness of automata.[5]

Dr Ernst Jentsch was born in 1867. The diversity of his cultural and psychological interests can be seen in his published works. His study of mood (1902)[6] includes a sympathetic account of affect in the *Studien über Hysterie* of Freud and Breuer;[7] in his two-part *Musik und Nerven* (1904 and 1911),[8] he notes how uncanny effects are readily produced in music;[9] and, among other works, he produced German translations of Havelock Ellis and Cesare Lombroso. Reference has often been made to Jentsch's essay on the uncanny, in the vast secondary literature of psychoanalysis after Freud, as if its content were already known, familiar and thus not requiring to be read. The essay had never before been translated into English; inasmuch as it now appears both familiar and unfamiliar, its reappearance here can be called 'uncanny'.

This translation first appeared in *Angelaki* 2.1 (1995), and I remain deeply grateful to Sarah Wood, the issue editor and one of the founders of the journal. For their advice, I would also like to thank Peter Krapp, Robert White and especially Forbes Morlock – whose 'Doubly Uncanny', which immediately followed my translation on its first publication,[10] remains a good starting point for further research.]

I

It is a well-known mistake to assume that the spirit of languages is a particularly acute psychologist. Thanks to this spirit, gross errors and astonishing naiveties are often quite readily disseminated, or at least supported – errors and naiveties which are rooted partly in the uncritical tendency of observers to become caught up in their own projections, and partly in the limited lexical material of a particular language. Nevertheless, every language still often provides particular instances of what is psychologically correct or at least noteworthy in the way in which it forms its expressions and concepts. In a psychological analysis, it is always a good idea to make the terminology clear in one's own mind; something can often be learned thereby, even when one cannot always make use of the result of the investigation.

With the word *unheimlich* ['uncanny'],[11] our German language seems to have produced a rather fortunate formation. Without a doubt, this word appears to express that someone to whom something 'uncanny' happens is not quite 'at home' or 'at ease' in the situation concerned, that the thing is or at least seems to be foreign to him. In brief, the word suggests that a *lack of orientation* is bound up with the impression of the uncanniness of a thing or incident.

No attempt will be made here to define the essence of the uncanny. Such a conceptual explanation would have very little value. The main reason for this is that the same impression does not necessarily exert an uncanny effect on everybody. Moreover, the same perception on the part of the same individual does not necessarily develop into the 'uncanny' every time, or at least not every time in the same way. But this does not mean to say that it would be impossible to give a working definition of the concept of the 'uncanny', since one can perhaps suppose that the impression which generates the feeling will be constituted along the same lines for a certain psycho-physiological group. In the present state of individual psychology, though, one can scarcely hope for a step forward in knowledge by this path.

So if one wants to come closer to the essence of the uncanny, it is better not to ask what it is, but rather to investigate how the affective excitement of the uncanny arises in psychological terms, how the psychical conditions must be constituted so that the 'uncanny' sensation emerges. If there were people for whom nothing whatsoever is uncanny, then it would be a question of psyches in which such fundamental conditions are completely lacking. But since (with the exception of these conceivable extreme cases) opinions as to what in this or that case can be described as having an uncanny effect will greatly diverge, it is a good idea provisionally to limit the posing of the problem even further, and merely to take into consideration those psychical processes which culminate experientially in the subjective impression of the uncanny with some regularity and sufficient generality. Such typical events can be singled out from the observation of daily life with some precision.

If one takes a closer look at everyday psychology in this sense, it can easily be seen that a quite correct and simply confirmable observation underlies the image used by language that was noticed at the outset.

It is an old experience that the traditional, the usual and the hereditary are dear and familiar to most people, and that they incorporate the new and the unusual with mistrust, unease and even hostility (misoneism[12]). This can be explained to a great extent by the difficulty of establishing quickly and completely the conceptual connections that the object strives to make with the previous ideational sphere of the individual – in other words, the intellectual mastery of the new thing. The brain is often reluctant to overcome the resistances that oppose the assimilation of the phenomenon in question into its proper place. We will therefore not be surprised that misoneism will be weakest where these resistances are smallest, where for example associative activity in a corresponding movement is particularly prompt and lively, or where it takes its course in some particular way: in the case of youth, of high intelligence or of a permanent aversion to the well-tempered fashion of judging things and reacting accordingly (as happens in a hysterical disposition, for instance).

That which has long been familiar appears not only as welcome, but also – however remarkable and inexplicable it may be – as straightforwardly self-evident. No one in the world is surprised under usual circumstances when he sees the sun rise in the morning, so much has this daily spectacle crept into the ideational processes of the naive person since early childhood as a normal custom not requiring commentary. It is only when one deliberately removes such a problem from the usual way of looking at it – for the activity of understanding is accustomed to remain insensitive to such enigmas, as a consequence of the power of the habitual – that a particular feeling of uncertainty quite often presents itself. In the example mentioned above, this happens when one remembers that the rising of the sun does not depend on the sun at all but rather on the movement of the earth, and that, for the inhabitants of the earth, absolute movement in space is much more inconsequential than that at the centre of the earth, and so forth. The feeling of uncertainty not infrequently makes its presence felt of its own accord in those who are more intellectually discriminating when they perceive daily phenomena, and it may well represent an important factor in the origin of the drive to knowledge and research.

It is thus comprehensible if a correlation 'new/foreign/hostile' corresponds to the psychical association of 'old/known/familiar'. In the former case, the emergence of sensations of uncertainty is quite natural, and one's lack of orientation will then easily be able to take on the shading of the uncanny; in the latter case, disorientation remains concealed for as long as the confusion of 'known/self-evident' does not enter the consciousness of the individual.

Apart from the lack of orientation arising from the ignorance of primitive man, an ignorance which under usual circumstances is therefore hidden from him to a great extent by the everyday, some stirrings of the feelings of psychical uncertainty arise with particular ease either when ignorance is very conspicuous or when the subjective perception of vacillation is abnormally strong. The first case can easily be observed in children: the child has had so little experience that simple things can be inexplicable for him and even slightly complicated situations can represent dark secrets. Here is one of the most important reasons why the child is mostly so fearful and shows so little self-confidence; and bright children are in fact generally quite the most fearful, since they are clearer about the boundaries of their own orientational abilities than more limited children are – although, as must of course be added, the latter can become particularly impertinent and cheeky once they have managed to achieve a certain intellectual mastery over a particular area.

As a rule, a certain insight with regard to the estimation of one's own intellectual capacities in the assessment of a situation is generally present in healthy people, as long as strong passions or psychically harmful factors (such as narcotic substances, exhaustion and so on) are not involved. Such insight can be reduced, since excessive associative activity – and also, for example, a tendency to unusually strong reflexivity – do not allow one to complete the formation of a judgement at the appropriate time. But one's insight can be especially reduced because of a rampantly proliferating fantasy, as a consequence of which reality becomes mixed up in a more or less conscious way with the additions of the apperceiving brain itself. In the latter case, confusion must of course be the result in how one regards things and, equally, in how one intervenes appropriately in one's environment.

It is certainly not necessary that the processes in question be articulated very clearly in order for the well-characterised sensation of psychical uncertainty to be aroused. Indeed, even when they know very well that they are being fooled by merely harmless illusions, many people cannot suppress an extremely uncomfortable feeling when a corresponding situation imposes itself on them. In games, children strive by means of grotesque disguises and behaviour directly to arouse strong emotions in each other. And among adults there are sensitive natures who do not like to attend masked balls, since the masks and disguises produce in them an exceedingly awkward impression to which they are incapable of becoming accustomed. This abnormal sensitivity is not infrequently a phenomenon accompanying a generally nervous disposition. It should therefore ultimately not make a great difference whether the affective availability of a certain class of moderately unsettling influences that do not generally or persistently concern healthy people is to be ascribed to a particularly intensive and rapid proliferation of the potential chain of consequences of the phenomenon in question, or whether, in more causal terms, their availability represents an excessive combination of more or less apposite unsettling reasons for the origin of the images exciting the affect. In any case, a stronger tendency to bring about such sensations of uncertainty under certain external circumstances is created in the case of an abnormal disposition or merely a psychical background deriving from an abnormal base, as for example in light sleep, states of deadening of all kinds, various forms of depression and after-effects of diverse terrible experiences, fears, and severe cases of exhaustion or general illness. The breakdown of an important sense organ can also greatly increase such feelings in people. In the night, which is well known to be a friend to no man, there are thus many more and much larger chicken-hearted people than in the light of day, and many people are much relieved when they have left a very noisy workshop or factory floor where they cannot make out their own words.

This entire group of states of psychical uncertainty, already determined in many subsidiary ways by abnormal conditions, can show similarities with or transitions to the general disorientation that appears in psychical illnesses.

The affective position of the mentally undeveloped, mentally delicate or mentally damaged individual towards many ordinary incidents of daily life is similar to the affective shading that the perception of the unusual or inexplicable generally produces in the ordinary primitive man. This is the source of that characteristic wariness in relation to unusual people, who think otherwise, feel differently and act otherwise than the majority, and in relation to processes that for the time being elude explanation or whose conditions of origin are unknown. It is not always just the children who watch the skilled conjurer – or however he calls himself now – with a certain nervous feeling. For the more clearly the cultural value of an enigmatic process strikes one, doubtless the more strongly the sensation aroused approaches the pleasant and joyful feeling of admiration. The appearance of this stirring always presupposes the individual's insight into a certain higher form of expediency of the phenomenon in question. So the remarkable technique of a virtuoso or a surgeon is simply admired, while an 'artist' who has huge stones crushed on his head, swallowing bricks and petrol, or a fakir who has himself buried or walled up, do not receive the genuine admiration of the majority, but rather leave behind a different impression. A slight nuance of the uncanny effect does also come to light now and then in the case of real admiration, and can be explained psychologically in terms of one's bafflement regarding how the conditions of origin for the achievement in question were brought about, on account of which such a nuance is generally lacking in those who are special experts in the field at stake.

II

Among all the psychical uncertainties that can become a cause for the uncanny feeling to arise, there is one in particular that is able to develop a fairly regular, powerful and very general effect: namely, doubt as to whether an apparently living being really is animate and, conversely, doubt as to whether a lifeless object may not in fact be animate[13] – and more precisely, when this doubt only makes itself felt obscurely in one's consciousness. The mood lasts until these doubts are resolved and then usually makes way for another kind of feeling.

One can read now and then in old accounts of journeys that someone sat down in an ancient forest on a tree trunk and that, to the horror of the traveller, this trunk suddenly began to move and showed itself to be a giant snake. If one accepts the possibility of such a situation, this would certainly be a good example to illustrate the connection indicated above. The mass that at first seemed completely lifeless suddenly reveals an inherent energy because of its movement. This energy can have a psychical or a mechanical origin. As long as the doubt as to the nature of the perceived movement lasts, and with it the obscurity of its cause, a feeling of terror persists in the person concerned. If, because of its methodical quality, the movement has shown its origin to be in an organic body, the state of things is thus explained, and then a feeling of concern for one's freedom from personal harm arises instead – which undoubtedly presupposes, however, a kind of intellectual mastery of the situation as far as all other intensity is concerned.

Conversely, the same emotion occurs when, as has been described, a wild man has his first sight of a locomotive or a steamboat, for example, perhaps at night. The feeling of trepidation will here be very great, for as a consequence of the enigmatic autonomous movement and the regular noises of the machine, reminding him of human breath, the giant apparatus can easily impress the completely ignorant person as a living mass. There is something quite related to this, by the way, when striking or remarkable noises are ascribed by fearful or childish souls – as can be observed quite often – to the vocal performance of a mysterious being. The episode in the Robinsonade[14] where Friday, not yet familiar with the boiling of water, reaches into simmering water in order to pull out the animal that seems to be in it, is also based on an inspiration of the writer that is psychologically very apposite. Likewise, the timidity of many animals may originate in the fact that they actually see the living object of their terror (the principle of the scarecrow), and the impression concerned produces in this case a particularly baroque effect, since the associative activity which usually provides a transition into another affective sphere is here very slight. This 'weakness' in beasts of burden is therefore treated successfully by, for instance, presenting or holding out to them the suspicious object so that they can see it or smell it, whereby a kind of intellectual classification of the object exciting the affect is undertaken by the animal and the object is at the same time turned into something familiar which, as mentioned above, easily loses its terrors for them. So when a few years ago, on the occasion of a great carnival procession, some tame elephants forming part of it took to their heels and created considerable confusion when faced with the dragon Fafner spewing fire and flames, this does not seem so remarkable in view of the fact that the elephants had not read the trilogy.[15]

The unpleasant impression is well known that readily arises in many people when they visit collections of wax figures, panopticons and panoramas. In semi-darkness it is often especially difficult to distinguish a life-size wax or similar figure from a human person. For many sensitive souls, such a figure also has the ability to retain its unpleasantness after the individual has taken a decision as to whether it is animate or not. Here it is probably a matter of semi-conscious secondary doubts which are repeatedly and automatically aroused anew when one looks again and perceives finer details; or perhaps it is also a mere matter of the lively recollection of the first awkward impression lingering in one's mind. The fact that such wax figures often present anatomical details may contribute to the increased effect of one's feeling, but this is definitely not the most important thing: a real anatomically prepared body does not need in the least to look so objectionable as the corresponding model in wax. Incidentally, it is of considerable interest to see in this example how true art, in wise moderation, avoids the absolute and complete imitation of nature and living beings, well knowing that such an imitation can easily produce uneasiness: the existence of a polychrome sculpture in wood and stone does not alter this fact in the least, and nor does the possibility of somewhat preventing such unpleasant side effects if this kind of representation is nevertheless chosen. The production of the uncanny can indeed be attempted in true art, by the way, but only with exclusively artistic means and artistic intention.[16]

This peculiar effect makes its appearance even more clearly when imitations of the human form not only reach one's perception, but when on top of everything they appear to be united with certain bodily or mental functions. This is where the impression easily produced by the automatic figures belongs that is so awkward for many people. Once again, those cases must here be discounted in which the objects are very small or very familiar in the course of daily usage. A doll which closes and opens its eyes by itself, or a small automatic toy, will cause no notable sensation of this kind, while on the other hand, for example, the life-size machines that perform complicated tasks, blow trumpets, dance and so forth, very easily give one a feeling of unease. The finer the mechanism and the truer to nature the formal reproduction, the more strongly will the special effect also make its appearance. This fact is repeatedly made use of in literature in order to invoke the origin of the uncanny mood in the reader. Not the least pleasure of a literary work, or a stage play, and so on, lies in the empathy of the reader or audience with all the emotional excitements to which the characters of the play, or novel, ballad, and so forth, are subject. In life we do not like to expose ourselves to severe emotional blows, but in the theatre or while reading we gladly let ourselves be influenced in this way: we hereby experience certain powerful excitements which awake in us a strong feeling for life, without having to accept the consequences of the causes of the unpleasant moods if they were to have the opportunity to appear in corresponding form on their own account, so to speak. In physiological terms, the sensation of such excitements seems frequently to be bound up with artistic pleasure in a direct way. However strange it may sound, there are perhaps only very few affects which in themselves must always be unpleasurable under all circumstances, without exception. Art at least manages to make most emotions enjoyable for us in some sense. For we can observe in children that they often show a certain preference for ghost stories. Horror is a thrill that with care and specialist knowledge can be used well to increase emotional effects in general – as is the task of poetry, for instance. In storytelling, one of the most reliable artistic devices for producing uncanny effects easily is to leave the reader in uncertainty as to whether he has a human person or rather an automaton before him in the case of a particular character. This is done in such a way that the uncertainty does not appear directly at the focal point of his attention, so that he is not given the occasion to investigate and clarify the matter straight away; for the particular emotional effect, as we said, would hereby be quickly dissipated. In his works of fantasy, E. T. A. Hoffmann has repeatedly made use of this psychological artifice with success.[17] The dark feeling of uncertainty, excited by such representation, as to the psychical nature of the corresponding literary figure is equivalent as a whole to the doubtful tension created by any uncanny situation, but it is made serviceable by the virtuosic manipulation of the author for the purposes of artistic investigation.

Conversely, the effect of the uncanny can easily be achieved when one undertakes to reinterpret some kind of lifeless thing as part of an organic creature, especially in anthropomorphic terms, in a poetic or fantastic way. In the dark, a rafter covered with nails thus becomes the jaw of a fabulous animal, a lonely lake becomes the gigantic eye of a monster and the outline of a cloud or shadow becomes a threatening Satanic face. Fantasy, which is indeed always a poet, is able now and then to conjure up the most detailed terrifying visions out of the most harmless and indifferent phenomena; and this is done all the more substantially, the weaker the critical sense that is present and the more the prevailing psychical background is affectively tinged. This is why women, children and dreamers are also particularly subject to the stirrings of the uncanny and the danger of seeing spirits and ghosts.

This possibility will be especially close, once again, when the imitation of an organic being is itself given. The boundary between the pathological and the normal is crossed here with particular ease. For people who are delirious, intoxicated, ecstatic or superstitious, the head of a pillar (or the figure in a painting, and so on) comes alive by means of hallucination: it addresses them, carries on a conversation with them, or mocks them, showing familiar traits. These means of arousing uncanny effects are also often exploited by poets and storytellers. It is a favoured and quite banal trick to come up with the most hair-raising things and then to reveal all that happened to the reader in three lines at the end as the content of a wild dream vision – favoured, because in this case it is possible to push the play with the reader's psychical helplessness very far with impunity.

Another important factor in the origin of the uncanny is the natural tendency of man to infer, in a kind of naive analogy with his own animate state, that things in the external world are also animate or, perhaps more correctly, are animate in the same way. It is all the more impossible to resist this psychical urge, the more primitive the individual's level of intellectual development is. The child of nature populates his environment with demons; small children speak in all seriousness to a chair, to their spoon, to an old rag and so on, hitting out full of anger at lifeless things in order to punish them. Even in highly cultivated Greece, a dryad still lived in every tree. It is therefore not astonishing if that which man himself semi-consciously projected into things from his own being now begins again to terrify him in those very things, or that he is not always capable of exorcising the spirits which were created out of his own head from that very head. This inability thus easily produces the feeling of being threatened by something unknown and incomprehensible that is just as enigmatic to the individual as his own psyche usually is as well. If however there prevails sufficient orientation with respect to psychical processes, and enough certainty in the judgement of such processes outside the individual, then the states described – under normal psycho-physiological conditions, of course – will never be able to arise.

Another confirmation of the fact that the emotion being discussed is caused in particular by a doubt as to the animate or inanimate state of things – or, expressed more precisely, as to their animate state as understood by man's traditional view – lies in the way in which the lay public is generally affected by a sight of the articulations of most mental and many nervous illnesses. Several patients afflicted with such troubles make a quite decidedly uncanny impression on most people.

What we can always assume from our fellow men's experiences of ordinary life is the relative psychical harmony in which their mental functions generally stand in relation to each other, even if moderate deviations from this equilibrium make their appearance occasionally in almost all of us: this behaviour once again constitutes man's individuality and provides the foundation for our judgement of it. Most people do not generally show strong psychical peculiarities. At most, such peculiarities become apparent when strong affects make themselves felt, whereby it can suddenly become evident that not everything in the human psyche is of transcendent origin, and that much that is elementary is still present within it even for our direct perception. It is of course often in just such cases that much at present is generally accounted for quite well in terms of normal psychology.

But if this relative psychical harmony happens markedly to be disturbed in the spectator, and if the situation does not seem trivial or comic, the consequence of an unimportant incident, or if it is not quite familiar (like an alcoholic intoxication, for example), then the dark knowledge dawns on the unschooled observer that mechanical processes are taking place in that which he was previously used to regarding as a unified psyche. It is not unjustly that epilepsy is therefore spoken of as the *morbus sacer* ['sacred disease'], as an illness deriving not from the human world but from foreign and enigmatic spheres, for the epileptic attack of spasms reveals the human body to the viewer – the body that under normal conditions is so meaningful, expedient and unitary, functioning according to the directions of his consciousness – as an immensely complicated and delicate mechanism. This is an important cause of the epileptic fit's ability to produce such a demonic effect on those who see it. On the other hand, the hysterical attack of spasms generally has a limited alienating effect under ordinary conditions, since hysterics usually retain consciousness, falling over and hitting out so that they do not (or only slightly) harm themselves – whereby they reveal precisely their latent consciousness. Then their type of movement again frequently reminds one of hidden psychical processes, in that here the muscular disturbances follow a certain higher ordering principle; this stands in relation with the dependence of their fundamental affliction on processes of imagination (in other words, processes that once more are psychical).

In the case of an expert, the corresponding emotion will occur only rarely or perhaps be completely lacking, for to him the mechanical processes in the human mind are no longer a novelty; and even if he is still exposed in particular cases to numerous errors with regard to their course, at least he knows that they exist and rediscovers their trace so often elsewhere that their appearance no longer has the power to affect him to any extent. The situations mentioned are also naturally quick to lose their emotional effect if someone is or has become otherwise used to such incidents, as is the case with a nurse, for instance, and – if one can speak of them in this way – with sick people themselves.

The uncanny effect which an insight into the deranged system of a sick person produces for most people is doubtless also based on the fact that a more or less clear idea of the presence of a certain urge to associate – that is, a mechanism – appears in man which, standing in contradiction to the usual view of psychical freedom, begins to undermine one's hasty and careless conviction of the animate state of the individual. If clarity regarding the relevant conditions is established, then the special character of the peculiar emotional state disappears – a state whose roots are to be sought simply in people's current disorientation with regard to the psychological.

The horror which a dead body (especially a human one), a death's head, skeletons and similar things cause can also be explained to a great extent by the fact that thoughts of a latent animate state always lie so close to these things. Such a thought may often push its way into consciousness so that it is itself capable of giving the lie to appearance, thereby again setting the preconditions for the psychical conflict that has been described. It is well known that such stirrings tend more or less to become lost in the case of those belonging to particular professions who are continually exposed to the corresponding impressions. Apart from the force of habit, the associative working through of the awkward affect that mostly occurs in such cases plays a very significant part in the affect's disappearance. Whether this working through is factual or not is of no great importance, as long as its final result is accepted by the individual. In intellectual terms, for example, the superstitious person also masters in his fashion a great part of his imaginative field, and he too has his doubts and his certainties: the inappropriateness of his entire judgement does not alter this psychological fact at all.

The human desire for the intellectual mastery of one's environment is a strong one. Intellectual certainty provides psychical shelter in the struggle for existence. However it came to be, it signifies a defensive position against the assault of hostile forces, and the lack of such certainty is equivalent to lack of cover in the episodes of that never-ending war of the human and organic world for the sake of which the strongest and most impregnable bastions of science were erected.

Notes

1. 'Zur Psychologie des Unheimlichen' was published in the *Psychiatrisch-Neurologische Wochenschrift* 8.22 (25 Aug. 1906): pp. 195–8 and 8.23 (1 Sept. 1906): pp. 203–5 (the bibliographical references in the Freud editions do not make it clear that Jentsch's essay is spread over two separate issues of the weekly). As far as I can tell, the German text has never been reprinted.

2. Sigmund Freud, 'The "Uncanny"', in *The Standard Edition of the Complete Psychological Works of Sigmund Freud*, vol. 17, trans. and ed. James Strachey et al. (London: Hogarth, 1955), pp. 217–56; or in *The Pelican Freud Library*, vol. 14, trans. James Strachey, ed. Albert Dickson (Harmondsworth: Penguin, 1985), pp. 335–76. For Freud's German text, see the *Gesammelte Werke*, vol. 12, ed. Anna Freud et al. (London: Imago, 1947), pp. 227–68; or the *Studienausgabe*, vol. 4, ed. Alexander Mitscherlich et al. (Frankfurt: Fischer, 1970), pp. 241–74.
3. Freud, 'The "Uncanny"', p. 219.
4. See Freud, 'The "Uncanny"', pp. 221 and 230–1.
5. See Freud, 'The "Uncanny"', pp. 226–7 and 233. For more on Freud's Jentsch, see the definitive study by Nicholas Royle, *The Uncanny* (Manchester: Manchester University Press, 2003), pp. 39–42 and 52.
6. Ernst Jentsch, *Die Laune: Eine ärztlich-psychologische Studie*, Grenzfragen des Nerven- und Seelenlebens 15 (Wiesbaden: Bergmann, 1902); this is the series in which Freud's *Über den Traum* (1901) had first appeared.
7. Ibid., pp. 49–51.
8. Ernst Jentsch, *Musik und Nerven*, vol. 1, *Naturgeschichte des Tonsinns*, Grenzfragen des Nerven- und Seelenlebens 29 (Wiesbaden: Bergmann, 1904); vol. 2, *Das musikalische Gefühl*, Grenzfragen des Nerven- und Seelenlebens 78 (Wiesbaden: Bergmann, 1911). On the uncanny in music, see Richard Cohn, 'Uncanny Resemblances: Tonal Signification in the Freudian Age', *Journal of the American Musicological Society* 57.2 (2004): pp. 285–323.
9. Jentsch, *Musik und Nerven*, vol. 2: pp. 56–7.
10. Forbes Morlock, 'Doubly Uncanny: An Introduction to "On the Psychology of the Uncanny"', *Angelaki* 2.1 (1995): pp. 17–21.
11. Interpolations in square brackets, and all notes, are mine. Trans.
12. 'Dislike of novelty' (*OED*), a novel word that is first found in English in 1886.
13. See Freud, 'The "Uncanny"', p. 226.
14. This episode may be found in the free version of Daniel Defoe's *Robinson Crusoe* by Joachim Heinrich Campe, *Robinson der Jüngere* (Hamburg, 1779), 17. Abend (available on line at http://gutenberg.spiegel.de/campe/robinson/robinson.htm).
15. Jentsch's joke refers to the *Nibelungenlied*, among the most well-known modern versions of which were trilogies by Friedrich de la Motte Fouqué, Friedrich Hebbel, and of course Richard Wagner (whose *Ring* consists of a prologue and three subsequent operas).
16. At this point the essay breaks off, to be resumed in the next issue of the *Wochenschrift*.
17. See Freud, 'The "Uncanny"', p. 227; this leads Freud into his analysis of Hoffmann's 'The Sand-Man'.

Index

aesthetics, 2, 45, 53, 61, 62, 66, 179, 182
Afghanistan, 203–8 *passim*
alienation, 1, 2, 11, 18, 38, 41, 53, 54, 55, 57, 59, 65, 93, 104, 108, 184, 202
  see also dislocation
allegory, 36
Amenábar, Alejandro, (*The Others*), 112–13, 115, 118, 120–2, 126
anima, 156
animate/inanimate, animation, 19, 21, 27, 51, 60, 83–4, 87, 162, 221–5
animism, 188
Antze, P., 116
anxiety, 4, 92, 93, 104, 108
'Apt Pupil, *see* King, Stephen
Asendorf, C., 17
atmosphere, 19
aura, 18, 21, 43
autre nuit, 61, 62, 66
Austerlitz, *see* Sebald, W. G.
authenticity, 92, 98–9, 102, 107
automatism, automaton, 26–7, 216, 223, 224–5
awakening, 40, 58, 60, 62, 66, 113, 119–20, 121, 125, 126

Baer, U., 112
Balzac, Honoré de, 44
Barnes, Djuna, 19–24
Barr, C., 28
Bass, E., 124
Batchen, G., 37, 38
Baudelaire, Charles, 10, 46
Baudrillard, Jean, 15, 209
beliefs, surmounted, 3, 32–3, 35, 68, 72, 75, 83, 85, 160–1, 182
Benchley, R., 96
Benjamin, Walter, 1, 17, 19, 37, 43, 109, 184, 187, 188, 192, 194
Bersani, L., 211
Bettelheim, Bruno, 148, 155
black bodies, performers, 96–7, 98–9
Blanchot, Maurice, 61, 66
Borderline (film), 94, 95, 99–106, 110
boundaries, 2, 4, 12, 14, 17, 21, 30, 34, 42–4, 103, 168, 171–2, 186
Bresnick, A., 31
Breton, André, 134, 182–197, *passim*, 198–9
Bronfen, E., 10, 14–15
Brooks, P., 116
Bryher, 94, 100, 107

Cadava, E., 9, 18, 37
camera, *see* photography
Carby, H., 104
Caruth, C., 115–26 *passim*
Castle, T., 3–4, 35, 36, 38, 81, 132, 143
castration complex, 3
categories, 11–12
Cavell, S., 54
caves, 203–10 *passim*
Chattopadhyay, S., 179
CIA (Central Intelligence Agency), 205, 207
cinema, *see* film
city, the, 1, 5, 53, 57–9, 62–3, 65–6, 169–70, 172–9 *passim*
Cixous, H., 16
Clark, S. W., 80
Clarke, S., 168
Close Up (film journal), 94–99, 105, 107
Coleridge, Samuel Taylor, 213
commodities, *see* objects
community, 4
confession, 114, 116, 129
Conrad, Joseph, 201–2, 212
cosmopolitanism, 94–5, 98, 102, 104, 105, 106, 110
creativity, 15, 18, 29, 32
cultural imaginary, the, 26, 128

Dalí, Salvador, 183
darkness, 39–40, 207, 208
 see also night
Dasein, *see* Heidegger
Davis, L., 124
death, 6, 13, 15–16, 18, 43, 44, 52, 59–60, 61, 119–20, 155, 160, 227
death-drive, 4, 34, 156, 157
decadence, 18
'Dead Terrorist, A.', *see* Jiao Shou Pan De
defamiliarization, *see* alienation; homely/unhomely
déjà vu, 21, 70, 73, 83, 203, 212, 213
depth/surface, 14–15, 16
Derrida, Jacques, 1, 27, 44, 50, 114, 126, 173, 176–7, 178, 179, 206
Descartes, René, 76, 77, 173, 174–6, 178
determinism, *see* mechanism
Diagnostic and Statistical Manual (American Psychiatric Association), 133, 140
Dick, Philip K., 183–4, 189–94, 196, 197
disenchantment, 181–4 *passim*
 see also alienation; Weber, Max
dislocation, 91, 170, 175, 178
 see also alienation
dissociation, 132–43 *passim*
Dolar, M., 97, 107, 111, 132
doll, doll's house, 19–20, 21, 24, 26, 223
Dolores Claiborne, *see* King, Stephen
domestic sphere, the, 17, 29
Donald, J., 5
Don't Look Now, *see* Roeg, Nicholas
Doolittle, Hilda, *see* H. D.
doubling, 5, 7, 36, 38, 39, 44, 51, 53, 59–60, 63–4, 65, 161, 173, 176, 203
dream, the, 40, 51, 52, 54–6, 58, 60–1, 62, 118–20, 187, 193–4, 198–9, 213–14
Dream Novella, *see* Schnitzler, Arthur
Dufrenne, T., 116–17
Dyer, R., 104

Eco, Umberto, 183–4, 194–7
Elkins, J., 43
Ellerman, Annie Winifred, *see* Bryher
Ellison, D., 3, 49
Enlightenment, 3–4, 26, 32–4, 37, 39–40, 75, 76–7, 132, 207
epilepsy, 226
eroticism, 53, 57, 60
estrangement, *see* alienation
everyday life, 28, 182, 184, 187, 190, 193, 194
experience, 11, 12, 20–1, 42, 45–6, 175, 176–7, 178–9
 see also modernity
eyes, 21–2, 23, 30–1, 77

false memory syndrome, *see* memory, recovered
familiar/unfamiliar, 92, 169–72, 177, 178–9, 202, 204
 see also homely/unhomely
family relations, identities, 23, 24, 30, 142, 169, 201
Fantastic, the, 70–4 *passim*, 78–87 *passim*
fantasy, 101, 103–4, 105
feeling, structure of, 5, 45
 see also sensation
feminine, the, 4, 24, 58, 59, 60, 64, 163
 see also gender
feminism, 128, 133, 139, 142
Ferenczi, Sandor, 130, 151, 155, 157, 158
Fetchit, S., 95, 98
figuration, figure, 5, 10, 32, 34–5, 38, 39, 41–6, 170, 202
film, 61, 62, 65, 66, 74, 82, 84–5, 87, 112, 117–8, 181–2, 184, 187
 see also ghost films
flâneur, the, 53, 57–9, 63, 65
Fraser, S., 128
Freud, Sigmund, 1, 2–3, 11, 27, 32, 51–3, 56, 58, 64, 66, 67, 68–9, 73, 75, 82–3, 86–7, 91–2, 94, 105, 109, 113–15, 116–17, 118–19, 120, 131, 132–3, 134, 146–63 *passim*, 165, 166, 167, 169, 171, 179, 181–7 *passim*, 193, 197, 210, 211, 213, 216
 ideas developed via Jung, 152–3, 159–62

ideas developed via Spielrein, 156–7
see also psychoanalysis

Gautier, Théophile, 79, 81
Gay, P., 155, 166
gaze, cinematic, 62, 64–5, 66
see also film
gaze, the, 22, 26, 62, 64, 65, 66
gender, 32–4, 54–5, 62–3, 92, 101, 106, 110, 139–42, 157, 162–3, 166
Gerald's Game, *see* King, Stephen
ghost films, 113, 118, 120–6
ghosts, ghost beliefs, 2, 3, 4, 10, 16, 19, 36, 39, 44–5, 49, 50, 121–3, 125, 131, 173–6, 224
see also Pepper's Ghost; spectral, the
Gilbert, S., 21
gnosis, *see* knowledge
Gordon, A., 27, 50
Gothic, 3, 4, 113, 130, 134, 135, 136, 142
Gubar, S., 21
Gunning, T., 5, 39
Guys, Constantin, 10, 12

Haaken, J., 131
hallucination, 3, 33, 36
Harlem Renaissance, 95, 96
haunting, 2, 18, 44
see also ghosts; spectral, the
H. D.(Hilda Doolittle), 94, 100, 102–4, 105, 106, 109, 110
'Two Americans', 106–9
Hegel, G. W. F., 54, 55, 56,
Heidegger, Martin, 92–93, 102, 104, 109, 173, 177–8
Dasein, 92–3
heimat (homeland), 93
see also home
heimlich/unheimlich, *see* homely/unhomely
Herman, J., 130–1
Herring, Robert, 95, 99, 100, 108
Highmore, B., 5
Hillman, J., 205
Hirsch, J., 118, 124–5
Hitchcock, Alfred, (*Vertigo*), 20, 24–5, 26–7, 28, 29–30, 43, 48
Hitler, A., 207
Hoffmann, E. T. A., 72, 77, 78–9, 81, 158, 224
'The Sandman', 20, 22–4, 25–7, 29, 30–4, 70, 78, 83, 126, 228
Hollywood, 97, 98
home, homely/unhomely, 2, 17, 20, 29, 46, 52, 57, 63, 68–9, 91–2, 93, 95, 99, 102, 104–5, 106, 110, 142, 146, 162–3, 169, 189, 202, 217
homelessness, *see* home
see also alienation
Hopper, E., 48
Huet, M.-H., 30

image, imagery, 3–4, 11, 12, 14–15, 36–7, 43–4
imagination, sympathetic, 4–5, 32, 45
see also cultural imaginary
immigrant, 202
irony, 31

Janet, Pierre, 133–4, 140
Jay, M., 1
Jentsch, Ernst, 69, 131, 216–27
Jiao Shou Pan De, 209–11
Jonathan Strange and Mr Norrell, *see* Clarke, S.
Jung, Carl Gustav, 146–63 *passim*, 164, 165, 166–7

Kant, Immanuel, 2, 40
Kerr, J., 146, 151, 158, 166–7
King, Stephen, 135–44
'Apt Pupil', 137
Danse Macabre, 136
Dolores Claiborne, 139, 143
Gerald's Game, 136, 140–1, 142, 143
'The Body', 135–6, 137
'The Library Policeman', 137–9, 141
The Shining, 136–7, 138, 141
Klein, Melanie, 211
knowledge (uncanny as source of), 181–97 *passim*

Lacan, Jacques, 119, 120, 206
Lambek, M., 116
Laub, D., 117, 118, 120, 124
'Library Policeman, The', *see* King, Stephen
Lifton, R. J., 130, 133
'Limbo', *see* Coleridge, Samuel Taylor
liminality, 168
  see also boundaries
literature, 53

machine, *see* automaton; mechanical uncanny; technological uncanny
Macpherson, Kenneth, 94–106 *passim*
magic, 68–85 *passim*
manipulation, 27–8
Marcus, L., 23–4
marvellous, the, 3, 71, 73, 79, 182, 183–4, 185
Marx, Karl, 1, 27
masculine, the, 15, 29, 63–4, 92, 101, 106
  see also gender
mass culture, 181–97 *passim*
Maurice, A., 97, 108
McNally, R., 116
mechanical uncanny, the, 13, 96–7, 221–2
mechanism, causal, 26–8
media, 5, 6
medium, *see* spirit world
Méliès, Georges, 76, 78, 84–5
memory, recovered, 113, 116, 122, 123, 124, 128–30, 131, 135
Mendoza, E., 75, 83–4
Milner, M., 78
mind, 3, 4, 36, 38, 51, 53, 57, 61, 66, 185–6
Mirawdeli, Kamal, 203–4, 205, 214
mirrors, 43, 63–4, 65, 72, 77–82 *passim*, 85, 123
modernism, 4, 11, 20, 24, 95, 104
modernity, 4, 5–6, 11, 26, 39, 40–1, 131–2, 173–4, 181, 184, 186, 188, 192, 206–7, 211
  experience of, 2, 38, 43, 75–7, 93–4, 109–10, 143, 172, 173–4, 175, 177
  project of, 39, 46
Møller, L., 30
mother, 52, 92, 105
Myers, F., 134
Mysterious Flame of Queen Loana, The, *see* Eco, Umberto

narrative, 70, 73, 74, 86
narrative/image contrast, 16
nature, 18, 21–2, 37, 177–8
neurosis, 4, 92, 93, 102–3, 105
'New Woman, The', 162
  see also feminism
Nietzsche, Friedrich, 93, 98, 105, 107
night, 51–2, 53, 55, 59, 61, 63, 66, 220
  see also darkness
Nightwood, *see* Barnes, Djuna
nothingness, 54–5, 57, 59, 61, 66

objects and powers, 17–20, 25–7, 184, 187–8, 191, 195, 197
occult, the, 147, 150–2, 159–60, 185, 190
  see also uncanny, the
optics, uncanny, 5–6, 22–3, 25–6, 30–1, 69–86 *passim*
Osama bin Laden, 206, 207
otherness, 1
Others, The, *see* Amenábar, Alejandro
'Oval Portrait, The', *see* Poe, Edgar Allan

Pabst, G. W., 94
painting, 12, 13, 16
parapsychology, *see* occult, the
past, the, 83
  as repetition, insistence, 10–11, 23, 25, 41, 91
  see also déjà vu; memory, recovered
Peel, E., 161–2
penumbra, 40–4
Pepper's Ghost, 79, 82
perception, 73–4, 76–7, 79, 86
phantasmagoria, 1, 28, 36, 37, 55, 56, 59, 60, 61, 63, 64–5, 66, 75, 76, 78, 79, 81
phantom, *see* ghosts
Philipsthal, P. (*alias* Philidor), 75, 76
Phillips, J., 92–3
philosophy, 53–4

photography, 5–6, 12, 17, 37–8, 43, 83
Plato, 208–9
Poe, Edgar Allan, 13–14, 16, 81, 206
Pons, P., 172–3, 175, 178
POOL group, the, 94–5, 99–102, 106
positivism, 181, 182, 185, 186, 193, 197
postmodern, the, 6
post-traumatic stress disorder (PTSD), 113, 115, 117, 128, 131, 133, 134
Potamkin, H., 96, 99, 108
powers, *see* objects and powers
presence, 6, 10–13, 34–5, 39, 42, 46
procreation, 15, 29, 30
  see also reproduction
prostitute, the, 57, 62, 114, 163
psychoanalysis, 2–3, 112, 116–17, 131, 132–3, 134, 143, 147, 150–63 *passim*, 165, 167, 181–2
  see also Freud, Sigmund
Pudaloff, R. J., 35
Punter, D., 135, 137
Putnam, F., 133

race, racism, 62–4, 95–108 *passim*
Ragland, E., 119
Rampo, E., 68, 79
Rancière, J., 11, 40
Rank, Otto, 86–7, 117–18
rationalism, rationality, 2, 34, 41, 53, 72, 75, 181–6 *passim*, 190, 197
realism, 28, 73, 86
reality, real/unreal, 14, 16, 19, 34, 35–6, 184, 188, 189
reflection, 2, 4
reflexivity, reflexive grasp, 4, 5, 12, 38–9, 41, 46, 62, 64–5, 174, 175, 219
repetition, *see déjà vu*
repetition compulsion, 51, 54, 114–15
representation, 10, 13, 14, 16, 30, 37, 42, 179
reproduction, 29–30
  see also procreation
revenant, *see* ghosts
Richardson, Dorothy, 96, 109
Richardson, J., 44
Robert-Houdin, J.-E., 72, 74, 76, 79
Robeson, Eslanda Goode, 94–5, 100, 104, 106, 108, 109
Robeson, Paul, 94–5, 100, 104, 105, 106, 107–8, 109
Rodley, C., 44
Roeg, Nicholas, 169–70, 171, 173, 178
Romanticism, 31–2, 37, 72, 78, 81
  Romantic psychology, 52–3, 66, 67
Royle, N., 17, 21, 118, 131–2, 157

Salem witch trials, 35
'Sandman, The', *see* Hoffmann, E. T. A
Sayers, J., 152
Scarry, E., 45
Schelling, F. W. J., 91–2
Schivelbusch, W., 132
Schnitzler, Arthur, (*Dream Novella*), 53–66 *passim*
science fiction, 189, 190, 192, 193
science, 77, 85, 181, 183, 186–7, 190
Sconce, J., 5
Scorsese, Martin, (*Taxi Driver*), 53–4, 61–6 *passim*
Scot, Reginald, 80
Sebald, W. G., 129–30
Secret Agent, The, *see* Conrad, Joseph
secrets, 147, 149–50, 154, 155, 158, 166, 206–7, 208
self, the modern, 3–4, 14–15, 19, 29, 33, 36, 38–9, 116, 177, 178, 179, 194
self-identity, self-presence, 23, 26, 43
Seltzer, M., 132, 142
sensation (feeling), the uncanny as, 1, 11, 42, 45, 85, 217–18, 220
sensibility, 2
sentimental, the, 17, 18
serial killers, 142
sexuality, 54, 55, 56–7, 95, 103, 104
shadow, *see* penumbra
Shining, The, *see* King, Stephen
sight, *see* eyes
simulacrum, 6, 15, 86, 209
Smiley, J., 129
social, the, 4
sound, 5
  disembodied, 6, 97, 107, 111
  film, 6, 96, 97
  gramophone, wireless, 6, 97
  telephone, 83, 97

special effects, 70, 74, 82, 86
spectacle, the, 1, 4, 78, 82
spectral, the, 3, 4, 5, 10, 15, 18, 35–6, 39, 44, 49
spectre, *see* ghost
Spielrein, Sabina, 147–63 *passim*, 166–7
spirit world, spiritualism, 4, 39, 76
stage, the, 53, 57, 61, 66
Steinmeyer, J., 79, 82, 84
Stewart, S., 20
subject, subjectivity, 41, 54, 55, 93, 97–8, 101, 105, 130, 131, 132, 170–9 *passim*, 186
supernatural, the, 2, 3, 35, 45, 72–4, 75, 130–1, 134, 137, 150–2, 156, 159–60
Surrealism, 4, 182–3, 185–8 *passim*, 193
survivals, 114, 119–20, 122, 124, 125–6, 129, 130
  see also beliefs, surmounted

Tasso, 115
Taxi Driver, *see* Scorsese, Martin
technological uncanny, the, 1, 5, 6, 13, 68, 79, 83, 97, 222
telegraph, 6
telephone, *see* sound
Terr, L., 135–6
Terror, 201–3
terrorism, 201–3, 208, 209–12, 214
therapy culture, 112, 116–17
'third sex', the, 19–20
Thousand Acres, A, *see* Smiley, J.
time, as unstable, 83
  as experience, 83
  the uncanny as belatedness, 56, 114, 171
  see also past, the; *déjà vu*
Todorov, T., 71–2, 75, 77, 81, 86
Tora Bora, 203–6, 207
transgression, sexual, 20, 23, 55, 57
trash, 185, 190, 192, 194
trauma, 29, 112, 114–15, 116–20, 122, 124, 126, 128–43 *passim*
triviality, 213–14
trope, *see* figure
'Two Americans', *see* H.D.

uncanny, the, 1–2, 11, 21, 42–6, 51–3, 58, 60, 61, 68–70, 71, 82–3, 85, 86, 113–15, 131, 158–62, 163, 169–72 *passim*, 177, 181–2, 210, 213, 217–27
  and modernity, 2, 3–4, 6, 10–13, 28, 35, 43, 46, 68, 85, 97, 110, 131–2, 173–4, 183–94 *passim*, 197, 213–14
  theories of, *see* Freud, Sigmund; Heidegger, Martin; Jentsch, Ernst
  uncanny, the technological, *see* technological uncanny
  see also doubling; ghosts; haunting; occult, the
'Uncanny, The', *see* Freud, Sigmund
uncertainty, intellectual, 69, 71, 74, 85, 216, 217, 218–25, 227
  see also Jentsch, Ernst
unconscious, the, 16–17, 38–9, 52–3, 55, 117, 134, 163
  collective, 52, 161
unhomely, *see* homely

Venice, 168–70
Vertigo, *see* Hitchcock, Alfred
Vietnam War, 116, 133
vision, *see* gaze, the; insight
Virilio, Paul, 207
Vivien, Renée, 17

Walton, J., 104
Warner, M., 42–3
Weber, Max, 2, 181–2, 183, 184, 185, 198
Weber, S., 163
What Lies Beneath, *see* Zemeckis, Robert
Winfrey, Oprah, 129
wireless, *see* sound
witchcraft, *see* Salem witch trials
witness, witnessing, 113, 114, 115, 117–18, 120, 122, 124–6, 171
Wolfreys, J., 44

X-Files, The, 129

Zemeckis, Robert, (*What Lies Beneath*), 112–13, 115, 118, 120, 122–5, 126
Žižek, Slavoj, 43